The
LHASA APSO

Anna Katherine Nicholas

Title page: Group winning Ch. San Jo's Kian Kandi Kan, ROM, by Ch. Zoro-shah Morific of San Jo ex Ch. San Jo's Tamara of Rob-Tell, ROM. Owned by Lois H.and Paul S. Voight and Leslie Engen.

Cover photo: by Isabelle Francais

Contents

A Word About Kennel Names — Anbara — Art-Est —
Barjo — Barker's — Bel-Air — Bhe Jei — Billie's Follie
Brynwood — Chen — Chizari — Danrew — Donicia —
Gold N Lhasas — Ja-Ma — Joni — Joyslyn — Juell —
Kachina — Kar-Lee — Knol-Wood — Lamoc —
Magestic — Marlo — Mio — Misti Acres — Mohican —
Mor-Knoll — Norbulingka — Potala — Ralda — Rhu-
Ha — Rimar — Ruffway — San-Jo — San Lo —
Sharpette — Shukti Lingka — Summerhill —
Sunshine — Tabu — Taglha — Takashi — Tammering —
Tn Hi — Wellington — Wynwood — Zijuh

Lhasa Apsos in Canada — Lhasas in Australia — Lhasas
in South Africa

AKC Standard for the Lhasa Apso — The British
Standard — Lhasa Apsos Through a Judge's Eye

About the Author

Since early childhood, Anna Katherine Nicholas has been involved with dogs. Her first pets were a Boston Terrier, an Airedale, and a German Shepherd Dog. Then, in 1925, came the first of the Pekingese, a gift from a friend who raised them. Now her home is shared with two Miniature Poodles and numerous Beagles.

Miss Nicholas is best known throughout the Dog Fancy as a writer and as a judge. Her first magazine article, published in *Dog News* magazine around 1930, was about Pekingese, and this was followed by a widely acclaimed breed column, "Peeking at the Pekingese," which appeared for at least two decades, originally in *Dogdom*, then, following the demise of that publication, in *Popular Dogs*. During the 1940s she was a Boxer columnist for *Pure-Bred Dogs/American Kennel Gazette* and for *Boxer Briefs*. More recently many of her articles, geared to interest fanciers of every breed, have appeared in *Popular Dogs*, *Pure-Bred Dogs/American Kennel Gazette*, *Show Dogs*, *Dog Fancy*, *The World of the Working Dog*, and for both the Canadian publications, *The Dog Fancier* and *Dogs in Canada*. Her *Dog World* column, "Here, There and Everywhere," was the Dog Writers' Association of America winner of the Best Series in a Dog Magazine Award for 1979. Another feature article of hers, "Faster Is Not Better," published in *Canine Chronicle*, received Honorable Mention on another occasion.

In 1970 Miss Nicholas won the Dog Writers' Association Award for the Best Technical Book of the Year with her *Nicholas Guide to Dog Judging*. In 1979 the revision of this book again won this award, the first time ever that a revision has been so honored by this organization. Other important dog writer awards which Miss Nicholas has gained over the years have been the Gaines "Fido" and the *Kennel Review* "Winkies," these both on two occasions and each in the Dog Writer of the Year category.

It was during the 1930s that Miss Nicholas's first book, *The Pekingese*, appeared in print, published by the Judy Publishing Company. This book, and its second edition, sold out quickly and is now a collector's item, as is *The Skye Terrier Book* which was published during the 1960s by the Skye Terrier Club of America.

During recent years, Miss Nicholas has been writing books consistently for T.F.H. These include *Successful Dog Show Exhibiting, The Book of the Rottweiler, The Book of the Poodle, The Book of the Labrador Retriever, The Book of the English Springer Spaniel, The Book of the Golden Retriever, The Book of the German Shepherd Dog, The Book of the Shetland Sheepdog, The Book of the Miniature Schnauzer, The World of Doberman Pinschers,* and *The World of Rottweilers.* Plus, in the newest T.F.H. series, *The Maltese, The Keeshond, The Chow Chow, The Poodle, The Boxer, The Beagle, The Basset Hound, The Dachshund* (the latter three co-authored with Marcia A. Foy), *The German Pointer, The Collie, The Weimaraner, The Great Dane, The Dalmatian,* and numerous other titles. In the KW series she has done *Rottweilers, Weimaraners,* and *Norwegian Elkhounds.* And she has written American chapters for two popular English books purchased and published in the United States by T.F.H., *The Staffordshire Bull Terrier* and *The Jack Russell Terrier.*

Miss Nicholas's association with T.F.H. began in the early 1970s when she co-authored for them five books with Joan Brearley. These are *The Wonderful World of Beagles and Beagling* (also honored by the Dog Writers Association), *This is the Bichon Frise, The Book of the Pekingese, The Book of the Boxer,* and *This is the Skye Terrier.*

Since 1934 Miss Nicholas has been a popular dog show judge, officiating at prestigious events throughout the United States and Canada. She is presently approved for all Hounds, all Terriers, all Toys and all Non-Sporting; plus all Pointers, English and Gordon Setters, Vizslas, Weimaraners, and Wirehaired Pointing Griffons in the Sporting Group and Boxers and Dobermans in Working. In 1970 she became only the third woman ever to have judged Best in Show at the famous Westminster Kennel Club event at Madison Square Garden in New York City, where she has officiated as well on some sixteen other occasions over the years. She has also officiated at such events as Santa Barbara, Chicago International, Morris and Essex, Trenton, Westchester, etc., in the United States; the Sportsman's and the Metropolitan among numerous others in Canada; and Specialty shows in several dozen breeds in both countries. She has judged in almost every one of the United States and in four of the Canadian Provinces. Her dislike of air travel has caused her to refrain from acceptance of the constant invitations to officiate in other parts of the world.

Multi-Group winning Ch. Sharil Patent Pending finishing his American title at Beaver County in 1983 judged by the author. Handled by Becki Kraus, co-owner with Bill Kraus, Arkay Lhaso Apsos, Detroit, Michigan.

One of Bob Sharp's earliest Lhasas, Sugar, who was a McFadden bitch and is pictured getting Best of Opposite Sex to Best of Breed at Long Island K.C. from judge Jim Trullinger in 1964.

Chapter 1

Origin of the Lhasa Apso

The Lhasa Apso is one of four breeds of dog whose history lies in the country of Tibet, a land of rugged, high mountains and deep valleys. The intensity of the heat and the bitterness of the cold make it a land in which only the hardy could possibly dare hope to survive.

The other dog breeds of Tibet are the huge and ferocious Tibetan Mastiff, the Tibetan Terrier, and the Tibetan Spaniel. The two which most closely resemble one another are the Lhasa Apso and the Tibetan Terrier, which share numerous, similar characteristics. It is interesting to note that two characteristics shared by all four breeds are extremely heavy coats (one of their chief means of survival against the elements) and tails tightly curled over their backs.

The Tibetan Lhasa Apso is a very special dog. Raised from earliest times in the lamaseries and in the villages of the sacred city of Lhasa, the breed has a most distinctive heritage.

In Tibet, Lhasa Apsos are never sold. Rather, they are given as gifts, only to those people whom a high lama considers as his good friends. It is believed that the gift of a Lhasa Apso will bring good luck to the recipient.

The ancestors of our modern Lhasa Apsos were kept as inside guard dogs to protect the interior of a dwelling, while the Mastiffs guarded the property outside. As the latter were usually kept

The great Best in Show winning Ch. Khan of Norbulingka, ROM, the background and foundation for Phyllis Marcy's Norbulingka Lhaso Apsos at Thetford Hill, Vermont. A very important and influential Lhasa of the 1960s.

chained, it was not unusual for an enemy to slip past and gain entry; this is when the Apsos would greet the intruder with a very competent "welcome."

There are two theories regarding the origin of the breed's name. One is that it was derived from the early Tibetan name for the breed, "Apso Seng Kye," meaning "Bark, Sentinel Lion Dog."

The other is that the word "Apso" was derived from the Tibetan word for "goat," which is "rapso," the logic being that the Apso's coat and that of the goats kept by Tibetan herdsmen were of similar quality and appearance.

It was during the early 1930s that the Tibetan breeds made their appearance in England. While not their *first* appearance, it was at this time that they really caught the public's interest, as was not the case in the past. The Honorable Mrs. McLaren Morrison, a very loyal breeder whose interest and involvement with the Apsos spanned several decades, had shown Lhasas prior to World War I. She did some winning, especially with a dog called Little Dargee. Mrs. William Corfield was also an exhibitor in early British shows, and a Mrs. Webster had a champion dog named Rupso. Still, the support necessary to call attention to the breed was sadly lacking.

When visiting England in 1935, I was astonished not only by the number of Lhasas I saw, but by their beauty as well. They were new to me then, as I had not yet had the pleasure of seeing any here at home.

The Tibetan Breeds Association was founded in England in 1934 to establish standards for the breed. Initially, there was indecision in choosing between *Lhasa Apso* or *Lhasa Terrier* as a breed name.

The controversy spread to the United States as the breed, although listed in the Terrier Group, alternated back and forth between the two names. The breed was recognized in the United States in 1935 as the Lhasa Apso. It then became the Lhasa Terrier for a period, after which time it reverted back again to Lhasa Apso. The switch from the Terrier Group to the Non-Sporting Group took place in the mid-1950s, since which time the dogs have been known consistently as Lhasa Apsos.

In Canada, as well, the Lhasa Apso started out in the Terrier Group, then later was transferred to Non-Sporting.

Ch. Karma Rus-ti, noted winning Lhasa of the 1960s, owned by Mrs. Dorothy Cohen of Las Vegas, Nevada. This handsome dog, a son of Ch. Karma Dmar-Po ex Hamilton Gyo-tru was bred by owner and was born on June 8, 1965. Photo courtesy of Mrs. Jane Forsyth, Rus-ti's handler in the East.

Chapter 2

Lhasa Apsos in the United States

Lhasa Apsos were introduced to the United States in the 1930s by Mr. and Mrs. C. Suydam Cutting, owners of Hamilton Farm at Gladstone, New Jersey. Mrs. Cutting had formerly, as Mrs. J. C. Brady, been a prominent fancier of German Shepherd Dogs in the 1920s. The family interest in dogs continues to the present day in yet another breed, the Jack Russell Terrier; Mrs. Cutting's granddaughter, Mrs. Ailsa Crawford, is the foremost American fancier of that breed.

It is well known that in Tibet the Lhasa Apso is held in religious reverence and may not be sold. During an exploration visit to Tibet in the 1930s, Mr. and Mrs. Cutting became acquainted with the Dalai Lama, who presented them with a gift of two Lhasa Apsos. These dogs, the first two ever seen in the United States, must have been the black and white male, Taikoo, and the blond bitch, Dinkie. Both exquisite specimens of the breed, they produced offspring in all of the following colors: grizzle and white, honey, gold, and brown and white.

In the 1937 Westminster catalog, eight Lhasa Terriers (as they were then known) were shown in the Terrier Group classification. These included a bitch named Hamilton Bidgy, Goby (exhibited by Mrs. William D. Thomas), and Hamilton Sarong. Particulars of parentage or birth for the three were not included. The remainder of the Lhasa entry was made up of Hamilton Tundu, Hamilton Tashi II, Hamilton Lhunpo, Sarong II, and Hamilton Bidgy II, all of these (born July 15, 1936, at Hamilton Farm) from the original Bidgy. Four were sired by Tundu, born July 1935, and he in turn was sired by Hamilton Tsaring.

The Hamilton dogs continued to dominate the Lhasa Apso scene in the United States into the 1950s. Sticking strictly to the direct descendants of the dogs the Dalai Lama had originally presented to them, the Cuttings carried on an extensive Lhasa breeding program. The last two Lhasas they received (in 1950), Le and Pehma, were carried by yak across the Himalayas to India, then flown to the United States. Pehma lived to be fourteen years old; Le, owned by Dorothy Benitez at South Plainfield, New Jersey, was still going strong in 1964. He was the last survivor of the dogs who came to this country as gifts from the Dalai Lama.

Le was one of the ten Lhasas exhibited by the Cuttings at Westminster in 1952, which was just prior to the breed's changeover from the Terrier Group to Non-Sporting. He was entered in Open dogs, his statistics as follows: date of birth, November 1948; breeder, Dalai Lama; sired by Nanchan ex Lucknow.

Pehma, born in November 1948, by Kuen Lun ex Gartok, was entered in the same Westminster show.

The other entries from the Cuttings included three sired by Le, these being from three different bitches. Hamilton Homburg was ex Hamilton Prome; Hamilton Urga was ex Hamilton Muni; and Hamilton Osh was ex Hamilton Lolo.

Other Cuttings entries included Hamilton Tatsienlu (Hamilton Yangchen—Hamilton Nova), born in May 1949; Hamilton Sandur (Hamilton Yangchen—Hamilton Kyichu II), born in 1946; Hamilton Lachen (Hamilton Dakmar—Takla), born in 1949; Tengri Nor (Hamilton Kodur—Hamilton Tughar), born in 1950; and Hamilton Novo (Hamilton Dakmar—Hamilton Maru), born in 1944.

There were other interesting Lhasa exhibitors at Westminster 1952 in addition to the Cuttings. They included Mr. and Mrs. Leo Arnaud with their dog, Chato, bred by the Chinese Catholic Mission, born in 1949 by Nehu ex Chamalhari, and Frank T. Lloyd, Jr. with his specials dog, Champion Ming Changnopa, born in June 1947, by Pedro from Champion Ming Lu.

The picture had grown considerably by the end of the 1950s,

judging from the Westminster catalog for 1959. Hamilton Farm was still in with a big entry—twelve of them to be exact—including Champion Hamilton Katha with Californian Mitch Wooten handling; Champion Hamilton Kung; and Champion Hamilton Tatsienlu. Tatsienlu was the sire of Katha, born in 1955 from Hamilton Docheno, and Kung, born in 1955 from Hamilton Dobra. Tatsienlu and another of his offspring were entered in the Brace class.

In addition to the three Cutting-owned specials, there were two others, a dog and a bitch, owned by Mrs. Dorothy Cohen, who was in the process of establishing her legendary Karma Kennels. These were the male, Champion Karma Getsun, by Champion Hamilton Kung ex Champion Hamilton Karma, and Karma herself, by Hamilton Maroh ex Hamilton Docheno, who had been purchased as a foundation bitch from the Cuttings.

Mrs. Marie C. Stillman had an American-bred bitch entry, Americal's Lona, by Champion Licos Kula La ex Champion Americal's Torma Tsing. Mrs. Stillman was doing well at this period with her Group-winning Champion Hamilton Torma.

In 1960, Hamilton was still the dominant kennel represented at Westminster. The Cuttings had a dozen of their dogs in competition including, as was their custom, multiple entries in both the Brace and the Team classes. In addition, there were several other Lhasas either carrying the Hamilton prefix or bred from their dogs. The Hamilton Farm title-holders entered that year included Champion Hamilton Kung; Henry C. Lum's Champion Hamilton Jimpa (handled by George Payton); Mrs. Cohen's Champion Karma Getson (by Kung) in specials; and Champion Hamilton Katha, owned by Mrs. John Licos.

As the 1960s moved along, Lhasa entries became increasingly competitive. Hamilton Farm remained very much in the picture at eastern dog shows, and there was increased activity among other Lhasa fanciers.

Mrs. Licos, a highly respected breeder, was coming on strong with Champion Hamilton Katha and her homebred Champion Licos Kulu La. Mrs. Cohen had her son and daughter of Kung (Champion Karm Getson and Champion Karma Gyapso) still out. Mrs. Dorothy Benitez had Champion Hamilton Namsa in the limelight. Anna M. Griffing, a Boston Terrier lady who was to become a great friend of the Lhasa, had a special going, Champion

15

Ming Toy Nola, by Champion Ming Changnapa ex Champion Americal's Nino.

Numerous additional names which would become important in Lhasa history started to appear. Champion Tibet of Cornwallis was born in 1966, bred by Paul Williams and then co-owned by Mrs. Leon (Keke) Blumberg and Carolyn Herbel. Mr. Williams co-owned Champion Karma Kan Sa, bred by Mrs. Cohen, with Mrs. Blumberg, whose Potala Kennels grew to become among the breed's best known. Raena Welks started out her lovely bitch, Licos Namni La, daughter of Champion Licos Chapila La and Champion Licos Nyapso La, who had gained points from the author along the way as a special.

Mrs. Licos had a gorgeous dog in Champion Licos Omorfo La, who represented the fifth generation of her breeding program which had begun in 1952. Omorfo was by Champion Licos Kula La from Champion Hamilton Pluti.

Champion Karma Rus-ti, by Champion Karma Dmar Po ex Hamilton Gyo-Reu, began to carry the banner for Dorothy Cohen. Bob Sharp was getting Champion Kyi Chu Friar Tuck under way, and Allen Lieberman was out with specials.

A very notable kennel was Tsung Lhasas Apsos at Hialeah, Florida, owned by Maria Aspuru and Angela Rossie, a truly dedicated pair of Lhasa fans. The two had many exciting dogs in their kennels, and I had known them to put as many as two dozen entries in the ring at a single show. Some of the East Coast top handlers would scramble like crazy to see that none missed their classes, while Maria sat proudly at ringside watching her furry treasures put through their paces. Her handlers included Houston and Toddie Clark and Barbara Alderman on a fairly steady basis, with help coming from wherever obtainable when the going got too frantic. In the late 1960s, Tsung Kennels was going strong with Champion Karma Frosty Knight O'Everglo (Champion Karma Kushog—Champion Hamilton Sha-Tzu, bred by Dorothy Cohen, born July 1963) and Champion Drax Ni-Ma Me (Champion Coralies Shan Bangalor—Champion Ramblersolt Shahnaz, bred by Drax Kennels).

At the beginning of the 1970s, Maria and Angela purchased the grandson of their so highly esteemed Champion Karma Frosty Knight O'Everglo, ROM, with whom they had racked up an overwhelming total of 11 All-Breed Bests in Show, setting a new re-

Group winning Ch. San Jo Shenanigan, ROM, at age 15 months. The sire of 22 champions, he was the American Lhasa Apso Club's Grand Futurity Winner, Western Division, 1976. Bred and owned by San Jo Lhasas, Marianne L. Nixon, Bellevue, Washington.

Ch. Jomo Dkar-Po of Abbotsford in 1963 winning a Best of Breed and a Group 2nd. Dam of the first Sam Jo champion and foundation stud, Ch. Gyal Khamnag of San Jo. Shown by Marianne L. Nixon, San Jo Lhasas, Bellevue, Washington.

cord. This grandson of Frosty was a two-year-old, Champion Sharno Ziju Zer Khan, bred and owned by Sharon Rouse, who had handled him in California. Bee Loeb, Zijuh Lhasas, was co-owner. Zer Khan sired 14 champions. His lineage, like that of many of our most respected Lhasas, goes back to Hamilton Farm and Karma breeding.

I never had the pleasure of meeting Maria Aspuru until we started regularly going on the Florida Circuit in the 1970s. She had a colorful personality and was obviously a great dog lover, along with being a most thoroughly sporting exhibitor. It is sad now to judge Lhasas in the South and no longer look up to see Maria smiling at ringside, looking proud and happy—win, lose, or draw. Her death was a loss to all who travelled the Southern circuits.

The Westminster catalog of 1969 detailed a sizable number of Lhasa specials. Entries included two from Ellen Lonigro's Kinderland Kennel: Kinderland's Zimba (by Hu Kahboh of Pickwick—Tabu of Norbulingka, bred by Mrs. Phyllis Marcy) and Kinderland's Kandy (by Champion Willy of Cornwallis—Champion Jo Khang of Norbulingka, bred by Mrs. Marcy and owner). Maria and Angela entered Frosty Knight and Champion Everglo's Zun Zun, Frosty's daughter from Champion Kyima of Everglo, bred by Gloria Fowler. Entrants from Mr. and Mrs. Alan Stang were Champion Chu Shu (Champion Shangri-La Rajan of Glen Pines—Champion Honey of Sharjimpa, bred by Carolyn Burkinshaw) and Champion Chu Shu's Honeybunch, Chu Shu's homebred daughter by Champion Hamilton Namsa.

Mrs. Dorothy Cohen had her handsome Champion Karma Rus-Tigu (homebred son of Champion Karma Rus-ti ex Karma Mantra) and, in co-ownership with Allen Lieberman, Champion Hamilton Sha-Tru (Champion Hamilton Sandupa ex Hamilton Charpa, bred by the Cuttings). Carolyn G. Sledzig had a single special, Champion Pon Go (by Champion Kham of Norbulingka—Champion Ha Ya Chi), who was bred by the Alexander Holsers.

As you start to read about U.S. kennels, be sure to note the many that are based on the Hamilton bloodline, either directly or through dogs from other kennels (Karma, Americal, Licos, etc.) who were originally bred from Hamilton dogs. It is quite safe to state that the majority of Lhasas bred in the United States and Canada are, indeed, direct descendants of those dogs who were presented to the Cuttings by the Dalai Lama.

Am. and Can. Ch. Magestic Po Nya, by Ch. Karma Rustilomar ex Magestic Cari, owned by Magestic Lhasa Apsos, Lois M. and Pamela Magette, Long Beach, California.

Chapter 3

United States Lhasa Kennels

There is no better way to describe the progress of a breed than by telling you of the individual breeders and kennels who have contributed along the way, having established or being in the process of establishing their own lines of outstanding members of the breed. We have selected a cross section of them with which to supplement our chapter on breed history, presenting many current winners and summarizing the backgrounds from which they have been produced.

On the following pages we pay tribute to some of our long-established prominent breeders and to newer ones who are on the way to joining their ranks. The newer breeders are of special importance since on their shoulders squarely rests the responsibility of carrying on and preserving what has already been accomplished. We feel that the Lhasa Apso is well owned, and that a brilliant future awaits these dogs whose past successes may well be equaled or even excelled. The Lhasa Apso has much on the ball to lead to continued achievement.

A WORD ABOUT KENNEL NAMES

A kennel name is important to a breeder; it should be selected and used from the time of one's first homebred litter. Kennel names are chosen in many different ways. Sometimes the name of the street on which a breeder is located is the choice. Some breeders use their own name or a coined combination of the names of family members. Often a kennel is named for a child who is especially enthusiastic about the dogs. Many breeders use the name, or a combination of the names, of their foundation dogs (either the proper names or call names of these dogs). Whatever strikes your fancy is appropriate, as long as the name does not have an excessive number of letters (remember that the number of letters in a dog's name is limited for registration purposes and the kennel name is included in the count) and does not infringe on anyone's prior rights. Your kennel name will identify you and your Lhasas through future generations.

A kennel name can be registered with the American Kennel Club (or the governing kennel organization in the country where you live), thus becoming exclusively your own for a stated period of time. A kennel name thus registered may not be used by any other person when registering a dog with the American Kennel Club unless you, in writing, specifically permit another person to do so (as would be the case with a puppy you have sold). Information about kennel name registration in the United States is available from the American Kennel Club, 51 Madison Avenue, New York, New York 10010). There are specific requirements regarding the type of names that are eligible and a fee is charged.

Of course there is nothing to stop you from coining and using a kennel identification name without having it registered, as long as it does not infringe on another's rights. The only problem with an unregistered name is that you are not protected against someone else using that same name too.

To be of greatest value, kennel names should be applied to all dogs bred in your kennel as then the dog and its background are immediately identified. A good method of registering each of your dogs is to start each name with your kennel title if the dog is a homebred, and to end the dog's name with the kennel title if it is a dog you have purchased.

AL-MAR

Al-Mar Lhasa Apsos are owned by Marjorie Lewis at Independence, Missouri. Famous as a professional handler, Marjorie is also an admired Lhasa breeder-owner. To her credit are literally hundreds of important show wins, made with her own or her clients' magnificent members of the breed.

A dog from this kennel who carved a special niche in breed history is the famed Best-in-Show-winning, American and Canadian Champion Orlane's Be Sparky of Al-Mar. "Big Red," as this handsome dog was known, had a host of admirers and was a strong influence on his breed. A multiple Best in Show winner with three such victories in both the United States and Canada, his group firsts reached the enviable total of 43, backed up by numerous placements.

A son of Champion Orlane's Dieh Bieh ex Orlane's Holly Berry, Sparky sired ten known champions with numerous other offspring pointed. He was bred at O. K. Lohman's Orlane Kennels.

A "Red" grandson, sired by Champion Al-Mar's Ala Kazam, won well under Marjorie's handling in the mid-1970s; upon occasion she piloted Sparky's son, the handsome Champion Mikado's Tobias of Apku, to some splendid wins.

ANBARA

Anbara Lhasa Apsos, among the most famous and consistent in America, are owned by Barbara Wood, Cranford, New Jersey. Barbara acquired her first of the breed, a little bitch called Buttons, as a gift from an actress friend who was about to tour with a national road company and felt it unfair to her pet to expect it to lead a life of constant travel. Barbara quickly fell in love with Buttons, the shaggy dog of her dreams.

Also at this point in her life, Barbara began a new career as a stage manager, working on anything to do with theater which in turn would lead her to meet those people who might utilize her talents. Buttons proved to be a perfect canine companion, accompanying her owner on the rounds of whatever she might be doing, then sleeping quietly at her feet if she was working in one place.

Barbara then became a sound effects artist for Sesame Street and at the same time established permanent residency in New York City. It was at that time that her interest in Lhasas started to really develop. Feeling that Buttons would be happier with a canine friend in the household, Barbara purchased a beautiful champion dog. Luck was with her, for although she was not yet sufficiently experienced with the breed to realize it, she had acquired an ideal male for line breeding to Buttons, as both dogs were from the Chig and Hamilton lines.

In due course they were bred. The resulting litter consisted of four boys, a gold and three whites (like their dam). As these puppies matured, Barbara became increasingly in love with the breed; by the time they were fully matured dogs, she was forever hooked on owning Lhasas. The puppy she kept from the first litter became Bo-Jangles C.D., of whom she says, "he has been the light of my life for 13 years."

Attending every match she could find within a reasonable distance of her home area, Barbara came to understand and enjoy dog shows. Handling classes and obedience classes also gave Bo and his mistress experience and expertise. Barbara started making friends in the Lhasa fancy, one of them being Keke Blumberg, who started Barbara on the process of learning what is correct (and what is not) in show-type Lhasas. As she learned more about the dogs, Barbara realized that Bo was not a show prospect, but an absolutely marvelous pet who also did well in obedience, as evidenced by his C.D. degree.

By then Barbara knew that she also wanted a show Lhasa with whom she could win. Sensibly, she returned to the breeder of Bo's sire and purchased a promising bitch from the Ellen Lonigro and Anna Griffing lines. This was the future Champion Rgyal Khetsa-Po, ROM, who went on to produce those marvelous show dogs for which Barbara was eager, and who herself became, as well, Barbara's first champion.

From Khetsa-Po's second litter, sired by the Best in Show Champion Rimar's Rumpelstiltskin, ROM, came group-winning Champion Anbara's Abra-Ka-Dabra, ROM. Barbara describes Abby, who loved shows, as a "breeder's dream come true." From only the second litter Barbara had ever bred, this bitch finished from the Bred-by-Exhibitor class in seven shows, becoming, as well, a Grand Futurity winner. Then with her litter brother, Champion Anbara's Ruffian, Khetsa Po became half of the Top-Winning Lhasa Apso Brace of all time, winning no less than six Best Brace in Show awards and remaining undefeated in group competition on all nine occasions when she and Ruffian were shown as a Brace.

A Lhasa Apso whom Barbara admired enormously was Champion Tabu's King of Hearts, ROM, owned by Steve Campbell.

Marjorie Lewis handling Ch. Lover's Chim Zu Tu to Winners Dog en route to his title back in 1975. By Ch. Donicia's Chim-Zu-Tu El Torro ex Dar-Roc's Ama Lilli Dew Drop.

Ch. Anbara-Rimar The Magic Marker, by Am. Ger. Int. Ch. Anbara Justa Teddy Bear ex Ch. Rimar's The Frivolous Fox, ROM, completed his title with a Group 2nd and a Best in Specialty Show from the classes.

Considering the dog to be the epitome of breed quality, Barbara bred Abby to him, producing the outstanding male, future Champion Anbara's Hobgoblin. "Goblin" became the Top Lhasa Apso of 1980 and 1981, all systems, and had Bests in Show to his credit.

During the time when Goblin was maturing, Steve placed a bitch, Foxy, with Barbara. The dog seemed of an unusually timid nature and Steve felt that if she became accustomed to city life, this obstacle would be overcome. Foxy was a daughter of "Rumpy's" litter sister, Champion Rimar's Penny Candy, and was sired by a King son, Best-in-Show–winning Champion Rimar's J. G. King Richard. Barbara's efforts were repaid when Foxy became a champion and later the dam of Anbara-Rimar's Footloose Fox.

Although Barbara bred a few dog champions in her early litters, she had placed them as pets upon completion of their titles. Thus after five years of breeding, she had only the one stud dog, Goblin, to whom Foxy was bred. Anxious to again breed Goblin's dam, Abby, Barbara thought about locating a stud for her who would strengthen those areas in which she felt her own stock was lacking. On the advice of Marianne Nixon, whom Barbara had met when the former judged the Midwest Futurity in Cincinnati and who had become a good friend, it was decided to breed Abby to an outcross, the group-winning American Best in Show and Canadian Champion San Jo's Raaga Looki Mei, ROM, who produced Champion Anbara Justa Teddy Bear and Champion San Jo Anbara Cuddle Bug, ROM. The value of this breeding is eloquently proven by the fact that Teddy Bear was bred back into the original Anbara line, producing the widely admired Best in Show Champion Anbara-Rimar Grin 'N Bear It, ROM, and Best in Specialty Show winner Champion Anbara-Rimar The Magic Marker. "Cuddles," bred to her brother, affirmed the success of her breeding when she produced two champions. The next generation to both lines produced two Grand Futurity winners.

Group-winning American and Canadian Champion Anbara's Abra-Ka-Dabra, ROM, most of whose accomplishments we have already discussed, deserves additional credit for winning Anbara's first Non-Sporting Group on the day that she also won their first Best of Breed. It was she who, bred to Champion Tabu's King of Hearts, ROM, gave Barbara her great Champion Anbara's Hobgoblin. Handled by his mistress to his championship, he then embarked on the career which brought him to Top Lhasa of 1980 and 1981 under the handling of Jean Lade and Betty Jo Bowman.

Best-in-Show–winning Champion Anbara-Rimar Grin 'N Bear It swept through to an exciting show career under the handling of Doug Holloway for Dr. and Mrs. Thomas Weil, and was in the top five Lhasas for 1982. As a producer, he has sired five champions, a C.D., and some six other dogs who are on the way to their titles. Among his progeny is the 1983 Region 2 Grand Futurity winner, Anbara San-Jo Scal-A-Wag, co-owned by Barbara and Rita Holloway.

Barbara adds the following comment to her kennel story: "Part of the fascination that keeps this complex dog game alive are the dreams and fantasies of breeding that quality dog who will take you to the top at the end of the dog show day. When it happens, there is no way to describe the thrill and pride of having achieved that dream. Best-in-Show–winning Champion Anbara-Rimar Mary Puppins (by Best in Show Champion S. J. W. Waffle Stomper, ROM, ex Champion Anbara-Rimar's Footloose Fox, ROM) became my partner in that dream, and is the culmination of 12 years of breeding. This typey little bitch possesses those qualities that enabled her to command attention at all levels of competition. She was always breeder-owner-handled by me, and has to her credit an all-breed Best in Show, five Specialty Bests of Breed, and was the top-winning breeder-owner-handled Lhasa Apso in 1984. She is now approaching motherhood with the same enthusiasm she exhibited in the show ring."

Another dog in whom Barbara takes particular pride is Champion Anbara Rimar Raisin' A Ruckus, by Best in Specialty Show Champion San-Jo's Rusty Nail ex Champion Anbara-Rimar's Footloose Fox, ROM. Barbara made him a champion undefeated in three Specialty Shows, including that of the National Specialty (American Lhasa Apso Club) in the 9-12 month Puppy Dog class. She looks for him to develop into an outstanding special.

Anbara breeds on a very limited basis, producing only a litter or two each year. Although the challenge to produce beautiful show dogs is still exciting to Barbara Wood, judging has started to pull her in another direction. Having bred and owned 38 champions, Barbara finds that judging is adding another dimension to the enjoyment and sport of purebred dogs and hopes it will prove equally rewarding in years to come.

ARKAY

Arkay Lhasa Apsos, established in Detroit, Michigan in 1980, are the result of Bill and Becki Kraus's involvement with the breed. From the beginning the Krauses realized that because of a shortage of space, it was necessary to limit their breeding program and also to start with the best foundation stock that they could find.

Following these guidelines, they have succeeded in producing at least one champion from each litter they have bred.

Arkay Lhasas are a combination of the Gunga Din English line and the Everglo-Hamilton line. Bill and Becki try to breed for an elegant style of Lhasa with a free-floating movement, comprised of equal reach and drive. To quote them, "We are most indebted to Gloria Fowler (Everglo) and Winifred Graye (Joymarc) for helping to instill these qualities in our line."

Arkay has been fortunate in acquiring some outstanding Lhasa Apsos on which to develop their breeding program. These dogs include the Krauses' first Lhasa bitch, Joymarc's Lai Dieh Kai of Arkay, as well as their first show quality bitch who became multi-Group–winning American and Canadian Champion Joymarc's Arkay Terra Cotta. Terra Cotta, bred by Winifred Graye, was born in January 1979, by On-Ba Lho-Bho O'Joymarc (sire of nine champions) ex Joymarc's Casaba. She completed her Canadian championship with a Group First from the classes, her American championship with three majors. She is now a multiple group winner and placer in both the United States and Canada.

Champion Everglo Arkay Paper Lion, born June 1979, is by Everglo Copper Carol ex Everglo Megan and was bred by Gloria D. Fowler, Bakersfield, California. This silver and cream was a Group winner from the Open class for his second major. He is the sire and grandsire of specialty-winning and group-winning Lhasas. From his first litter, ex Lai Dieh Kai, Paper Lion sired American and Canadian Champion Arkay Lai Dieh Jane, a specialty winner. When Jane was bred to Champion Everglo Ku Su, their litter produced three puppies who were pointed from the Puppy classes, as well as a Canadian Champion and group winner, Arkay Tsuro the Energizer, who finished at seven months old.

Recently the Krauses have moved primarily in the direction of exhibiting Lhasas, with their own breeding program becoming somewhat of a sideline. In 1982 a Lhasa was sent to them to be shown in whom they were most fortunate to eventually acquire co-ownership. This dog, American and Canadian Champion Nexus Lam Kam Chin (called Casper), enjoyed a tremendously successful United States show career, which culminated with winning Best of Breed at the 1985 American Lhasa Apso Club National Specialty. Born in September 1979, he is a son of Canadian Champion Innsbrook's Kha Zas ex Canadian Champion Orlane's Topaz; was bred by Anthony and Gerri Viklicky, Islington, Ontario; and co-owned with the Krauses, by Lillian K. Woods of Ontario. Interestingly, he was the only puppy sold from the only litter the Viklickys ever bred.

Casper completed his Canadian Championship in 1981 and his American Championship in 1982 on the highly competitive Florida Circuit. At Westminster in 1982, following his Florida triumphs, Casper was moved up from the Open class to specials, in which he was awarded Best of Breed. He won his second major back in November 1981 at the Oakland County Kennel Club, Detroit, by taking Group First from the classes. He is the only Canadian Lhasa to win an American all-breed Best in Show and the ALAC roving National Specialty. His combined show record in the United States and Canada includes approximately 130 Best of Breed, 35 Group Firsts, and numerous other placements.

Another Lhasa which Becki and Bill have been fortunate in acquiring is American and Canadian Champion Sharil Patent Pending, a pure Hamilton line male whom they easily finished in both countries and who is now just beginning a specials career in both the States and Canada. This dog was born in November 1981 by Ocon Joymarc's Daredevil ex Everglo Mary Mary and bred by Cherlynn Jozwick, who is now co-owner with Becki Kraus. A grandson of multi-Best-in-Show–winning Champion On-Ba Khabhul Khan of Sharbo, Patent Pending is a multiple Best of Breed and group placer from the Open classes. He is the sire of four champions, including the 1984 Midwest Grand Futurity winner, Champion Dan-Ba Sharil Natural High.

A promising young Lhasa, born in January 1985, is group-winning Canadian Champion Arkay Tsuro the Energizer, by Champion Everglo Ku Su ex American and Canadian Champion Arkay Lai Dieh Jane (daughter of Paper Lion and Lay Dieh Kai). Owned by Roger and Susan Hild, this young golden dog is handled by Susan and Bill Kraus. A Canadian Champion in four

Group winning Can. Ch. Arkay Tsuro The Energizer, age eight months, winning Best Puppy in Breed at the October 1984 Lhasa Apso Club of Ontario Specialty under judge Stella Luftus. Handled by Bill Kraus; bred by Bill and Becky Kraus; owned by Susan and Roger Huld, Bowmanville, Ontario, Canada. "Ricky" is the son of Am. and Can. Ch. Arkay Lai-Dieh-Jane and the grandson of Group winning Am. Ch. Everglo Arkay Paper Lion.

Ch. Art-Est Genteel Gizmo, born September 1981 by Best in Show winning Ch. Anbara's Hobgoblin, ROM, ex Ch. Art-Est She-Ma, ROM, bred and owned by Esther DeFalcis, is the foundation stud dog at Art-Est Kennels. Handled by Miss Lani Howell, he gained his championship in eight weeks of showing, winning six shows, five of them consecutively.

shows at age seven months, he was Best of Breed Puppy at the Lhasa Apso Club of Ontario Specialty in 1985 and a Group winner at ten months of age.

ART-EST

Art-Est Lhasas Apsos are located in Lawrenceville, Georgia, a suburb east of Atlanta. The kennel is owned by Esther and Art DeFalcis, who started out—as do so many others—with the purchase of a pet prior to being bitten by the "dog show bug." Since Esther did not have much luck trying to locate and purcase a nice, show-quality Lhasa at an affordable price without a lot of strings attached, she decided to get a brood bitch and establish her own line of homebred champions.

At a meeting of the Lhasa Apso Society of Atlanta, Esther became acquainted with Gene Poss, who was willing to let her have a three-year-old brood bitch. Three months later, Gene's Flaming Mame was bred to Best-in-Show–winning Champion Qua-La-Ti's Makara. That union produced a litter of seven puppies, two of which are Champion Art-Est Technics and Champion Art-Est She Ma.

Champion Art-Est She Ma, ROM, was pointed before she was a year old, and, upon completion of her championship, was bred to the famous Champion Tabu's King of Hearts, ROM. Their mating produced six puppies: Champion Art-Est King of the Road, Champion Art-Est Shin-Ko, Champion Gene's Victor of Art-Est, Champion Gene's Han-som of Art-Est, champion-producing Art-Est Lotz of Pizazz, and South American Best in Show winner Art-Est Takashi King.

She-Ma's next litter was sired by Best-in-Show–winning Champion Anbara's Hobgoblin. This time she produced Champion Art-Est Genteel Gizmo and Champion Art-Est Sher Kahn.

Then bred to Champion Mor-Knoll Chok's Grand Slam, ROM, She-Ma produced group-winning (from the Open class) Champion Art-Est Most Valuable Player.

With beginner's luck like this, Art-Est hopes to continue to produce more champion quality Lhasa Apsos with the sweetest temperaments and showiest attitudes around!

She-Ma is descended from some very outstanding lines. Her sire, Best-in-Show–winning Champion Qua-La-Ti's Makara, ROM, is a son of Champion Ruffway T'ang Chu, ROM (Champion Reiniet's Royal Chanticleer—Champion Ruffway Kham Chung) ex Champion Tiffany's Yolanda La-Tsu (Best-in-Show–winning Champion Barcon's The Avenger ex Champion Tiffany's Tami La). Her dam, Gene's Flaming Mame, is a granddaughter of Champion Gene's Adak; Champion Gserbo, Champion Dunkleha-ven Ama Lil-Boi, and Champion Kamba Bombo of Gar-Ten are among her great-grandparents. The good judgment of Art and Es-ther DeFalcis in breeding this bitch to King of Hearts, Hobgob-lin, and Grand Slam confirms the fact that a quality bitch is a new kennel's greatest asset, and that breeding her to top quality stud dogs from good-producing bloodlines is the best way to go in es-tablishing a strong line of one's own.

BARJO

Barjo Lhasa Apsos at Schaumberg, Illinois, belong to Barbara Jo Lipsky, a lady who has been admirably successful as a breeder-owner-exhibitor.

Among the stars from this kennel one finds Champion Brandy's Singtuk of Gold, known to friends as "Tuk," who has enjoyed an excellent show career which has included notable Best of Breed and group placements.

Tuk is a son of American and Canadian Champion Tiffany's Gold Cadillac (by Sakya Me and My Shadow, son of Best-in-Show–winning Champion Everglo's Spark of Gold, ROM, and American and Canadian Champion Sakya Mila, ROM, a daughter of Champion Orlane's Dulmo, ROM). Tuk's dam is B and B Brandy Mine, a great-granddaughter of Best-in-Show–winning Champion Tibet of Cornwallis, ROM.

Along with his accomplishments in the show ring, Tuk has dis-tinguished himself as a valuable stud dog as well; a point proven in his handsome son, Champion Barjo's Excalibur, or "Timmy." Born on December 1, 1983, Timmy was the result of a union be-tween Tuk and Barbara Jo's noted winning bitch, Champion Qua-La-Ti's Max-Min's Mol-Le-Qui, ROM. The latter is a daughter of Best-in-Show–winning Champion Tiffany's Qua-La-Ti, ROM, ex Champion Haji's Liberated Lady-Ki-Sulo, ROM, and a de-scendant of a star-studded pedigree.

The same breeding combination which produced Timmy also had produced, a year earlier, Champion Barjo's Chin Te of Max-Min, or "Wags," also an admired winner.

Ch. Brandy's Singtuck of Gold in an informal pose. Bred, owned and handled by Barbara Jo Lipsky, Barjo Lhasa Apsos.

Ch. Barker's Sugar Lace, ROM, completing title owner-handled at Somerset Hills K.C., September, 1981. Sired by multiple Best in Show winning Ch. Potala Keke's Candy Bar ex Ch. Potala Keke's Kind-A-Krimson. Bred and owned by Drs. Randolph and Sandra Barker.

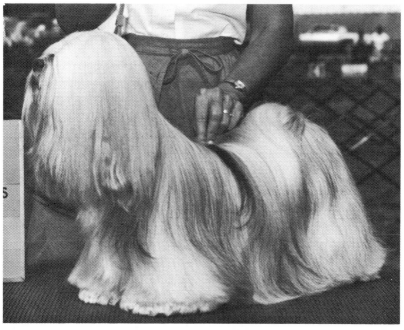

BARKER'S

Drs. Randolph and Sandra Barker of Charleston, West Virginia, began their small kennel with a bitch from Keke Blumberg's Potala Kennels, Champion Potala Keke's Kind-A-Krimson. A line breeding to multi-Best-in-Show–winning Champion Potala Keke's Candy Bar produced Champion Barker's Sugar Lace, who has been the foundation bitch for Barker Lhasa Apsos. The Barkers breed their dogs selectively and limitedly, but have been very successful in combining the Potala lines with Joan Kendall's Orlane dogs. Champion Barker's Sugar Lace, ROM, was bred twice. Her first breeding, to American and English Champion Orlane's Intrepid, ROM, produced three pups, two of which became the Barker's first homebred champions. These littermates won both the 12-18 month classes at the 1983 Lhasa Apso Club of America Eastern Futurity as they matured to become Champion Barker's Guilty As Charged and Champion Barker's Capital Offense.

The second breeding of Sugar Lace was to another Orlane dog, English import Saxonsprings' Earle, an Intrepid son. This time she produced Champion Barker's Sugar Coated, a multiple breed winner from the classes and winner of the 12-18 month bitch class at the 1985 ALAC Midwest Futurity, thus carrying on in the family tradition. Littermate Barker's Sheer Elegance is nearing her championship.

Champion Barker's Capital Offense was bred to Dorothy Sweeney's Champion Dorjon's Champagne Edition, ROM, a dog going back to Orlane and Potala lines. This breeding produced Champion Barker's A.W.O.L. O'Babs and Barker's Crime of Passion, a multiple group-placing bitch who is close to championship.

In their nine years of breeding and showing, the Barkers have bred only four litters, finishing six champions primarily owner-handled, with three more pointed and soon to finish.

BEL-AIR

Bel-Air Lhasa Apsos are widely known for Lhasas of outstanding quality. Their owner, Mrs. Lorraine R. Cole of Grain Valley, Missouri, has credit due her for a successful breeding program.

The original Lhasas of Bel-Air combined the Hamilton and Miradel bloodlines. To that lineage have been added the lines of

Best-in-Show–winning Champion Orlane's Be Sparky of Al Mar, introduced through Sparky's handsome son, Champion Mikado's Tobias of Apku.

Mrs. Cole's foundation stud dog was Champion Bel Air's El Toro Romeo, by Champion Zizun El Toro ex Beck's Parti Doll. Romeo has sired at least six champions, including the also extremely admired and well-known Champion Donicia's Chim Zu El Torro, a sire of considerable prestige himself, who was a source of pride and pleasure to his owner, the late Pat Stewart. Romeo's progeny also includes Champion Bel-Air's Kee Kee Dee, an owner-handled group winner and the dam of two sons who are champion producers.

It is interesting to note that Joyce Hadden's multi-group winner and Best of Breed at Westminster in 1981, Champion Cameo's Khor-Ke San O'Honey Dew is one of Chim Zu's sons and thus a grandson of Romeo.

Mrs. Cole has numerous fine Lhasas who are close to the title. Her daughter, Sherri Baker, is also a breeder-exhibitor of Lhasas.

BHE JEI

Bhe Jei Lhasa Apsos at Menlo Park, California, started in the early 1980s when owner Barbara J. Ling became involved with this breed. Her first champion, a homebred, was a multiple group winner who received one of these awards while still in the classes. He is Champion Bhe Jei Beau Jolais, a dog of the lovely, deep red color so greatly admired but seldom seen nowadays. His littermate, Bhe Jei's Dom Perignon, also a truly lovely dog, needs just a point to finish, which is true as well of Bhe Jei's Cleo-Patia (a bitch) and Bhe Jei's Ko Koa of Morgas, another bitch.

All four, from Na-Tasha Ling III, are a mixture of bloodlines, principally Orlane and Hamilton.

In 1985, Barbara became interested in breeding pure Hamilton lines. For this purpose she acquired several dogs from Sharon Rouse-Bryant, noted for Hamilton (and Sharbo) lines. Sharon is now no longer breeding, and Barbara is delighted at having been chosen to continue with some of her dogs.

Ch. Mikado's Tobias of Apku, son of Best in Show winning Orlane's Be Sparky of Al-Mar ex Tasha Gae Lady, is an important stud dog belonging to Mrs. Lorraine R. Cole.

Ch. Billie's Follie Ezekiel, by Sharbil My Boi O'Dolsa ex Chiz Ari Billie's Follie Belle, ROM, ranked No. 7 Lhasa Apso in 1983. Bred and owned by Billie A. and Dr. Samuel L. Shaver. He is shown making one of his many wins.

Barbara has done quite well with her Hamilton lines, especially so when one considers that they were puppies when shown and one of them was a brood bitch.

Sharbo Bhe-Jei's T'Summer Wine was born in December 1984. She won a four-point major from the 9-12 month puppy class at age nine months at the Lhasa Apso Club of Northern California Specialty. Many of the oldtimers in the breed who have seen Summer have been very enthusiastic about her, so hopes are high for her future.

Sharbo Tyngso Sirius of Bhe Jei, a littermate of Summer, is also pointed. Sharbo Topaz of Bhe Jei is expecting her first pure Hamilton litter and will be brought out following her maternal duties.

BILLIE'S FOLLIE

Billie's Follie Lhasa Apsos at Charlotte, North Carolina, are owned by Billie A. and Samuel L. Shaver, M.D., Ph.D.

Their first Lhasa was obtained in 1973 by Billie as a surprise for Sam, who did not really fancy dogs. After living with Khalif, a pet, for three months, Sam himself purchased a bitch, Shana, who was also a pet. The Shavers became equally involved with the Lhasas, and when Khalif died at age seven years, both parties decided to buy no more dogs because of their total involvement and devotion to their first pets.

Within two months, however, they had obtained four show Lhasas, two of which finished their championships, and one becoming a Top Producing bitch.

The Shavers remark that they are forever grateful to Mattie Chizever who entrusted to their care the two parti-color bitches, Chiz Ari Billie's Follie Bella, ROM, and Champion Chiz Ari Billie's Follie Doll. The former is a splendid producer, the latter an excellent show dog.

The Shavers next purchased two other specials Lhasas, multiple group-winning Champion Sharbil My Boi O'Dolan and multiple Best in Show Champion Shi Sedo's Moli. Following her show career, Moli was returned to her breeder, Sandy Nyberg (who retained co-ownership with the Shavers).

Bella was bred to Champion Sharbil My Boi O'Dolsa, producing the Shavers first two homebred champions, Billie's Follie

Ezekiel and Billie's Follie Heidi. Bella was next bred to Sharon Russett's Champion Sharbil Dolsa Fleetfoot Mac, producing two more champions, Billie's Follie Triple Crown and multiple Best-in-Show–winning Champion Billie's Follie Preakness. "P. K.," as Preakness is called, is still going strong in the specials ring. Her owners tell me that at less than three years of age, she held the most records for Lhasa bitches of any Lhasa bitch in history. She has won 32 groups in only 16 months of showing, Bests in Show, and holds a great many additional group placements.

Billie's Follie specializes in parti-color Lhasa Apsos.

BRYNWOOD

Brynwood Lhasa Apsos, owned by Denise and Anne Olejniczak at Loves Park, Illinois, have been in existence since 1983. Denise and Anne first started showing in December 1983 with a young homebred puppy who, unfortunately, did not turn out to be of show quality.

They then purchased (in January 1984) their first show prospect, an eight-month-old dog who became Champion Jolee's Got To Be Lucky. He finished his title in May 1985, just ten days short of his second birthday.

The other show dogs at this kennel are Jolee's Phanton of Brynwood (11 points), Jolee's Basic Black (13 points), and Jolee's A Touch of Class (4 points). Denise and Anne have not, as yet, done any active breeding because they are anxious to finish both of their bitches first.

Champion Jolee's Got To Be Lucky is by Best-in-Show–winning Champion Orlane's Span-Kieh, C.D., ROM, ex Saxonsprings Carisma. He was born in May 1983 and bred by Jolene Cazzola. Being their very first champion, and owner-handled most of his points (except for one weekend with Patricia Martella piloting him to back-to-back majors), Denise and Anne take very special pride in this lovely dog. He has had Best of Breed wins from the classes en route to his title, and many Junior Showmanship awards with Anne.

Jolee's Basic Black, born in November 1983, is by Champion Jolee's Spike Jones ex Jolee's Witchy Woman. She, too, was bred by Jolene Cazzola, and is the first Spike Jones offspring to be pointed. Only a major is lacking to finish her championship.

Jolee's Phantom of Brynwood is by Champion Kikyru Quentan

Jolee's Basic Black shown by owner-handler Denise Olejniczak for herself and co-owner Jolene Cazzola.

Bhe-Jei's Don Perignon, by Best in Show winning Ch. Sho-Tru's The Main Event ex Na-Tasha Ling III, taking Best of Winners at age nine months from the Puppy Class, Sacramento 1983. Bred, owned and handled by Bobbie Ling.

Tzu ex Saxonsprings Carisma, again bred by Jolene Cazzola. At 16 months of age, he needed only a major to finish, having acquired nine of his points from the Puppy class (including an owner-handled major). His outstanding temperament and showmanship have made him a splendid dog for his co-owner Anne Olejniczak to work with in Junior Showmanship.

CHEN

Chen Lhasa Apsos, owned by Mrs. Patricia Chenoweth of Saratoga, California, have been an extremely successful and dominant force in the breed.

It was back in 1961 that the first of the Chenoweth Lhasas, Champion Chen Makalu Nor of Dzunger, completed his title. From then, through the years of its activity, the Chen Kennel was the home of a whole series of successful winners, perhaps crowned by glorious little Champion Chen Korum Ti, a fourth generation homebred, who took the country by storm, coast-to-coast, during his exciting career. "Kori" sired 24 champions, surely leaving an impressive mark on the breed.

Born in October 1967 and co-bred by Francis Harwell and Mrs. Chenoweth, Kori was a son of Champion Chen Nyun-Ti ex Champion Chen Karakorum. He was one of 21 champions sired by Nyun-Ti, a dog in whom Pat Chenoweth also took special pride.

This kennel was also the home of Champion Chen Krisna Nor, ROM, another who sired 21 champions. Among the bitches, Champion Chen Krisna Tsoma Nor, ROM, produced five champions; Chen Himalayan Hanah Nor, ROM, produced four.

Pat Chenoweth had, at one time in the early 1970s, seventeen dogs at home, including three who were retired, ten champions, and four others (among them three champions) co-owned with her mother.

A tragic fire destroyed Mrs. Chenoweth's home and some of her dogs several years back. It was a heartbreaking experience which brought deep sadness to Lhasa fanciers and to dog lovers everywhere.

CHIZARI

ChizAri Lhasas Apsos were established in 1969 by Madeline P.

Durholz (formerly Chizever) and her daughter Joanne P. Baker. ChizAri's route to success started in the obedience ring with Chiz Ari Kheley, C.D.

Shortly thereafter, ChizAri acquired five-month-old "Sheli," a double Sparky grandson, and "Winnie," a bitch bred from the Hamilton line, both from Ellen Lonigro of Kinderland Lhasas. Madeline and Joanne thereupon commenced on months of blood, sweat, and tears, never dreaming that multiple Best-in-Show–winning Champion Little Fir's Shel Ari of Chiz, ROM***, sire of 17 American Champions, and Kinderland's Winne of Chiz, ROM*, would be the results of their efforts when their puppies became grown Lhasas. (Note: In Lhasa pedigrees one frequently notes one or more asterisks [*] following the name of a dog. These indicate the number of champions produced by that dog or bitch.)

Their hard work and training continued to be rewarding. In 1976 Joanne made an exciting win with Bandit, one of their Lhasas, when she piloted him to the first Best Puppy in Lhasa Apso Specialty Show ever awarded in the United States. In 1977 she earned her place as the American Lhasa Apso Club's Top Junior Handler. Joanne's victories climaxed in 1979 when she handled "Shelli" to two Bests in Show, and in 1980 handled Champion Chiz Ari Autumn to the American Lhasa Apso Club's Eastern Grand Futurity award.

Since ChizAri's activities began with obedience, it is easy to understand that the kennel's highest priority in its breeding program is fine temperament without sacrificing type, structure, soundness, and movement.

Madeline and Joanne have bred 20 Lhasa champions, including Best in Show champion Chiz Ari Wellington Shofar, ROM*.

ChizAri became a registered kennel prefix with the American Kennel Club in 1978. The kennel was awarded the American Lhasa Apso Club's coveted Register of Merit Breeder Award in 1980. It's crowning achievement came in 1985 when Champion Chiz Ari Sehilot, ROM*****, became the Top-Producing Lhasa Apso female in the world, with 16 American champions to her credit, and several more of her progeny still being exhibited, having already gained their major points.

ChizAri Kennels, located in Westminster, Maryland, is now into its sixth generation of homebred Lhasa Apsos of outstanding type and quality.

DANREW

Danrew Kennels, although new to Lhasa Apsos, actually belong to a couple who are far from new in dogs, Enid and Andrew Londis, of Montgomery, New York.

Enid recently arrived here from London, England, where she was a breeder of Corgis and Irish Setters.

The aim of Danrew is to breed for sound and typey dogs with outgoing, happy personalities.

The foundation Lhasas at Danrew are Talimer Ja-Ma Just In Time, Talimer Danrew Gee Whiz, Talimer Second Time Around, and Ja-Ma Danrew Cadbury Bar.

The first litter at Danrew, from of Champion Potala Keke's Candy Bar's daughter and sired by Ja-Ma's Infra Red, is now on the ground.

DONICIA

Donicia Lhasa Apsos at Kansas City, Missouri, were owned by the late Pat Stewart and her husband, Don Stewart. The kennel came into being in the early 1970s when the Stewarts started out by purchasing a pet puppy who then died, leaving them with a large vet bill and empty hearts.

With fierce determination not to make a similar mistake again, the Stewarts set about finding a replacement. And what a replacement it turned out to be! Purchased from Lorraine R. Cole, Bel Air Kennels, and bred by Kenneth Sharpton, Cameo Acres Lhasas, that replacement dog grew up to become Champion Chim Zu El Torro, foundation stud for Donicia's Lhasas.

Bought actually as a pet, Chim soon captured his owners' hearts completely. Having been told of Chim's quality when they made the purchase, Pat, of course, bragged of her beloved Chim's royal ancestry. It wasn't too long before someone made the mistake of telling the Stewarts that Chim "didn't look as though he was all that great," which set Pat off to prove that person wrong. This she did quite eloquently.

Seeking out the assistance of professional handler Marjorie Lewis, Pat quickly finished Chim to his title. She repeatedly stated that "to the day he finished, her heart would be in her throat every time he won," the reason being that one of the very first tricks Chim had learned to perform as a puppy was to play dead when pointed to!

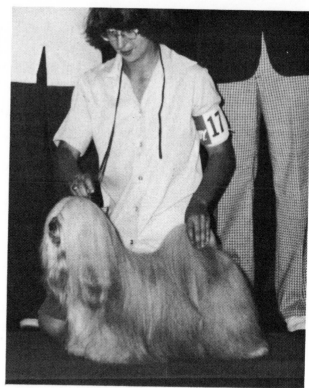

Multi-Best in Show winning Ch. Little Fir's Shez Ari of Chiz, ROM, by Group winning Champion Ruffway Marpo, ROM, ex Champion Orlane's Meling of Ruffway, was bred by David Van Kline. Owned by Madeline P. Durholz and Joanne P. Baker.

Left, Talimer Danmere Gee Whiz, handled by Enid Landis, co-owner, Winners and Best of Winners at Monticello K.C. in March 1985 under judge Barbara Wood, Anbara Lhasas. *Right,* Talimer Second Time Around, handled by Janet Whitman, taking reserve. Both Lhasas owned by Enid and Andrew Landis.

Ch. Donica's Chim Zu El Torro, by Bel Air's El Toro Romeo ex Golden Rule's Mel-O-Ne O'Everglo. The sire of 11 champions, including Ch. Cameo's Khor-ke-San O'Honey Dew who was Best of Breed at Westminster in 1981. Owned by Pat and Don Stewart, Donicia's Lhasa Apsos.

Ch. Gold N Kismet winning Best of Breed at Mohawk Valley in 1979. Handled by Bonnie Sellner for owner Virginia H. Snare.

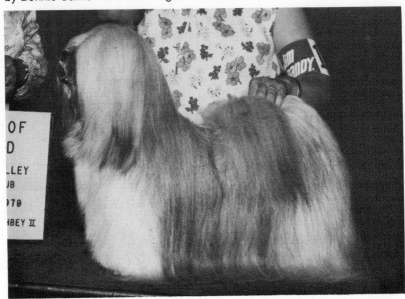

Not being all that fond of the show ring, Chim was not campaigned extensively. Within a short time, his potential as a sire became obvious, and he left his mark on the breed with eleven champions, four of them homebred.

Pat, having by then been bitten by the dog show bug, set about finding a suitable bitch who would go with Chim and whom she could show as well. So into her life came Champion Donicia's Tai Suki Lu, who was purchased from Janet Whitman of Ja-Ma Lhasas. Pat was pleased at having acquired Suki, as she was the only bitch in the litter and it was necessary to do some real negotiating in order to get her.

Finishing her championship quickly with back-to-back, five-point majors, Suki produced as well four champions for Pat and Don. They are Champion Shi Shedo Soo Lai Mon, Champion Donicia's Rhe-Ghan San, Champion Donicia's Kha-Sha Kieh, and Champion Donicia's Ja-Ma Scirrocco. Three of these finished almost entirely owner-handled, as Pat was superb in the ring and finished Lhasas for others as well as her own.

Pat Stewart was the mainstay of Donicia's Lhasas, with a lot of help and support from Don. She brought a great deal of knowledge, showmanship, and wisdom to many in the fancy. She was a breeder of Lhasa Apsos in the truest sense of the word, continually striving for improvement. She is now gone, but her passing will not be forgotten by the Lhasa world, as her beloved dogs continue to make their mark on the breed.

GOLD N LHASAS

Gold N Lhasa Apsos, owned by Virginia H. Snare, are situated at Voorheesville, New York.

Virginia completed title on her very beautiful bitch, Champion Norbulingka's Gold N Glory, who was campaigned for her during 1985 mostly by professional handler Bonnie Sellner.

Gold N Glory is a truly lovely bitch carrying the finest bloodlines with which to enhance the breeding program at this kennel. She is sired by Champion Potala Keke's Golden Gatsby ex Norbulingka Falluca, was born in 1981 and bred by Phyllis Marcy. Her puppies are to be looked forward to with keenest anticipation.

Gold N Glory is the latest of the champions to finish from this kennel, but she has been preceded by some dogs of beauty and excellence over recent years.

When Virginia Snare wanted a new breed back in the 1970s, her specifications were not easy! She was looking for a dog with the intelligence of a German Shepherd Dog, good temperament, and outgoing personality. She was told, "Then you must get a Lhasa Apso." At this point, Virginia had not the slightest idea even of what a Lhasa looked like, nor was she experienced with the coated breeds. But she went looking at them anyway, and purchased Gold N Silver Patch, a light red with a white patch on her shoulder. Her breeder had wanted to call her "Pumpkin Patch" as she was at the time the color of a ripe pumpkin, but Virginia had to get fancy, as she says, and that is how the kennel name "Gold N" came about.

"Patch" was to be allowed one litter, but Virginia did not feel herself to be sufficiently well informed on the subject and chose to get her evaluated first and then breed her to the best available and most suitable stud. It was then that she had the tremendous good fortune of meeting Bob Sharpe, to whom she remains eternally grateful.

Bob examined Patch and her pedigree, and said "We'll breed her to Kori," which is how she came to have a litter by Best-in-Show–winning Champion Chen Korum Ti. When the pups were six weeks old, Bob said "Don't sell that one," and so Virginia didn't. "That one" grew up to become Champion Gold N Kismet, one of the top Lhasa bitches in the country with very little showing.

While Kismet was still growing up, Bob offered Virginia his share of Champion Krisna Hylan Krissie, whom he then co-owned with Wendy Harper. The arrangement worked out well until, as Kismet matured, Virginia realized that she had two top specials competing with each other, which was unfair to both. She was not about to get another handler as Bonnie Sellner handled Gold N Lhasas exclusively (except in case of illness or other emergency), so Krissie was sold to Colin Williams of Nova Scotia, under whose ownership he became one of the Top Canadian Lhasas, finishing his career in 1984 by winning Best in Show at a prestigious Canadian event for veterans only.

Not long after Virginia's acquisition of Krissie, Bonnie Sellner phoned to say "Mrs. Snare, you must get this puppy." The puppy she was referring to was a very elegant daughter of Krissie from a bitch of Bob Sharp's breeding. This one became Gold N Elegance, finished very rapidly, and was bred to Best-in-Show–winning Champion Rimar's J. G. King Richard, producing a super litter of eight. Most, of necessity, were sold as pets. One went to California where she took a Group First after coming out of the classes that same day with a five-point major. One is Gold N Princess Royal whom Mrs. Snare soon hopes to finish. Princess Royal took time out of her show career to raise a litter of five by her uncle, Champion Sharpette's Nip N Tuck (a litter brother to Gold N Elegance). Mrs. Snare's pick of this litter was Gold N Bib N Tucker.

JA-MA

Ja-Ma Lhasa Apsos, ROM, are owned by Janet and Marv Whitman at Spring Valley, New York. This kennel had its beginnings in 1970. Nine years later it became an American Lhasa Apso Club Register of Merit (ROM) kennel by having bred at least ten champions. As of January 1986, the total stood at more than 25 champions bred here.

Ja-Ma Lhasas is a home, not a kennel. The Whitmans feel that this fact is evident by the excellent termperament of their dogs. They have found much success in combining Hamilton and Sparky lines. They strive for quality, not quantity.

Foundation stud dog at Ja-Ma was Multiple Best in Show Champion Arborhill's Rapso-Dieh. He is the winner of seven Bests in Show in the United States and Canada, and is, as well, a Best in Show producer and the sire of over twenty champions. These include Best in Show Champions Arborhill's Rah-Kieh and Ja-Ma's Rah-Bieh of Karlan; American and Canadian Champions Ja-Ma's Rhe-Bel-Len and Ja-Ma's Bohemian Rapso Dieh; plus American Champions M'Lou's Bacchus Kahn, Lee's London Fog, Oro's Bani-Leu, Ja-Ma's Fancee Footwork, Irlee's Shangrelu Cajun Pride, Vir-Lyn's Sasparilla, Tra-Mar Ja-Ma Standing Ovation, Light Up's Chewbacca, Ja-Ma's Kristal Lea of Tammering, Ja-Ma The Wiz, Tra-Mar Beau Coup De Chance, Light Up's Tara of Rho-Mhi, Haltbar's Pepsi Cola, and Ja-Ma's Sun Dance of Rho-Mhi.

Ja-Ma's foundation bitches have been show winners and top producers as well. Champion Joval's Midnight Lace, ROM, is the dam of Best in Show Champion Ja-Ma's Rah-Bieh of Karlan, and the following additional champions: Ja-Ma's Fancee Footwork, Ja-Ma's Kristal Lea of Tammering, Ja-Ma's The Wiz, Ja-Ma's Sundance of Sho-Mhi.

Champion Lifelong's Stolen Sugar, ROM, for her part has produced American and Canadian Champions Ja-Ma's Bohemian Rapso-Dieh and Ja-Ma's Rhe-BelYon, plus Champions Ja-Ma's Mee-Tu of Kai-Bi and Donicia's Tai Suki Lu.

Another excellent producer for the Whitmans has been Champion Ja-Ma's Scarlet of Dolsa Syung.

Among additional champions bred at Ja-Ma are Ja-Ma's Flor-escent, Ja-Ma's Infra Red, Ja-Ma's Joslyn Starbar, Ja-Ma's Scarlet Ribbons, Ja-Ma's Donicia Tatiana, Ja-Ma's A Little Night Music, and the newest addition, Ja-Ma's Peach of a P'Earl, who finished from the Bred-by Exhibitor Class, owner-handled all the way.

The Whitmans strongly believe that the successful future of the Lhasa Apso lies in breeding for correct size, structure, type, and excellent temperament—a dog sound in both body and mind.

JONI

Joni Lhasa Apsos are owned by Joanne Pavlik at Newburgh, New York. This kennel is the home of the famous Best-in-Show–winning American, Bermudian, and Canadian Champion Blahopolo's Norbulingka Ke-Ko, a son of Best-in-Show–winning Champion Everglo's Spark of Gold, ROM, ex Secunda Kye.

Ke-Ko is a multiple Best in Show winner in the United States. A rare and true showman, this gold and white son of Best-in-Show–winning Champion Everglo's Spark of Gold, ROM, ex Secunda Kye has been widely admired for his exceptionally fine movement and is everybody's friend. Not only is he a proven winner, he is reproducing his quality with the result that several of his offspring are pointed and on their way to their titles.

For 1978, Ke-Ko was No. 2 dog, all systems, as printed in the *Lhasa Apso Reporter*. He is now retired, enjoying life at home and at stud.

Then there is the young Champion Ceala's Hustler, by Champion Ceala's Fuzzbuster ex Champion Syung's Ceala Shea Lady,

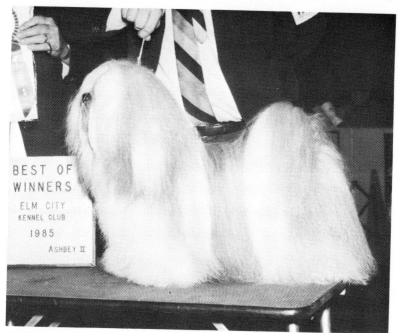

Joni's Ke-Ko Dee is handled by Marc Canter for Joanne Pavlik, Joni Lhasa Apsos. This Lhasa Apso is a son of Best in Show winning Am., Bda. and Can. Ch. Blahopolos Norbulingka Ke-Ko.

Am. and Can. Ch. Ja-Ma's Kristal Lea of Tammering was bred by Janet and Marv Whitman. Owned by Elaine Scharf for whom Dee Sheppard is handling. Winning the breed at Wachusett in 1980.

who started his show career at 12 months of age as the Midwest Grand Futurity winner, completely owner-handled. He won back-to-back majors and finished at the Chicago International with a five-point major, going Best of Opposite Sex over five well-known male specials.

Hustler is now a group-winning champion, and a champion producer with other pointed offspring. He is a sound red-golden male with a fantastic personality, beautiful texture, and easily-cared-for coat. Joanne Pavlik say of him, "he is a joy to love and own." Hustler is being handled as a special by John A. Mohr.

JOYSLYN

Joyslyn Lhasa Apsos are the result of Lynn and Joyce Johanson, David City, Nebraska, having purchased their first Lhasa puppy, a female, shortly after their marriage in 1972. Two months later a second female followed, Joyslyn's Miss Buffy Jo, who was to become their foundation bitch.

From Buffy's first litter came two champions. These were Champion Joyslyn's Raggedy Rebel and American and Canadian Champion Joyslyn's Piece of the Rock. The latter became their first champion, and much of Joyslyn's success can be attributed to his impressive achievements.

The Johansons take pleasure in the breeding and showing of their Lhasas. Each breeding is an attempt to improve the quality of the breed. Dogs are bred for correct size, structure, type, movement, and for loving, pleasing dispositions. Joyslyn's foundation lines go back to Champion Everglo's Spark of Gold, especially through Best-in-Show–winning American and Canadian Champion Arborhill's Rapso-Dieh, ROM.

Joyce and Lynn feel that the future of the breed lies in serious newcomers, and they stress the importance of educating novices, whether they be pet owners or potential exhibitors. Joyce's monthly *Dog World* column, which has appeared since 1976, is one such attempt at sharing knowledge. Lynn uses his artistic talents to sculpt Lhasa figurines.

Joyce is a member of the American Lhasa Apso Club.

Joyslyn Riunite, known as "Rio," is a Joyslyn Lhasa who has

the potential to become famous in the world of television viewers. Rio has been chosen to play Alexis's (Joan Collins's) pet dog on the popular *Dynasty* series, where his chief activity is to lie on Alexis's bed and look pretty. Rio was trained by a firm which supplies animals for movie and television appearances.

Rio's vital statistics are: sired by Champion Joslyn's Rachmaninoff ex Champion Joslyn's Elfin Magic O'Jokang. He was sold to Gary Gero who owns Birds and Animals Unlimited, and was trained for his role in the television series by Gwen Johnson.

JU-ELL

Ju-Ell Lhasa Apsos are owned by Julie K. Elliott and are located at Janesville, Wisconsin. Mrs. Elliott, in addition to being a Lhasa breeder and having a grown daughter who shares the interest of the dogs with her, is a full-time college student majoring in psychology and journalism, with the intent of going into the field of animal behavior. She attends the University of Wisconson-Madison. With this interest, her main goal in breeding Lhasas is to breed a dog that is as sound in mind as it is in body, temperament being her top priority. As she puts it, "After all the ribbons are won, and no matter how excellent the conformation is, what it boils down to is the fact that the Lhasa is a companion dog, and we must breed a dog that is a good companion."

Ju-Ell Lhasas are a rather new kennel, Mrs. Elliott having been showing since the late 1970s but only breeding since the early 1980s. She has been extremely conservative in her breeding program, planning for each litter carefully, as she feels that the world has enough dogs and that breeders must be conscious of where the pets that they breed go, rather than just be interested in turning out show dogs.

For her background breedings, Mrs. Elliott has been working with the best of Hamilton-Ruffway lines combined with Joan Kendall's Orlane lines. Toward this end, she had the good fortune in the beginning to obtain a lovely black dog from Shirley Scott as her foundation sire. He is Champion Shyr-Lyz Shan Mar, who is producing beautiful, consistent puppies no matter who is bred to him because he is a brother-sister breeding and linebred out of

Ch. Joyslyn's Rachmaninoff, by Am. and Can. Ch. Joyslyn's Piece of the Rock, ROM, ex Ch. Sinka's Sironna Khan, ROM, completed title at age two years in March 1985. Born in August 1982, he was bred and is owned by Joyce and Lynn Johanson.

Ju-Ell's Pride and Prejudice winning a Group 2nd from the puppy class at 10 months of age. Bred, owned and handled by Julie K. Elliott.

SECOND IN GROUP
BURLINGTON K.C
MAY 19, 1984
PHOTO BY TERI

group-winning Champion Shyr-Lyz Shama Shama and American and Canadian Champion Shyr-Lyz Fabulous Flirt. Mrs. Elliott's foundation bitch is a new champion, having just completed her title with a Group First after having had a short time away from the shows for motherhood. She is Champion Orlane's Golden Girl, by English Best in Show Champion and American Best in Show Champion Orlane's Intrepid and Champion Orlane's Whimsey of Innsbrook.

Julie Elliott and her teenage daughter, Monette Thiele, have finished the following dogs: Champion Shyr-Lyz Shan Mar, Champion Jolee's Ring Around the Collar, Champion Jolee's Jubilee Juell, Champion Jas Phantasia Juell, and Champion Orlando's Golden Girl. Additionally, they only need majors on Juell's Vanity Fair, and one major on Juell's Pride and Prejudice (Golden Girl's first daughter and son, respectively). Vanity Fair has been shown from the Bred-by-Exhibitor class, as has Pride and Prejudice, who already has done some notable winning for so young a dog, having taken breed several times over Best in Show specials and, on one occasion, a Group Second from the Puppy class. Monette's Junior Showmanship dog, Amberwood's Alcheringa (out of Champion Shyr-Lyz Shan Mar) needs just one more point to finish.

Being especially sold on the type, soundness, and style of the Orlane dogs, Mrs. Elliott was recently delighted at being able to acquire another Intrepid daughter, Champion Light Up's Golden Graffitti, bred by Cynthia Klimas, Light Up Lhasas.

KACHINA

Kachina Lhasa Apsos at Sumter, S. Carolina, are owned by Sally Ann Vervaeke-Helf, publisher-editor of *The Lhasa Apso Reporter,* a lady in whose life dogs, one breed or another, have always played an important part. Lhasas, the only breed she now owns, entered her life in 1976. A few litters, perhaps one to three, are bred at Kachina's Place each year. Each breeding is carefully planned and is a part of Sally Ann's overall objective. Her Lhasas must fit the standard in all ways, including height.

Sally Ann writes, "Since I must show on a limited income, I have exhibited only a few of my Lhasas." She has done so with considerable success!

The first show Lhasa at Kachina was American and Canadian Champion Sharpette's Rumpie Dil Dox, Bob Sharpe's pick of the litter with whom he parted when he started judging. "Rumpie" has some very outstanding Lhasas to his credit, including his children: Canadian Champion Kachina Tu Rum-Pala Soyal SM; Canadian Champion Kachina RM Sabu Tecumseh; American and Canadian Champion Kachina RD Tauy-Jones; Canadian Champion Kachina RD Ma-Ra-Wu; Greeter's Son, C.D.; and the pointed Kachina RD Mi-Ha-Pah. His grandchildren include: American, Canadian, and Puerto Rican Champion of America for 1985 Kachina TKP Jim Thorpe TT; Canadian Champion Kachina TKP Poppy Seed; Canadian Champion Kachina Palatala Kambu; and Kachina Palasiva of San (pointed in the United States). Also, there is a great-grandson doing well for the family, Canadian Champion Carho's All The Right Stuff.

Sally Helf takes great pride in the Lhasas bred at Kachina's Place—particularly Tauy, whom she feels to be the epitome of the standard. Unfortunately this lovely dog could not be specialed as he really should have been. He is siring some especially nice puppies, one of whom, Kachina TJA Red Jacket, was retained for finishing.

A Kachina Lhasa who is making his mark is the delightful "Jimmy," American, Canadian, and Puerto Rican Champion of America for 1985, Champion Kachina TKP Jim Thorpe TT. He was sparingly specialed, but has made a major contribution to the breed when selected by Anick Benoit of Har Kala Rachi to visit Belgium. He is being shown elsewhere in Europe and used at stud. Jimmy, too, is a fitting representation of the standard.

Sally Helf comments, "My Lhasas have opened many doors for me, and I have made many friends through them. Because I possess the skill and desire to write, I have written magazine articles. One of my outstanding contributions to the breed was the creation of *Lhasa Lore*, winner of the 1983 Dog Writers Association of America Best Breed Book Award. In late 1984 I had the opportunity to become publisher of *The Lhasa Apso Reporter*, and I thoroughly enjoy it." As one of her readers, I can attest to the excellence of Sally Ann's work, and the very outstanding job she is doing with this magazine!

In the summer of 1984, Sally Ann became co-owner of Chen Kachina Jada-Lu. Since the very tragic fire that destroyed some of Pat Chenoweth's magnificent Chen Lhasas—and her home—in California, some of the survivors have been at Kachina's Place

Am. and Can. Ch. Sharpette's Rumpie Dil Dox finishing title with a 5-point major handled by Jean Lade for Sally Ann Helf, Kachina Lhasa Apsos. Foundation stud at Kachina Kennels.

Ch. Karlee's Golden Bandit, by Ch. Sharpette's Skeetzo ex Am. and Can. Ch. Dee's Sagittarius Girl, was bred by Carol Rose and Dolores Beamon. Born March 1980, pictured winning Best of Breed at Wampanaug K.C. in 1982. Owned by Wesley Rose and John Ioia.

with Sally Ann. Now these two ladies co-own Chen Sha-Rin Mika Nor, and are just starting what should be an exciting show career. Also, Chen Kachina Celeste is co-owned by them, and plans are being made for some future litters.

KAR-LEE

Kar-Lee Lhasa Apsos are owned by Carol and Wesley Rose at Scotia, New York, who started in the breed in the mid-1970s with the lovely American and Canadian Champion Dee's Sagittarius Girl as their foundation bitch and Champion Sharpette's Skeetzo as their foundation dog. Thus their bloodlines go back to such dogs as the great Best in Show winner, Champion Kyi Chu Friar Tuck (Skeetzo is his grandson) and outstanding Lhasas from Everglo, Rondelay, Sharbet, and other leading kennels.

These two foundation Lhasas have produced well for the Roses with such notable offspring as the excellent Champion Kar-Lee's Golden Bandit and Champion Kar-Lee's Tiger Lilly among them.

The Roses have become enthusiastic supporters of the Lhasa breed and it is very obvious that numerous coming champions will be added, as the years go by, to those they have already bred.

KNOLWOOD

Knolwood Lhasa Apsos are at Dunwoody, Georgia, where they are owned by Marion Knowlton. This is the home of two very well-known winners, both of whom seem destined to leave their mark upon the breed.

Best in Show Champion Tom Lee Manchu of Knolwood was bred, as well as being owned, by Marion Knowlton. He is a multiple Best in Show winner and he was No. 2 Lhasa Apso for 1983. As a sire, he is a proven producer of champions. Tom Lee Manchu is by Champion Orlane's Inimitable ex Champion Ruleo's Peppermint Patti.

Marion's other current star is also an Inimitable son (his dam is Innsbrook's Scarlett Lady). He is Champion Innsbrook's Patrician O'Sulan, and while his half brother is the great show star, Patrick has proven himself to be the great producer. Thirteen champions by him have finished by him, with several others major-pointed. But most exciting of all, he is the sire of the stunning Best in Show winner, Champion Sulan's Gregorian Chant, who has been piloted to a top place in the ratings by Emily Gunning.

LAMOC

Lamoc Lhasa Apsos, established in 1978, are owned by Mrs. Elizabeth Faust at New Braunfels, Texas. Several lovely champions have been produced here, blending Hamilton-Sparky lines along with pure Hamilton, and will shortly have its first ROM bitch.

Head man here is the multiple group-winning and multiple specialty winner, Champion Jolee's Spike Jones. A son of Best-in-Show–winning Champion Orlane's Span-Kieh ex Orlane's Goldberry, Spike Jones was bred by Jolene Cazzola and Linda Smith and born in 1981. Handled by Sandra Tremont, his accomplishments include three times Best in Specialty Show, Best of Opposite Sex at the National Specialty in 1984, and No. 1 American Lhasa Apso Club Group Placing dog in 1984.

Champion Hun Nee Glo Sinoi, by Tiffany's Yo Yo La ex Bhran Dhi, headed towards her ROM, is the dam of Champion Lamocs Lei Roi Sung Chu, sired by Champion Qua La Ti's Barracuda Bear; Champion Lamoc's Instant Mischief, sired by Champion Tabu's Hearts Are Trump; and Lamoc's Incantation, who needs only a major to finish, also by Champion Tabu's Hearts Are Trump.

Champion Fanci Gold Sunset, by Royal Crescent Lama Mai Ling ex Miss Poppy, is the dam of Champion Lamoc's Hallmark O'Fanci, sired by Champion Samural Bushido.

Champion Jolee's Windancer is by Champion Ruffway Mashala Chu ex Champion Talisman Jolee's My Dorothy.

Champion Tabu's Hearts Are Trumps is by Champion Tabu's Stars and Stripes ex Champion Tabu's Queen of Hearts.

And, last but not least, Lamoc's On The Town, by Tabu's Heart Throb ex Tabu's Dressed In Sable, is pointed.

MAGESTIC

Magestic Kennels have been breeding Lhasa Apsos on a very small, selective scale since 1969. These Lhasas are owned by Lois M. and Pamela Magette.

Magestic's foundation stock was purchased in the spring of 1968 from Mrs. Dorothy Cohen of Karma Kennels in Las Vegas, whose breeding stock stems from the foundation dogs given to Mr. S. Cutting by the Dalai Lama of Tibet. Mr. Cutting's kennel name was Hamilton Farm (he bred and showed these dogs as Lhasa Ter-

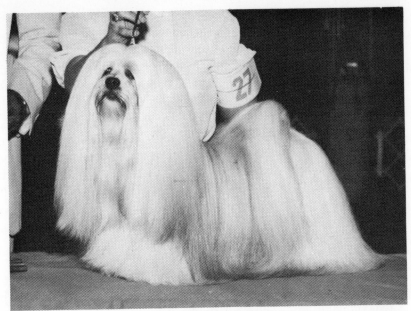

Ch. Jolee's Spike Jones winning Best in Specialty Show at the Lhasa Apso Club of Greater Houston. Elizabeth Faust, owner, Lamoc Lhasa Apsos.

Ch. Karma Skar Cen, by America's Sandar of Pamu ex Hamilton Chang Tru, the first bitch of the breed to her owner's knowledge to have won the Non-Sporting Group in stiff California competition over an entry of 298 Lhasas. She also was Best of Opposite Sex at the first West Coast Specialty supported by the American Lhasa Apso Club. Owned by Magestic Kennels, Lois M. Magette and Pamela Magette.

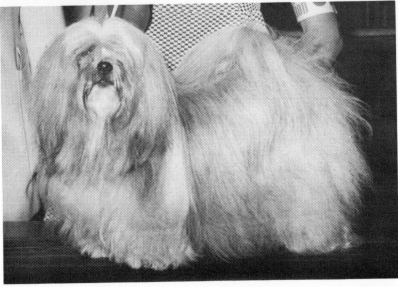

riers while they were relegated to Terrier classification by the American Kennel Club prior to the breed's change of name from Lhasa Terrier to Lhasa Apso, and group from Terrier to Non-Sporting), thus the pure Hamilton designation when referring to this particular pure line of Lhasa Apsos. This line, descended from Hamilton, still reflects the AKC standard for the breed from those times, including narrow skull, correct proportion of muzzle to skull length, and straight front legs. Due to the selective breeding program followed by the Magettes, Magestic Lhasa Apsos also reflect these most desirable qualities. Add to these particular attributes the overall type which Magestic Lhasas are known to represent and you will see a Lhasa that not only fits the Standard for the qualities listed by the AKC, but a Lhasa Apso of pure breeding who will be a wonderful pet, guard dog, and beautiful companion for many years. Lois Magette emphasizes that at Magestic Kennels only *pure* Hamilton bloodlines are used for breeding, based on a very carefully researched background.

All of the Magestic dogs, as well as puppies, live in a home atmosphere and are socialized with the family, assuring wonderful, sweet dispositions. The Magettes show many of their dogs themselves, although they do, upon occasion, have them professionally handled. Lois Magette reminisces about the exciting occasion on which one of their bitches, Champion Karma Skar-Cen, won an early Non-Sporting Group in stiff competition. To the Magettes' knowledge, this was the first time that a Lhasa bitch had been awarded this honor owner-handled in a stiffly competitive group in California (the Non-Sporting entry that day having totaled 298). Skar-Cen also was Best of Opposite Sex at the first West Coast Specialty supported by the American Lhasa Apso Club, this award attained against top dogs from all parts of the country.

Since those days, the Magettes have finished many dogs with the Magestic prefix. They have several American and Canadian champions, as well as their American, Canadian, and Mexican Champion Magestic Gyad Po, a dog who contributed tremendously to the Magestic line.

During more recent years, Magestic has had a top winning bitch, American and Canadian Champion Magestic Shigatse Po Cha Mo. Actively campaigned for less than a year, she made her presence strongly felt in breed competition.

The Magettes' most recent star is American and Canadian

Champion Magestic Po Nya, who finished very quickly in both Canada and the United States.

The Magettes are also proud to note the fact that they had a Top-Producing Bitch in the 1970s, Champion Karma Rustimala, who produced eight champion offspring sired by several different males.

MARLO

Marlo Lhasa Apsos are located in Beverly Hills, California, where they are owned by Lynn Lowy.

Lynn was born and raised in northern New Jersey. In 1958 widowed, she moved with her two children to Los Angeles. She had never owned a dog—neither as a child, nor as an adult—having been frightened by one when a youngster. Not until she was remarried and her children half grown and nagging her, begging her, did she even consider buying a dog. In 1969, she went to visit friends who owned a Lhasa, and promptly fell in love! They all went out and purchased the first Lhasa they could locate, a male named Simba. Lynn was told that he was not show quality. But later, after much experience, she realized that he was a very nice looking dog and could have finished easily. However, Simba remained at home, her favorite, and they lived happily together for 16 years.

A year after acquiring Simba, Lynn got her first pure Hamilton Lhasa, Champion Cordova Tom True, by Karma Kacho ex Champion Karma Sakyi. He finished very quickly and Lynn acquired another pure Hamilton dog, Champion Dolsa Krisna Khorog, by Champion Chen Krisna Nor, ROM, ex Cordova Sin-Sa, ROM. The two dogs did not get along, and Khory was sold. There was a long period of buying and selling dogs, looking for the "right stuff" on which to base her own breeding program.

About this time, Lynn and her husband divorced. Tom Tru was sold. Lynn then found what was to become her foundation bitch, Marlo's Tara of Dolsa, ROM, who is behind every Lhasa she has bred. Tara was a lovely cream bitch by Champion Zijuh Don-Ra Tsamten, ROM, and a little red Everglo bitch, Cameo's Densa Dobra. Tara's full litter brother, a black, International Champion Dolsa Marlo Matador, made breed history in Europe by becoming the Top-Winning Lhasa ever and also by being a Top Producer.

Lynn started to breed on a small scale in 1974, just one or two litters a year, in which fashion she still continues. Tara's dam, Densa, was bred one more time producing one white dog, the group-winning Champion Marlo's Icecream Man O'Rimmon. Icecream Man was used only a few times and produced four champions. Adrienne and Len Ripley co-bred and co-owned this dog and campaigned him on a limited scale. Nearly everything Lynn owns and has bred goes back to these few good dogs.

Lynn has done well for herself as an exhibitor and as a breeder operating on a small scale. She has had all colors—not too many black and some parti-colors—but still likes the golds and red-golds best. Lynn does not like her pedigrees too mixed, feeling that linebreeding is what has made her dogs stand out and really look like the type she admires—enough leg, good neck, beautiful heads with sweet expressions, and exceptional movement. She prefers a more elegant dog, and does not like too much nose or a "down" expression. Most important of all is a happy temperament.

Tara, a very sweet-tempered bitch, produced Champion Marlo's Melanie, Champion Marlo Kyi Chu Artful Dodger, and Champion Marlo's Flim Flam Man.

Champion Marlo's I Love Lucy (ROM-eligible) came from Flim Flam Man by Best in Show Champion Yojimbo Orion (Tara daughter, thus doubling up on Tara). Lucy, a beautiful, red-golden, small, typey bitch, was bred to Champion San Jo Soshome Up, ROM, producing group-winning American and Canadian Champion Marlo Rocky Road; Champion Marlo Mel-O-Dee; multiple Best in Show Japanese Champion Marlo Madame (Top Winning Lhasa in Japan in 1984), and Canadian Champion Marlo Pride and Joy.

Lucy was then bred to her son, Rocky Road, and now has a new champion daughter, Champion Marlo Unexpected Pleasure. Lynn says that particular litter has certainly given her a lot of satisfaction. Marlo Cinnamon Twist, from the same litter, is starting out.

Marlo's other foundation bitch, Champion Marlo's One Of A Kind, ROM, was a single puppy and is a Tara granddaughter from an Icecream Man daughter who was bred to a Hamilton-Abbotsford male, American and Canadian Champion Pawprints Pied Piper, ROM. Pawprints is owned by Jean Kausch.

One Of A Kind was bred to another Hamilton-Abbotsford

male, Champion Suntory Four On The Floor, and produced German Champion Marlo White On White, Champion Marlo Dolsa Coming Out Parti, Champion Marlo Ultrabrite, and the group-placing Champion Marlo Something Else, known as "Spiffy."

Lynn has always home-raised her puppies. She owner-handles them as youngsters, then gives them to professional handlers when they are ready. She took the big step with "Spiffy," finishing her from the Bred-by-Exhibitor class, under Norman Herbel, with Best of Breed. Spiffy now is a multiple Best of Breed winner and is campaigned on a limited basis. Flushed with success, Lynn started owner-handling Rocky Road whom she finished in eight shows with Best of Breed from the classes. Now she owner-handles when time permits, but also uses professional handlers.

Now that they are old enough, Lynn is breeding Lucy's children to Champion Marlo's One Of A Kind's kids with exciting results.

Lynn has several Lhasa "children" in Germany, including German Champion Marlo White on White, Marlo's Ma Cherie, and German Champion Marlo Dolsa Jazzercise.

Altogether Lynn has owned or bred 19 American champions. She has an ROM kennel and is a board member of the American Lhasa Apso Club. In addition, she publishes two dog magazines: *The Bichon Frise Reporter* and *The Great Dane Reporter*.

MIO

Mio Lhasa Apsos, owned by Joan Pettit of Woodmere, New York, began with the purchase of a pet for Joan's daughter in 1968. The family immediately became enchanted with the pet and thought it would be fun to try her out in the show ring. Joan Pettit's mother had shown dogs in England and had often told Joan about her favorite attention-getting call, "Mio," which is how Mio came to be selected for the kennel's name. Much to their disappointment, the Pettits soon learned that their adored family pet was exactly that and not of show quality.

The next acquisition, since by then the Pettits were determined to have some really competitive Lhasas, was their first true show puppy, purchased from Dorothy Cohen of Karma Kennels. This time they were on the right track, for the pup became Champion

This is the Marlo Foundation Bitch, dam of three champions, taking Best Puppy in the Lhasa Apso Club of Southern California Match Show in 1974. Marlo's Tara of Dolsa is owned by Lynn Lowy (handling) and her son Marc Lowy, on the right.

Mio's Dust Buster, by Ch. Mio's Clean Sweep ex Ja Mar's Talimer Tangerine, was handled by Christine Pettit Gates to Winners Dog and Best of Opposite Sex on his first time in the ring at Wilmington K.C. in 1985. Bred by Joan and Burt Pettit.

Karma Kasha. Even before they had finished Karma another purchase was made from Mrs. Cohen, the puppy who became the noted Champion Karma Rgyal Po-Chan. These two eventually were sire and dam of the Pettit's first homebred champion, Mio Pasha Kumara. Thus, the breeding program was begun on the purest Hamilton lines.

American and Canadian Champion Mio's Clean Sweep, called "Hoover" by friends, and his litter sister, Champion Mio's Shantooz, have both brought enormous pleasure to Joan Pettit, both as show dogs and as family members to be dearly loved.

"Hoover" has had an exciting career in the business world, as well as in the show ring. He has done magazine advertisements and television commercials and is very much in demand, being so sweet, gentle, and accommodating. Photographers truly enjoy working with him, knowing they can count on him to never let them down.

Hoover was a fun dog to show as well, always ready to go. He completed his Canadian championship in three days undefeated.

Shan-tooz was not shown until she had reached four years of age. Then she finished quickly, taking, among other honors, Best of Winners at the American Lhasa Apso Club National in Texas in 1984.

The newest star at Mio is Mio's Roses R Red, who has all the qualities Joan Pettit most admires in the breed. It is hoped that she will have a successful year when she really starts compaigning.

Christine Pettit Gates, the Pettits' daughter for whom that very first Lhasa was purchased in 1968, has retained her love for and interest in the breed. Recently Mrs. Pettit made her a gift of Mio's Dust Buster, by Clean Sweep from Ja-Mar's Talimer Tangerine, as a pet for her children. As her mother had done before her, Christine decided to give dog showing a try, and her first time in the ring with Dusty earned Winners Dog and Best of Opposite Sex. Mrs. Pettit comments "If she continues, she will be a third generation owner-handler."

MISTI ACRES

Misti Acres Lhasa Apsos are bred, owned, and handled by Beverly A. Drake of Glen Arm, Maryland, a small breeder who keeps her dogs not only to show but, even more importantly she tells us, as pets. Having always thought it important not to overproduce or to keep more dogs than to whom she could give proper care and attention, Beverly has sold a number as pets which she feels could easily have finished.

Everyone has goals in life and Beverly is no exception. Her goal was to get a Best in Show on one of her Lhasas, doing so entirely breeder-owner-handled. She finally realized her dream in July 1984 when American and Canadian Champion Misti's Play It Again Sam brought her this honor. He is a multiple specialty Best in Show winner as well.

Sam was bred to Champion Phancy Tiko's Abby. Ann which produced Champion Phaney Samson of Misti Acres and to Kinderland Ta Sen Isis which produced Champion Kinderland Ta Sen Mime O'Sam, Champion Kinderland Ta Sen Shade O'Tara, and Kinderland Ta Sen Amity O'Isis, who needs but one major to finish. A repeat breeding produced six bitches who are presently starting their show careers, two of whom have won Best in Sweepstakes at specialty shows.

Beverly Drake's foundation bitch was Schu Schu, whom she bred to Champion Sakya Kamaru (producing Champion Misti's Shesa Ladi) and to Champion Chiz Ari Ko-Khyi (producing Champion Misti I've Got Da Spirit). Somehow or other, Beverly just never found the right combination for Shesa until she bred her to Misti Acres Sailor. This proved highly successful, the litter including Sam and his litter sister, Champion Misti Acres Sindy Sue. Spirit was bred just twice in her lifetime: once to Champion Kinderland's Kishri Ruff, producing the 1979 Grand Futurity winner Champion Misti Acres Strutter; and to Champion Kinderland's Ta Sen Dakini which produced the 1981 Grand Futurity winner Misty Acres Gin Jo's Bambi.

Both Bambi and her litter brother, Misti Acres Sailor, were sold to friends of Beverly who eventually lost interest in showing. Both were pointed, with Bambi needing only a three-point major to finish. However, at that time both were cut down and Bambi was spayed.

MOHICAN

Mohican Lhasa Apsos at Fairfield, Connecticut, are owned by

Thelma G. Hartmann who is, in every sense of the word, a hobby breeder.

Mrs. Hartmann bought her first Lhasa, Pasha, in 1970. Mrs. Hartmann fondly calls him her "first mistake." He is the first Lhasa to carry her Mohican prefix. Shown as a young dog at match shows, Pasha won two Best in Match awards, and of course that did it so far as his owner's interest in showing was concerned. Unfortunately, despite his great beginnings, he turned out not to be championship quality material, being unsound in both mind and body. Mrs. Hartmann had him neutered then set forth to find herself a good foundation bitch.

The first requisite for this bitch was that she be sound both in mind and body, following the Hartmanns' experience with Pasha. After many months of patient searching, Mrs. Hartmann bought a five-month-old puppy who later became Champion Baijai's Tara Ling of Mohican. She was a sound, flashy gold going back to Licos on her sire's side, to Hamilton and to Rondelay. On her dam's side she was of similar lines. She was an excellent foundation bitch with fantastic temperament and also the only bitch Mrs. Hartmann ever bought.

At the time Tara was purchased the Standard was saying "golds preferred," making an uphill climb with a parti-color. None the less, Tara gained both her majors in a year when majors were hard to come by. Mrs. Hartmann was doing her own handling then, a job which her daughter now has taken over. Thus Mohican still remains a family affair.

Everything now owned or co-owned by Thelma Hartmann among her Lhasas comes down from the bitch Tara Ling. She died in October 1985 at 13 years of age.

In the Mohican breeding program, Thelma Hartmann has placed emphasis on quality bitches, having done so in the belief that in a breeding program one will eventually reap the returns of what one has invested—not necessarily in the first generation but in those which follow. In addition, as a small hobby breeder she is limited in the number of dogs to be kept, which means that only the best can stay with her. This reflects on her stud force which by now has become practically nonexistent (having owned only three males in fifteen years). Those following the original Pasha were Champion Mohican's Connecticut Yankee (from her very first litter), who is the sire of Champion Sammche Mohican Mi-

Ch. Misti's Shesa Ladi finished at 20 months. She is the dam of Champions Misti's Play It Again Sam and Misti Acres Sindy Sue. Beverly Drake, Glen Arm, Maryland.

Group placing Ch. Sammche Mohican Mirage, by Ch. Mohican's Connecticut Yankee ex Ch. Mohican's Pony Express, taking Winners Dog at Holyoke in 1984. Bred and owned by Sandra Pond and Thelma G. Hartmann.

rage and Mohican Yankee Goldsmith, the young star of the future. Mohican, thus, is really where quality bitches reign supreme.

From each generation, Thelma Hartmann has always kept a good bitch with which to carry on her line. Taking time to show each one to championship, she is now working on her fifth generation.

Champion Mohican's Pony Express is one of Mrs. Hartmann's best producers. She is co-owned with Sandra Pond, a friend whose help has been inestimable in permitting the Mohican breeding program to continue.

Mohican is very proud of Mohican X-Tra Tempting, C.D., who is the youngest known Lhasa to have earned a C.D. degree. She is owned by Marilyn Kain.

MOR-KNOLL

Mor-Knoll Lhasa Apsos are located at Florham Park, New Jersey, where they are owned by Liz Morgan.

Liz purchased her first Lhasa bitch in 1970, Champion Mor-Knoll's Victoria, ROM. Vickie quickly completed her championship, then was bred to Best-in-Show–winning Champion Tibet of Cornwallis, ROM. That breeding, and a repeat with the same two, produced five champions, one of which, Champion Mor-Knoll's Alex-A-Hente, ROM, gained title undefeated from the open class, owner-handled, at one year's age.

Shortly thereafter, Liz was fortunate to acquire, on a co-ownership with her breeder Carol Kuendel, Chok's Joppa Bu Mo, ROM. This bitch, "Josie," became one of the all-time top producers with 12 champions to her credit. Her last litter of three, sired by Best-in-Show–winning English and American Champion Orlane's Intrepid, produced Champion Mor-Knoll Chok's Grand Slam, ROM, who is a top producer with 15 champions to his credit; and group-winning Champion Mor-Knoll's Chok's Line Drive, also a producer of champions. Lindy is owned by Eileen MacLennan.

Recently, Mor-Knoll had another bit of good fortune in being able to acquire San Jo's Hussel Mei as a young bitch after she had won the Futurity. Mei Mei finished her championship with ease, and is now proving herself to be an excellent producer and an exciting addition to Liz's breeding program.

Basically, almost all of the Mor-Knoll dogs are owner-handled. Liz is proud that dogs bearing the Mor-Knoll prefix have been responsible for starting many other young kennels on their way in the breed.

Liz Morgan has bred or co-bred 25 champions, seven group-placing and group-winning dogs, and a Best in Show dog.

NORBULINGKA

Norbulingka Lhasas are owned by Phyllis D. Marcy at Thetford Hill, Vermont, which has been the home of some very memorable members of this breed.

From a litter whelped in Anchorage, Alaska, in 1961, Mrs. Marcy especially was impressed with one male puppy, which nobody wanted. She had faith in him however, and her judgment very definitely was correct as he grew up to become Champion Kham of Norbulingka, ROM, who was the Top-Winning Lhasa from 1963-1966, winning five all-breed Bests in Show.

His show success was only the frosting on the cake for this magnificent dog. The most important proof of his excellence is the fact that he sired 25 champions, including Champion Gindy of Norbulingka, who is the Top-Producing Lhasa bitch in history. She is owned by Norman and Carolyn Herbel at Tabu.

A son of Kham's, Champion Lingkhor Bhu of Norbulingka, ROM, was Best of Breed under the author in a huge entry including the leading Lhasas from coast to coast at Westminster in 1973. He followed through on this win with numerous group placements.

A son of Bhu's, American and Canadian Champion Minda's Tsong of Bhu, ROM, had many Best of Breeds and a few group placings. However, as he disliked showing, Mrs. Marcy retired him at a young age.

This dog, Josh, sired a lovely bitch, Champion Norbulingka Crazy Daisy, ROM, who has produced several champions, among them Champion Norbulingka Sherpa-Tenzing; American and Canadian Champion Norbulingka's Khyber, and Champion Norbulingka's Bella Bella.

A son of Josh, Champion Norbulingka Prosciutto, is also currently being shown (by Greg Strong).

Ch. Mor-Knoll'd Alex-A Hente, ROM is by Best in Show Ch. Tibet of Cornwallis, ROM, ex Ch. Mar-Knoll's Victoria, ROM. Owner-bred by Liz Morgan, Alex is pictured here completing his undefeated championship owner-handled.

Ch. Lingkhor Bhu of Norbulingka, Winners Dog at Westminster 1973, a group winner with many Group placements, owned by Phyllis Marcy. A son of the great Ch. Kham of Norbulingka ex Lui Gui's Tonka of Lingkhor, born January 1970.

POTALA

Potala Kennels, owned by Mrs. Keke Blumberg at Huntington Valley, Pennsylvania, were founded in the very early 1960s. This was a tremendously successful show kennel of Lhasas into the 1980s, producing 58 AKC Champions, many, many group winners, and six Best in Show dogs.

The kennel was a hobby venture, dedicated to the sport of purebred dogs and striving for excellence. Potala developed some very important breed characteristics, the first of which was bite. To quote Keke, "Bites were terrible in the early days, and by using Champion Tibet of Cornwallis wisely, these began to improve to the point that after eight years Potala had tight scissors mouths with good strong, straight teeth."

Also, by crossing lines, Potala produced beautiful, correct heads and eyes. Again quoting Keke, "The Lhasa head is unique, and today we need more breeders who will not settle for a head that borders on a Shih Tzu or a Tibetan Terrier, but will work to produce a correct Lhasa head."

Potala produced many wonderful, winning dogs. At the top of the list has to have been Champion Potala Keke's Yum Yum. She was whelped in 1968 and died in 1984. She was truly the fulfillment of a breeder's dream—a wonderful, loving pet and a super show dog, as well as a marvelous producer.

Yum Yum won two National Specialties back-to-back in 1975 and 1976. Plus, she was a Westminster Best of Breed winner and an all-breed Best in Show bitch. Yum Yum whelped a total of ten puppies of which six became champions. One of her sons was the most spectacular Lhasa ever born at Potala, Champion Potala Keke's Tomba-tu. He was a most exciting and gorgeous dog who won more than 50 Non-Sporting Groups, but never took a Best in Show, to the disappointment of his numerous admirers. His was a profuse and beautifully correct coat, which was used to develop the wrapping technique to grow a coat and care for it properly. Tomba's sire was the magnificent Champion Everglo Zijuh Tomba.

The list of handsome Potala dogs is quite long, and Mrs. Blumberg names just a few who were special favorites. They include: Champion Keke's Bam Loo (all of her dogs were registered "Keke's" prior to registration of "Potala"), Champion Potala Keke's Mystique, Champion Potala Keke's Zin Zin, Champion

Potala Japalan Camelot, Champion Potala Keke's Sharabara, Champion Potala Keke's Zintora, Champion Potala Keke's Kelana, Champion Potala Keke's Andromeda, Champion Potala Keke's Luckee, Champion Keke's Georgy Girl, Champion Potala Chiang, Champion Potala Keke's Fraser, Champion Potala Keke's Bhu-Tan, Champion Potala Pandan Apollo, and Champion Potala Keke's Kind-a-Krimson.

During the early 1980s, breeding at Potala came to an end owing to Keke Blumberg's heavy schedule of judging commitments. It became impossible to spend the proper amount of time breeding and raising puppies, and Mrs. Blumberg also felt that to own top-winning dogs creates conflict-of-interest problems. The last dog to carry the Potala banner was Candy Bar, a beautiful, happy, fun-loving dog and the winner of four all-breed Bests in Show during his show career. Candy Bar, unfortunately, died at age five, leaving behind only a few progeny.

Keke won her first Best in Show in 1966 under a very respected trio of judges: Henry Stoecker in the breed; Alva Rosenberg in the Group; and Ray Beale for Best in Show.

Can. Ch. Ralda's Venus Flytrap has both majors in United States, too. By Am. and Can. Ch. Rondelay Raja of Rjay ex Am. and Can. Ch. Ralda's Flowering Quince, bred, owned and handled by Arlene G. Dartt, Ralda Lhasa Apsos. Taking Best Puppy in Specialty in November 1984, Lhasa Apso Club of Canada, at the age of seven months.

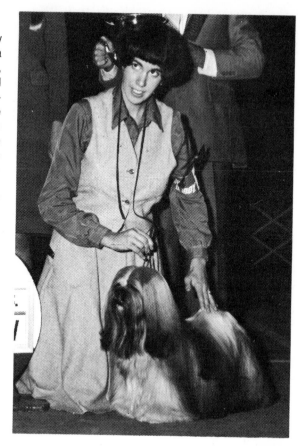

Multi-Best in Show winning Ch. Potala Keke's Candy Bar, owned by Janet and Marvin Whitman (Ja-Ma) and Keke Blumberg (Potala) here is winning one of those Bests in Show—this at Dan Emmet K.C. in 1978, handled by Emily Gunning.

RALDA

Ralda Lhasa Apsos, at Stowe, Vermont, are owned by Robert and Arlene Dartt. This is the home of American and Canadian Sharpette's Nip N'Tuck, Canadian ROM, who was bred by Robert Sharp and Dorothy Carpenter. He is the sire of six Canadian Champions (five of whom were bred by Mrs. Darrt in two litters). Two of his other children are pointed; several others are major-pointed in the United States. Tuck is the sire of littermates Canadian Champion Ralda's Cinnamon Shrub and Canadian Champion Ralda's Lady Prunella; littermates Canadian Champion Ralda's Golden Nugget, Canadian Champion Ralda's Knuuttila D'Erable, and Canadian Champion Ralda's Kiodisan Katie-Rae.

U.S.-pointed Canadian Champion Ralda's Squash Blossom is the dam of Canadian Champion Ralda's Cinnamon Shrub (who lacks a major to finish in the States). Blossom also has another pointed daughter from her first litter and two-year-old sons (from her second litter) who are pointed.

U.S.-pointed Canadian Champion Ralda's Apple Cider Man is the sire of two Canadian Champions, one of whom finished title at seven months and is a Puppy Group winner.

Major U.S.-pointed Canadian Champion Ralda's Cinnamon Shrub and her dam, Blossom, have been shown as a brace both in the United States and Canada where they have multiple wins, including a Lhasa Specialty Best Brace award.

Multi-Group–placing Canadian Champion Ralda's Kiodisan Katie Rae is owned by Colin Williams, Newfoundland, Canada.

Major-pointed, Group-placing Canadian Champion Ralda's Knuuttila D'Erable, a Puppy Group winner, owned by Joyce L. Bormann, Manchester, Massachusetts, is another who was bred by Mrs. Dartt, as is U.S.-pointed Canadian Champion Ralda's Prunella (co-owned with A. Bianchi, Swanton, Vermont) and Canadian Champion Ralda's Golden Nugget (co-owned with Shirley Royce, Nassau, N.Y.).

American and Canadian Champion Ralda's Flowering Quince is a multiple Group placer in Canada who finished her American title with three majors during 1983 with very limited showing. Flower is Mrs. Dartt's first homebred American Champion, and she is the dam of major-pointed Canadian Champion Ralda's Venus Flytrap, who needs just single points to finish her U.S. title having earned both majors (four points each) over one weekend during October 1985. At her first Canadian show, Venus went Best Puppy in Group and Best Puppy in Specialty (Lhasa Apso Club of Canada) in Montreal.

Mrs. Dartt lives right on the line between the United States and Canada, thus having easy access to shows in both countries. She is president of the Green Mountain Dog Club at Stowe, Vermont, membership chairman of the American Lhasa Apso Club, and has been in charge of handling instruction and training classes of several clubs. She has handled and pointed many dogs for others, especially of the toy breeds, in both countries.

RHU-HA

Rhu-Ha Lhasa Apsos, at Roanoke, Virginia, are owned by Ruth M. Hatcher, a very dedicated lady devoted to this breed. She

Ch. Rhu-Ha's Regal Ruffles completing her title in 1982. Jean Lade handling for Ruth M. Hatcher, Roanoke, Virginia.

thoroughly enjoys the planning, breeding, and whelping of a litter, watching the puppies develop, then either showing them to win or placing them in homes where they will be appreciated. She describes herself as "a very small breeder, very interested in keeping the Lhasa Apso true to Standard."

Ruth Hatcher's first Lhasa was named Hatcher's Mai-Ling Poppi (by a son of Champion Millamor's Golden Guy), her pedigree going back to Champion Cherryshores Bah Beeh Boi, Champion Neika's Minka Lee, Champion Chen Tag-Ser of Shahi-Taj, Champion Verle's Jigme Tru, and Champion Potala Vindicator.

Bred to Champion Thmilos Magic Dragon (by Best-in-Show–winning Champion Taglha Kambu ex Champion Joval's Geni Su Ding), Poppi produced Champion Rhu-Ha's Regal Ruffles, dam of a very exciting litter, a couple of which puppies are already winning points.

Rhu-Ha's Han Sha Te San O'Art-Est is by Best-in-Show–winning American and Canadian Champion Anbara's Hobgoblin (a Tabu son). From the background behind her dogs, it would seem that she is well situated to bring about many splended champions in the future.

RIMAR

Rimar Lhasa Apsos were established in 1970 by Stephen G. C. Campbell, and are located at Elizabeth, New Jersey. During the past 15 years, 25 champions have, to date, been bred by Steve. His foundation bitch was Champion Rimar's Tipit, ROM, who became the dam of Best-in-Show–winning Champion Rimar's J. G. King Richard. Steve's top stud dog, Champion Tabu's King of Hearts, ROM, was the sire of King Richard and of over 30 other noted champions. He is the third Top-Producing Stud Dog in the history of the breed, his progeny including at least three Best in Show winners.

Steve has bred four Best in Show Lhasas, which is certainly a record to view with satisfaction. They are Champion Rimar's J. G. King Richard, American and Canadian Champion Rimar's Rumpelstiltskin, ROM (co-bred with Barbara Wood), Champion Anbara-Rimar's Grin 'N Bear It, and Champion Anbara-Rimar's Mary Puppins.

Rumpelstiltskin, known as Rumpy, was the Top Lhasa in the United States in 1978. He won the American Lhasa Apso Club's Eastern Regional Specialty in 1977 and 1978, owner-handled by Steve in 1977 and by Jean Lade in 1978. During 1978 and 1979, Rumpy was campaigned by Jean Lade for Steve in partnership with William and Betty Jo Bowman. Since retirement, he is now Jean Lade's house pet, thoroughly enjoying life with her and her family. Born September 18, 1974, Rumpelstiltskin was sired by Champion Yeti's Paper Tiger ex Champion Arborhill's Lho-Lha of Rimar. He earned a total of three all-breed Bests in Show and six Regional Specialties during his ring career.

Champion Rimar's J. G. King Richard, known as Tricky Dick, was a Top Group-winning Lhasa in 1976, taking approximately 20 Group Firsts to his credit. He went Best in Show at the Mohawk Valley Kennel Club in January 1977 (after winning the Group there from the author). Tricky Dick was also Best of Breed and Group Second at Westminster in 1979, handled by Douglas Holloway for then-owners Mr. and Mrs. Thomas Weill. He was also owned during part of his show career by Susan Lefferts. King Richard is a son of Champion Tabu's King of Hearts (he by Champion Zijuh Seng Tru ex Champion Kinderland's Tonka) from Champion Rimar's Tipit.

Steve Campbell was the first American Kennel Club delegate

elected to represent the Lhasa Apso Club, taking office in 1974. He is also the first breeder to have been selected to judge the National when the club changed its former policy of two Regionals annually to just one National Specialty each year. Steve had this assignment at Kansas City in 1983.

Currently a judge of Lhasas and Poodles, Steve Campbell is a vice president and auditor of a bank on Staten Island, New York.

RUFFWAY

Ruffway Lhasa Apsos are owned by Georgia E. Palmer, Addison, Illinois, breeder or co-breeder of 37 champions.

After having started in a very small way with Collies, Georgia's husband and she bought the first of their Lhasas in 1956. Glenfo's Girga started her show career at the International in 1957 with a Best of Breed and finished her title of champion undefeated in her sex.

In 1957 a male puppy was added, Champion Miradel's Mong Fu-Tzu. Girga had her first litter in 1958, including one bitch puppy who became Champion Ruffway Solitaire. All three of these Lhasas were black and white parti-colors. A later litter from the same parents contained a gold and white parti, Ruffway Hon-Nee-Bun who went to Gloria Fowler and later became the grandam of Champion Everglo's Spark of Gold.

Georgia became interested in the Hamilton line after seeing Champion Licos Kulu La. In 1961 she purchased a red-gold female who greatly impressed her—Stittig's Moka-Cara-Deimar, whose sire and dam both had been bred at Hamilton Farm. Later the same year, she bought a puppy bitch, Karma Tagan, a blue-grey with black tippings from Dorothy Cohen. In early 1963 a male was added, Karma Rolpai.

Gloria Fowler, who like Georgia had started with Miradel stock, had also become interested in the Hamilton dogs, and she sent a little red female (from an unplanned breeding of Hamilton Norden to Champion Kai Sang's Clown of Everglo) who became Champion Ruffway Lholung. All of the present Ruffway stock is descended from these acquisitions, with a few significant additions.

Champion Karma Frosty Knight O'Everglo exerted his influ-

Ch. Rimar's Rumpelstiltskin waiting to return to the ring for the Best in Show judging after winning the Group at Boardwalk K.C. in 1978. Stephen G. C. Campbell, owner, Elizabeth, New Jersey.

Winner of the American Lhasa Apso Club Specialty Stud Dog Class, Kansas City 1983, under breeder-judge Steve Campbell. Ch. Ruffway Mashala Chu (*left*) with Georgia Palmer, with his get behind him: Best in Show, Ch. Ruffway Patra Paloling, owned by V. Cohen; Best in Show, Ch. Cameo's Beau Duke-J, owned by Dr. Charboneau; and Ch. Ruffway Patra Tashi Tu, owned by R. Lombardi.

ence through his son, Champion Ruffway Chogal, and his daughters, Ruffway Khanda and Champion Ruffway Kham Chung who was the dam of Champion Ruffway T' and Chu. T'and Chu was a Group winner and the sire of 18 champions including two Best in Show winners.

At a time when Georgia Palmer had nothing of her own tracing back to her original pair, she bred two bitches to Champion Everglo's Spark of Gold, both of them daughters of Lholung (Spark of Gold's half sister). One produced Champion Ruffway Byang-Kha; bred to a T'and Chu son she produced Champion Ruffway Tashi. The other Lholung daughter, Champion Ruffway Kara Shing, produced Champion Ruffway Norru, Champion Ruffway Marpa (sire of 14 champions), and Champion Ruffway Mashaka, Best in Show winner and sire of five champions.

Bred to a T'and Chu daughter, Mashaka produced Champion Ruffway Mashala Chu, sire of 20 champions, three of them Best in Show winners.

Tashi has one champion by Mashaka and eleven by Mashala Chu, including Best in Show Champion Ruffway Patra Pololing, Top Winner in the breed for 1982 and 1983; and Champion Ruffway Patra Dutch Treat, who was a Group winner in the U.S. and is a multiple Best in Show winner in South America.

Frosty Knight, Sparky, and T'and Chu all appear repeatedly in the Ruffway pedigrees.

SAN JO

San Jo was the prefix selected by Marianne Nixon for the Lhasas she bred and exhibited after acquiring her first of the breed in 1953. In more recent years she has shared the interest with her daughter, Leslie Ann Engen, and both are well-known breeder-exhibitors in the Pacific Northwest and across the country. San Jo is located at Bellevue, Washington.

With few exceptions, San Jo Lhasas have been owner-breeder-handled, and in a 25-year period more than 70 of these Lhasas have been shown to championship, primarily by Marianne and Leslie Ann.

San Jo's first registered Lhasa was purchased from Mrs. James Roberts of Abbotsford. This eventual champion, Jomo Dkar-po of Abbotsford, bred to her half brother, produced the foundation stud, Champion Gyal Kham-nag of San Jo, ROM. A multiple Group winner, he was the sire of nine champions in limited use at stud. Notable among his progeny was Chapion San Jo's Torgi whom Marianne showed to two Bests in Show during the 1960s. Torgi was the first Lhasa in the Northwest to achieve Best in Show status.

The record over the years speaks eloquently of San Jo's success in the Lhasa world. Since 1974, the kennel has competed in 12 American Lhasa Apso Club National Futurity events. At these events, ten San Jo Lhasas have come away with the title Grand Futurity Winner. On three occasions San Jo winners of Best Puppy and Best Adult had to compete against each other for Grand Futurity winner. All of these Futurity winners went on to championships, and a number of them have achieved special records, both in the show ring and as producers.

San Jo has bred and shown 15 Group-winning champions, three of which were bitches. Among these 15 are four Lhasas who attained multiple Best in Show honors. They include Champion S. J. W. Waffle Stomper, ROM, sire of nine champions; Champion San Jo's Shindig, *Kennel Review's* No. 1 Lhasa for 1984; and Champion San Jo's Hussel Bussel, ROM, dam of eight champions.

American and Canadian Champion San Jo's Soshome, ROM, achieved American Best in Specialty Show awards, and was No. 1 Lhasa in Canada for several years, with multiple Bests in Show to his credit. Multiple Group-winning American and Canadian Champion San Jo's Shazam attained his Canadian title with a Best in Show from the classes. A third Canadian Best in Show winner was Champion San Jo's Raaga Looki Mei, ROM, sire of 13 champions, who was Canada's No. 1 Lhasa in 1978 and, with five Bests in Show, was Canada's No. 4 Non-Sporting Dog as well. Looki Mei returned to the American show ring in 1979 and at age eight was the American Lhasa Apso Club's National Specialty Winner (Baltimore, Maryland) from the Veteran Dog class.

Several other San Jo Lhasas deserve special recognition. Waffle Stomper set a record by acquiring title in four days; Best of Winners at the 1981 National Specialty and points at the other three following shows. This magnificent young Lhasa achieved three All-Breed Bests in Show and one Best in Specialty Show prior to his untimely death. The high quality of his progeny ensures his continuing influence. A daughter, Champion Anbara-Rimar's Cobbi Cuddler is a Group winner, and her sister, Champion Anbara-Rimar's Mary Puppins, is a multiple Group and Best in Show winner.

Mention must be made of Champion San Jo Shenanigan, ROM, C.D. A Grand Futurity winner in 1976, he achieved special distinction by receiving the American Lhasa Apso Club's ROM award with a first-year total of 11 champions sired. As of 1985, he is the sire of 22 champions and, at eight years of age, has gained his C.D. degree.

Champion San Jo's Hussel Bussel, ROM, is probably the best known of the San Jo Lhasas, and will be long remembered for her effortless motion and eager attitude, along with her close adherence to the official Standard. She was the 1977 ALAC Grand Futurity winner, and took her first Best in Show that same year at less than two years of age. Being a bitch, her show career was intermittent, with time out for maternal duties. Despite this fact, she returned to the show ring in January 1983 for a total of 14 shows between then and retirement. At these shows she won Best of Breed 13 times, Best in Show eight times (four each all-breed and Specialty), Best of Breed at Westminster 1983, and Best of Opposite Sex at the AKC Centennial in 1984. She was Best of Breed at the 1983 National in Kansas City where two of her progeny from consecutive litters vied for Grand Futurity. Hussel Bussel repeated her Best of Breed win from the Veteran class in 1984.

San Jo, whose bloodlines are being incorporated into those of other well-known breeders with success, is a kennel which contributes enormously to the quality of its breed.

SAN LO

San Lo Lhasa Apsos are owned by Michael A. Santora and Alan J. Loso at Kendall, Florida, who have had the breed since 1973, have been breeding since 1975, and started showing their dogs in 1980. Not, however, until late 1984 did they really take up the challenge.

In 1977, Michael and Alan bred their pure Hamilton bitch to Champion Arborhill's Brandieh, ROM. The result was a litter of two, one dog and one bitch, both pointed, but the owners were

not yet serious enough exhibitors to bother finishing them. The bitch, Brandieh's Amaretta of San Lo, was bred to Best-in-Show–winning Champion Qua-La-Ti's Makara (the youngest Lhasa in history to win Best in Show), producing a litter of puppies line-bred to two pillars of the Lhasa breed, Champion Karma Frosty Knight of Everglo, ROM, and Champion Everglo's Spark of Gold, ROM, both of them Best in Show winners. Among the puppies were the two excellent littermates Champion Royal Cognac of San Lo and Remy Martin of San Lo, who needs just one major to finish, and probably has it by now.

Cognac is a gorgeously-headed dog with a heavy gold coat set off by black ear tippings. The author had the pleasure of awarding him points at Fort Myers in 1984, doing so with admiration. Along the way, he gained the approval of Edd Bivin, Merrill Cohen, and Mrs. Keke Blumberg, under whom he finished.

Litter brother Remy has the same loving disposition as Cognac and is also a handsome dog.

These two fanciers would seem to be off to a really fine start in the Lhasa world.

SHARPETTE

Sharpette Lhasa Apsos have been made very famous by their owner, Robert D. Sharp, a longtime Lhasa breeder and owner, a professional handler, and now a noted and popular AKC-approved multiple breed judge. Sharpette is located at Albany, New York.

When I first met Bob Sharp, he and his family were at Norwalk, Connecticut, and Bob was showing Boxers, I believe, for himself. It was not long after our introduction that he discovered Lhasas, and since that time his contribution to the breed has been inestimable.

The Sharps finished their first two Lhasa puppy bitches in 1964. One of them, I believe, was the youngest ever of the breed—at least prior to that occasion—to complete the title, and, making it even better, did so undefeated. This was Champion Kyi-Chu Whimsi of Sharpette, by Champion Karma Kanjur ex Champion Kyi Chu Kira, C.D. Bob acquired other Lhasas, too, in those days, but when he really hit the jackpot was with his acquisition, from Mrs. Ruth H. Smith, "the Kyi Chu lady," of her magnificent young Champion Kyi Chu Friar Tuck.

Remy Martin of San Lo, by Best in Show winning Ch. Qua-La-Ti's Makara, ROM eligible (Ch. Ruffway T' and Chu, ROM—Ch. Tiffany's Yolanda La-Tsu, ROM) ex Bhrandieh's Amaretto of San Lo (Ch. Arborhill's Bhran-Dieh, ROM—High Tide's Pum-Kin Pie). Taking Best of Opposite Sex at Blennerhassett, handled by Barbara Alderman for owners M. A. Santora and A. J. Loso, San Lo Kennels.

Tuck was born on January 30, 1965, bred by Mrs. Jay Amann and Mrs. Ruth Smith, sired by Champion Quetzal Feyla of Kyi-Chu ex Champion Colarlie's Miss Shandha. Bob Sharp owned Tuck, with the exception of one very short period, throughout the dog's long lifetime. Tuck became a record-holding show winner, the sire of many champions, and a beloved companion to all of the Sharps. He was a Champion in Bermuda, Mexico, South America, the United States, and Canada. His first Best in Show was won at age three years at the prestigious Bryn Mawr Kennel Club event. Tuck thus became only the second parti-color Lhasa in America to have gained this honor. Before long he had accounted for more than half a dozen Bests in Show, becoming, first, the all-time Top-Winning parti-color Lhasa in U.S. history, then No. 1 among all Lhasas of every color, and a placer among all Non-Sporting Group winners in 1968.

Bob was then asked if he would handle the great California-bred dog, Champion Chen Korum Ti, in the East for Mrs. Pat Chenoweth. He accepted and did so with historic results. Kori, smaller and a stunning red-gold in color, was quite different in appearance from Tuck. He became an immediate favorite with the judges, just as Tuck had done before him.

Two years after Tuck had won Best in Show at Boardwalk, Kori repeated his honor, his seventh at that time, including the great Trenton Kennel Club event. By 1971 he had become the Top-Winning Lhasa in the United States and the No. 3 Non-Sporting dog. Among the "goodies" to which Bob Sharp piloted him were a Group Second at Westminster (the highest ever received by a Lhasa at this event) and a formidable list of Best of Breed and Group victories. Kori did some great winning at home on the Pacific Coast with Mrs. Chenoweth too. He was a real super star.

Bob also has some fond memories of good winning with Champion Rimar's J. G. King Richard, Champion Korky of Kee-O, Champion Kinderlands Tonka, Champion Tabu's Triple Threat, and Champion Potala Keke's Zintora, to name just a few. Plus he fondly remembers the many, many Lhasas he finished to their titles.

Meanwhile, the breeding program at home is carrying on. One will find Sharpette-bred dogs and their descendants behind many winners, especially in the New York area.

The great Ch. Kyi-Chu Friar Tuck as a young dog with his owner-handler Robert D. Sharp, Sharpette Kennels, Albany, New York. One of the all-time "greats" of the breed, Tuck enjoyed a long and exciting show career during which he became the holder of important records.

SHUKTI LINGKA

Shukti Lingka Lhasa Apsos are owned by Kenneth and Harriet Silverman and are located at Marblehead, Massachusetts.

It was in 1970 that the Silvermans, answering an ad in a local newspaper, visited the kennel of Miriam Borofsky and purchased Yum Yum VII. The idea of a black dog appealed to Harriet, who felt that would be' the easiest color to keep clean, and so it was that Yum Yum started the kennel which has become known as "The House That Black Built."

The Silvermans' first litter from Yum Yum arrived on August 4, 1972, sired by the magnificent Champion Lingkor Bhu of Norbulingka. The pups were ideals of linebreeding as Yum Yum is a double granddaughter of the great Champion Kham of Norbulingka and Bhu is a Khan son, with Hamilton and English bloodlines behind him. Five puppies were whelped. Among them was the glorious American and Canadian Champion Tob Ci of Shukti Lingka, who, owner-handled to all of her wins except those in Canada, became a Group winner on two occasions and had many other prestigious awards to her credit. What a start in the breed— a Lhasa of such quality in one's very first litter.

Tob Ci was bred twice. The first time she produced seven puppies, an entirely red-gold and blond litter by Champion Tabu's King of Hearts. A bitch from this litter went to Ray Sledzik under co-ownership and became Champion Shukti Lingka Pongo Zim-Ze. The male kept by the Silvermans, Ko Ba (deep red in color) earned points but did not complete his title. He did, however, become the sire of American and Canadian Tai Koo, a stunning white and black parti-colored dog who made his owner realize that Tob Ci carried the parti-color gene which she had passed along to her son in her first litter. There were two other parti-color littermates of "TK" sired by Tob Ci's son, Ko-Ba.

For her second litter, Tob Ci was bred to Champion Reiniet's Royal Chanticleer (Hamilton - Lui Gi lines), from which came a parti-color daughter and a black and tan, Ka Ra. Thus the Shukti Lingka lines now carry the dominant black gene from Yum Yum; the parti-color and the black and tan from a Tob Ci daughter.

Yum Yum next produced seven Lhasas of pure Hamilton breeding by Champion Licos Shipki-La. From this came Jetta, who in turn was bred to Champion Chen Hy-Lan Jampal producing the superb stud, American and Canadian Champion Po-Ba-Ri and the lovely bitch Dakini, who carries a parti-color gene and is the dam of American and Canadian Champion Tai Koo and Champion Torma.

For her third litter, Yum Yum was bred to Champion Orlane's Cenpo Kabsad, bringing in a link to the Spark of Gold line. This breeding produced a litter of eight, two of which were bitches. One of those bitches was bred to Po and produced Champion Shukti Lingka Ltag, sold as a puppy to Lillie Bucci who showed him to championship. The other bitch from this Yum Yum litter was Me-Ri, who had earned three points when she unfortunately lost two front teeth, and so was never again shown. "Sis" did her bit for the kennel nonetheless, when bred to the black and tan Tob Ci grandson, To-Re, as she produced the major-pointed Sen-Ge and his black sister, Nam Che. This brother-sister team became parents of black and tan Me-Zi.

The Silvermans have bred five generations of Lhasas down from their original Yum Yum. Top winners bred by them include American and Canadian Champion Tob Ci of Shukti Lingka, Champion Shukti Lingka Pongo Zim-Ze, American and Canadian Champion Po-Ba-Ri of Shukti Lingka, Champion Shukti Lingka Ltag, American and Canadian Champion Tai Kee of Shukti Lingka, and Champion Torma of Shukti Lingka.

SUMMERHILL

Summerhill Lhasa Apsos, owned by Jan and Doug Bernards, are at Valencia, California. The Bernardses breeding program is based on the beautiful bitch Champion Sulan's Victorian Sonnett, who is the first champion daughter of multiple Best-in-Show–winning Champion Sulan's Gregorian Chant, ROM, and Jenifer Juniper of Sulan, ROM. Thus her grandsires are Champion Innsbrook's Patrician O'Sulan and Champion Shoga's Ben-Ming. Her distinguished great-grandparents are Champion Orlane's Inimitable, Champion Innsbrook's Scarlett Lady, Champion Orlane's Be Sparky of Al-Mar, Champion Shoga Pan Kizamu-Isha, C.D., Champion Joi San's Happieh Go Luckieh, and Champion Dunklehaven Red Cleuver. The last two were great-grandparents twice each, being sire and dam of both of Sonnett's grandmothers.

Following a successful show career, Sonnett settled down to

Yum-Yum VII, the foundation bitch at Shukti Lingka Lhasas, was born February 1970. She still, at the close of 1985, rules her owners' household. By Goldmere Dorji ex Tess-La, she was bred by Miriam Borofsky and belongs to Kenneth G. and Harriet A. Silverman, Marblehead, Massachusetts. This photo at age going on 15 years.

Ch. Sulan's Victorian Sonnett was born January 1982 by Ch. Sulan's Gregorian Chant ex Jeniffer Juniper of Sulan. Bred by Suzette Michele and Marlene D. Kimbrel, this lovely bitch is owned by Jan and Doug Bernards.

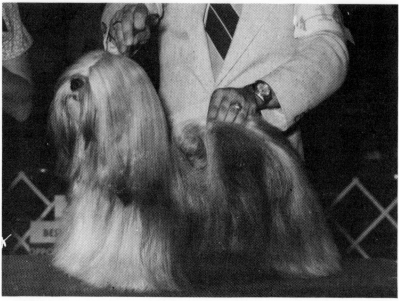

maternal duties, producing for her owners two beautiful litters sired by Champion San Jo's Out O'The Blue. The breeding was outstanding, Out O'The Blue being by Best-in-Show–winning Champion Anbara-Rimar Grin 'N Bear It ex multiple Best in Show and Best in Specialty Show Champion San Jo's Hussel Bussel, ROM.

The first litter included Summerhill's Dream Weaver, pointed and Best of Winners from the 9-12 months Puppy class and Summerhill's Spirit of Sulan, who was purchased by Suzette Michele (owner of Sulan Kennels). This fine Lhasa was the winner of a large Puppy class at the American Kennel Club Centennial Dog Show (the breed judged by Keke Blumberg) and in early 1986 had a three-point Bermudian major.

Summerhill's Keora was out in Open class, while the last member of the litter, the lovely black and tan bitch Summerhill's Pride of Joy, owned by Deanna Maxwell of Joy Lhasas, was Best of Breed at the Southern California Lhasa Apso Club A Match.

Sonnett's second litter produced Summerhill's City Slicker, Summerhill's C. Robin of Sulan (owned by Suzette Michele), and Summerhill's Tis For You Jill, all making their presence felt in the puppy classes. C. Robin went on to Reserve Winners Dog in a big entry his second time in the ring (from the 6-9 months class).

Summerhill has the young Champion Sulan's Minstral o'Summerhill out as a special with a number of breed wins and Group placements to his credit. His first litter looks to be especially promising and his owners are excited over its quality.

The ambition at Summerhill is to produce dogs of good balance, sound movement, correct expression, and good temperament. This kennel is surely succeeding. Summerhill dogs are trained, roadworked, and conditioned at home, where all are enjoyed as family friends.

SUNSHINE

Sunshine Lhasa Apsos, at Gary, Indiana, are owned by Mrs. Mary C. Soto, who began showing her dogs in 1980 after becoming fascinated and bewitched by her first Lhasa, Mopsy.

The genetics of breeding had always been interesting to Mrs. Soto who originally started out breeding cats—not on a professional level but purely as pets and with only a couple of litters.

Once she had acquired her first Lhasa she became so quickly captivated by the breed that nothing short of learning everything she could about these dogs satisfied her. She then tried to create her own line of what she considered to be ideal.

Mrs. Soto wisely feels that the only reason for ever breeding a litter is the desire to produce higher quality. To this end, she has bred only after careful consideration and then most cautiously. The parents must be as genetically free of faults as possible. An excellent disposition is a must. Good, sound bodies with keen minds is another important consideration.

Mrs. Soto's first bitch, Muffin's Mopsy, a black and white, was whelped on April 5, 1979. In her pedigree, one finds Champion Dunklehaven Tommy Gun and Orlane's Shadow Tag. She became the dam of one champion.

The second bitch at Sunshine Lhasas was Tashi Sunshine's Velvet Petal, by Champion Tashi Jim Nieh Kri-Ket (an Orion son) ex Tashi Huni Bear, granddaughter of Champion Orlane's Gold Standard. She was bred by Jeanne Holsapple, Tashi Kennels.

The third bitch Mrs. Soto owned became her first champion, who also produced a champion and two others who pointed toward the title. She is Champion Tashi Sunshine's Gold Melody, by Best-in-Show–winning Champion Yojimbo Orion ex Champion Kyber Rum Poppy.

Tashi Sunshine's High Society, a black dog with white chest and feet, became Mrs. Soto's foundation stud, siring a champion for her and others who are pointed. He is strong in Orlane bloodlines.

The first homebred champion finished by Mrs. Soto was Champion Sunshine's San Miquel, a golden dog with a most impressive pedigree. Sired by American and Canadian Champion Joyslyn's Piece of The Rock, ROM (by Best-in-Show–winning American and Canadian Champion Arborhill's Rah-Kieh, ROM), "Mikey" is from the Orion-Rum Poppy daughter, Champion Tashi Sunshine's Gold Melody.

Following Mikey, the second Sunshine homebred to finish was Champion Sunshine's Maris Stella.

With some very excellent youngsters coming on, there will undoubtedly be at least several more champions carrying the Sunshine banner.

TABU

Tabu Lhasas are owned by Norman and Carolyn Herbel, for-

Ch. Sunshine's Maris Stella takes his 2nd major on November 17, 1985 at Birmingham K.C. By Tashi Sunshine's High Society ex Muffin's Mopsy, "Star" is handled by Gary Doerge for owners, Sunshine Lhasas, Mary C. Soto.

merly of Langhorne, Pennsylvania, and now situated at Putnam, Kansas. Both of the Herbels have been active and enthusiastic Lhasa owners right from the first, building up a success record which is awe-inspiring to contemplate. The dogs they have owned, the success they have achieved with them, the many contributions they have made to the progress of the breed through giving of their time and effort—all have played their part in the story of Tabu.

When it was decided that the Herbels wanted to own and breed Lhasas, it was not a "spur of the moment, let's rush out and find one" sort of thing at all. Very careful groundwork was the start, such as watching breed judging at dog shows; reading every available word about breeding; developing their "eye"; and generally preparing themselves to recognize quality and potential when the time came to make a choice.

It was almost two years after the first decision to own Lhasas had been made when a young dog came to the Herbels' attention. His name was Tibet of Cornwallis, bred by Paul Williams of the Cornwallis Kennels and sired by Karma Tharpa. He was 14 months of age at the time he joined the Herbel family, and the success with which he met is now history.

So pleased were the Herbels with "Tibs" that later that same year they purchased another Karma Tharpa son. The Herbels' first two dogs became Best-in-Show–winning Champion Tibet of Cornwallis, ROM, and American, Bermudian, and Canadian Champion Ku Kah Bo of Pickwick.

Ch. Tabu's Queen of Hearts on the way to the title in 1979 taking Winners and Best of Opposite Sex at Grand Island, Nebraska, handled by Carmen Herbel Spears for owners Carolyn Herbel and Grace Vanden Heuvel. Daughter of the Group winning Ch. Tabu's King of Hearts ex Ch. Tabu's Cinnamon Stick.

The next to join the kennel, the following year, was the famed multiple Best-in-Show–winning American and Bermudian Champion Kinderland's Tonka, ROM, who was a Tibet daughter ex Champion Kinderlands Sang Po, ROM (daughter of Champion Kham of Norbulingka). Tonka's show career was highly successful, but even more important she proved to be a shining asset to the Tabu breeding program. In her first litter, sired by Champion Zijuh Seng Tru, ROM, came the also very famous Champion Tabu's King of Hearts, ROM, who appears in the pedigree of many a winning Lhasa and numerous noted kennels, earning for him the position of No. 3 Lhasa Apso Producer in breed history. Tonka's Tibet litter included a lovely bitch, Champion Tibet's Kiss Me Kate, who in her only litter produced a Group winner.

One more Lhasa played a role in the foundation of Tabu—one of the finest producing bitches one could possibly have hoped to obtain. This was the puppy who grew up to become Champion Gindy of Norbulingka, ROM, a daughter of Champion Kham of Norbulingka, ROM, who is who on the list of top-producing dams.

So well did they produce together that Gindy and Tibet were

bred for several litters. Their offspring include Champion Tabu's Rhapsody in Red, Champion Tabu's Raquel, Champion Tabu's Double or Nothing, and Champion Tabu's Dresdon Doll (the last two both point winners at the American Lhasa Apso Club Specialty Show en route to their titles). Tibet—Gindy also produced American and Canadian Champion Tabu's Appleseed Annie, Group-winning Champion Tabu's Fame and Fortune (a Westminster Winners Dog), Tabu's Rags to Riches, and Tabu's **Firebird**.

As of November 1985, the Herbels had bred 46 Lhasa champions, among them dogs of inestimable importance to the breed. It is certain that more will follow, as breeding still goes on at Tabu, although on a more limited basis now that the Herbels have increased their interest to include judging.

Both Norman and Carolyn are respected and popular judges who seem to thoroughly enjoy the task. Also, they have made an enormous contribution to the breed through their book, *The Complete Lhasa Apso,* and by their activities as very active and involved club members.

Carmen Herbel, Norman and Carolyn's daughter, in 1972 won the *Kennel Review* "Winkie" Award for more placements in Junior Handling than any other junior in the nation. She also was elected to receive the *Dog World* Award for first placement in Junior Showmanship and the Dog Writers Association of America Award for Good Sportsmanship. Carmen started out with terriers and had made her first champion, a Cairn Terrier, when nine years old. On more than one occasion she has been the No. 1 Junior Handler of Lhasa Apsos.

TAGLHA

It was during the 1960s, a period which produced many outstanding show Lhasas, that Taglha Lhasa Apsos were established by Mrs. Wilson J. Browning, Jr., of Norfolk, Virginia, whose interest in the breed very quickly became a commitment.

Mrs. Browning had purchased a pet which kept her on the run between the vet, groomers, and a local obedience class as she tried to learn everything possible about the breed.

Mrs. Browning's next step was, very wisely, to contact Jane Kay, who was handling some of the most important winners of that time, including such dogs as Champion Kham of Norbulingka and Champion Frosty Knight O'Everglo, both Best in Show dogs, and ask her for assistance in finding a bitch for show and breeding. Mrs. Kay arranged for Mrs. Browning to purchase Kimrick's Jeh Sah Cah at Westminster, where "Jessie," as she was called, won Best of Winners. This lovely bitch went on to gain championship in both the United States and Canada. Hers was an "open" pedigree of which Mrs. Browning says, "not pure Hamilton, but impressive."

The first breeding by Mrs. Browning was of Jessie to Best-in-Show–winning Champion Tibet of Cornwallis who was co-owned by Mrs. Keke Blumberg. The first litter produced Champion Taglha Dum Cho, who finished with all majors from the puppy classes, and Champion Taglha Muni, who was co-owned with Ellen Lonigro and leased to Carolyn Herbel. Muni finished and subsequently was bred to Champion Pan Chen Tonka Sonan. Mrs. Browning owns one champion bred from Muni, Champion Kinderlands Tila of Taglha.

Meanwhile, a Sparky bitch, from Champion Ruffway's Marpa, was purchased from Ellen Lonigro. This little girl, Champion Kinderlands Tonka Tu, produced Group-winning Champion Taglha Sinsa of Kinderland and Champion Taglha Bee Uti, the latter a Tibet daughter.

Dum Cho, who remained with Mrs. Browning, was bred to Best-in-Show–winning Champion Korum Ti and produced Mrs. Browning's specials bitch, Champion Taglha Pokhara of Nottoway. "Poke" loved the show ring and placed twice in the Group from the classes. She finished in a big way by going Best of Winners at Trenton in 1973 (138 entries) for the American Lhasa Apso Club National Specialty. She was then retired and bred to Champion Tabu's King of Hearts. In her only litter, she produced Best-in-Show–winning Champion Taglha Kambu, Champion Taglha Kusu, and Champion Taglha Puckyi. Mrs. Browning now was ready to start a closer program of linebreeding.

Kusu, who was Best of Opposite Sex at Westminster in 1977, produced Champion Taglha Kubo, winner of the Southern Futurity Adult Division in 1979; Champion Taglha Kusuma, who was Winners Bitch at the Eastern American Lhasa Apso Club Specialty in 1977 and Winners Bitch at the Garden in the same year; Champion Taglha Mi Tambu, Best of Opposite Sex at the Garden in 1981; and Champion Taglha Linto who was Best of Opposite Sex at the Northern California American Lhasa Apso Club Spe-

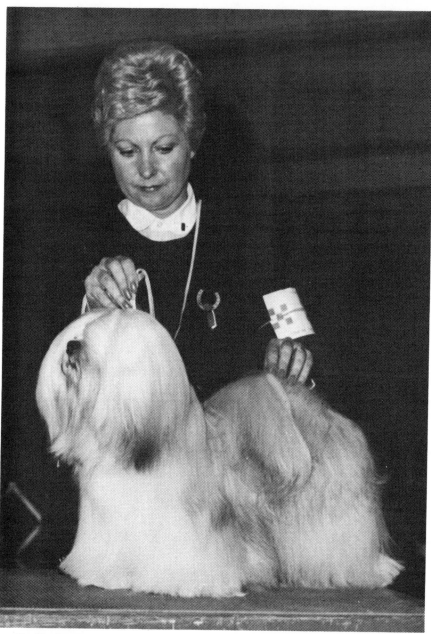

Ch. Taglha Pari of Tao Yin taking points toward's the title at Tuscaloosa in 1980. Owned by Jean Buck in Cincinnati, along with several others from the Taghla breeding program developed by Mrs. Wilson J. Browning, Jr., Norfolk, Virginia.

Ch. Donicia's Rhe Gan San, by Ch. Donicia's Chim Zu El Torro, ROM, ex Donicia's Tai Suke Lu, ROM, bred by the late Patricia Stewart. Owned at time of photo by R. L. Crowder, Takashi Lhasas; now owned by Jerec Kennels.

Am. and Can. Ch. Ja Ma's Kris-Tal Lea O'Tammering owned by Elaine Scharf, Tammering Lhasa Apsos.

cialty in 1982. This was certainly a lineup in which to take pride.

Tambu has already produced Champion Mi Taglha Tom Bu, Champion Mi Taglha Pebbles Rambu, Champion Taglha Mi Sok Tsu, and Champion Mi Taglha Tulip, who is the first Lhasa to go Best in Show in Japan. During the 1980s, Mrs. Browning has worked closely with Joan Buck in Cincinnati, who owns Tambu and many other Taglha dogs, including Champion Taglha Pari of Tao Yin.

During the past few years, Mrs. Browning has been doing less breeding in retirement. But she has finished Champion Taglha Valentine and Champion Taglha Nama Su of Thimilo. She is now enjoying working with an increasing number of wonderful breeders, including Evelyn Bigman in Boston and Laurie Turner in Raleigh.

TAKASHI

Takashi Lhasa Apsos at Independence, Missouri, are owned by Ronnie L. Crowder, a most enthusiastic and devoted member of the Lhasa fancy.

Takashi's El Capitan is an example of what Mr. Crowder likes in a Lhasa. His dogs are based on leading bloodlines from the Missouri area. El Capitan, who was bred by Linda White, goes back into the Bel-Air lines of which Mr. Crowder is a great admirer.

It was Ronnie Crowder who sent us the kennel story of the Donicia dogs, the handsome and influential winners owned by the late Patricia Stewart.

TAMMERING

Tammering Lhasa Apsos are a small kennel at Santa Barbara, California, owned by Elaine Scharf, who is a strong believer in breeding only when welcome homes are assured for each puppy which may be born, and/or when she herself is in need of a new show dog. Elaine places great emphasis in the breed on elegance, showiness, and beautiful, graceful movement.

In 1977, Elaine received the puppy who became American and Canadian Champion Ja Ma's Kris-Tal Lea O'Tammering as her Christmas gift. Born on December 14 of that year, bred by Janet and Marvin Whitman, "Krissy" was the pick of the litter, Elaine's shining star in the show ring, and her foundation bitch. She was owner-handled to her Canadian championship in 1979, then the following year completed her American title under the guidance of her breeder and good friend Janet Whitman.

Krissy is a daughter of Best-in-Show–winning Champion Arborhill's Rapso-Dieh, ROM (Best in Show Champion Everglo Spark of Gold—Champion Arborhill's Lee Sah, ROM), ex Champion Jovan's Midnight Lace, ROM (American, Canadian, Mexican, and Bermudian Champion Potala Chaing—Champion Tabu's Rhapsody in Red).

Sho True The Mud Pie, a handsome, pointed male, was selected as the sire to whom Krissy should be bred. (Sho True was sired by Best-in-Show–winning Champion Orlane's Vindicator, ROM, from Sunji Laitse of Krisna.) From their breeding came four lovely puppies, three females and one male. The male became American Champion Tammering's Samara Lea who completed his championship in late 1985. One female, Tammering's Natalea, is Canadian pointed. The other puppies went to pet homes.

Samara obtained his first Canadian point in July 1984 while on a holiday in Ontario, Canada. He began his American career in Texas with his good friend Sandy Trement, who handled him to his American championship.

As a sire, this handsome dog is off to a good start with litters numbering six and seven puppies, gold and red-gold, with a striking black overlay and mask.

Samara's sister, "Natasha," the smallest of the Sho True— Krissy litter, would fall asleep before she finished eating then would have to be aroused and urged to eat. It took awhile for her to catch up, but catch up she did! Her owner describes her as "a talky character who can spend ten minutes conversing with a piece of kibble before devouring it!" She received three points on a Canadian holiday in 1984, and will begin her American campaign in 1986. She has not yet been bred.

TN HI

Tn Hi Lhasa Apsos are owned by Mrs. Joyce Hadden of Stanfordville, New York, who established the kennel in 1966 and since that time has been a highly successful breeder whose Lhasas are noted for their sweet temperament and good health, in addition to their beauty.

Champion Tn Hi Zeus the Dethroner is the result of eight generations of Tn Hi Lhasas. A striking silver and white parti-color and a multiple Group winner, he is known for his devotion to his handler and for his vivacious, affectionate nature.

The deep red and golden-red color which prevails at Tn Hi Kennels assures good black pigment in puppies. Two champion sisters, Tn Hi I've Got Pizazz and Tn Hi Pixie Minx, have bouncy, happy offspring of their coloring who carry on the Tn Hi winning tradition in the show ring. When at home and retired, these Lhasas make magnificent companions, constantly offering their love and attention.

When retired from show competition in 1982, Champion Cameo's Khor-Ke San O'Honeydew was No. 5 Lhasa Apso in the nation. His offspring at Tn Hi Kennels are following in their sire's paw prints by winning in the show ring and winning hearts with their happy dispositions.

WELLINGTON

Wellington Kennels are owned by Paul S. Voight and Lois H. Voight of Burnsville, Minnesota, who purchased their first Lhasa Apso in 1972.

Several years later, the Voights decided that they would like to have a Lhasa of show quality, so in February 1976 they traveled East to the National which was being held in Louisville. Very sensibly, they wanted to see what dogs were being exhibited and to decide what "type" of animal appealed to them. They fell in love with a little red bitch who went Winners that day under a Dr. Berndt. Her name was Chiz Ari Shiloh, owned and bred by Madeline Chizever Durholz.

The Voights puchased "Lili," as she was called, from Maddie, and she became the first champion bitch for the Wellington Kennel and the foundation of its breeding program. She is the Top-Producing Lhasa Bitch so far, the Voights tell us, with 16 United States Champion offspring and five others who are pointed. Some of her kids include Best-in-Show–winning Champion Chiz Ari Wellington Shofar, Champion Chiz Ari Autumn (an Eastern Grand Futurity winner), Champion Wellington's Comeuppance

(Best of Winners at the National Specialty in Kansas City under judge Stephen Campbell in 1983), Champion Wellington's Shady Deal, C.D. (Best Puppy in the 1982 Midwest Futurity and Lhasa high-point record holder for achieving the C.D.), Champion Wellington's Nice 'N Spicy (Winners Bitch at the Chicago International), and Champion Chiz Ari Wellington Zahar of Joval (Winners Dog at the Eastern National Specialty under judge Edd Bivin. Ten of Lili's 16 U.S. champions have had Group placements. Several of these 16 U.S. champions also have other international championships.

In July of 1977, the Voights traveled to the Northwest (Seattle) to visit Paul's father and meet Marianne Nixon. There they purchased Champion San Jo's Kian Kandi Kan, then still a puppy, from Marianne. Kandi, who became the second Wellington foundation bitch, was the Top-Winning Lhasa Apso Bitch in the United States in 1979.

Kandi produced seven champions, among them the multiple Best in Show Champion S. J. W. (Sun Jo Wellington) Waffle Stomper and Group-winning Champion S. J. W. Whipper Snapper.

A granddaughter of both Lili and Kandi, Wellington San Jo Tokyo Rose, was Reserve Winners Bitch at Westminster, Best of Winners at the Chicago International, and Winners Bitch at the Western Specialty, all in 1985.

The Voights have heavily used the outstanding stud dogs of Marianne Nixon's San Jo Kennel. Among them are Champion San Jo Shenanigan, C.D., ROM; Best in Show Champion San Jo's Raaga Looki Mei, ROM; Champion San Jo's Soshome Up; and Champion San Jo's Out of the Blue. They also have used their Lili and Kandi sons.

Since 1976, the Voights have had 31 Lhasas gain championship in the United States, 29 of which were bred at Wellington. Among those who are Wellington homebreds one finds two Best in Show winners, two Grand Futurity winners, 15 Group placers, and eight others who are pointed. Voight Lhasas have been specialed on the East and West Coasts and in the South, the Midwest, and the Northwest.

The goals in breeding at Wellington are (in the order named): excellent temperament, sound, healthy bodies, and fine type and excellent movement. The Voights breed and show Lhasas that

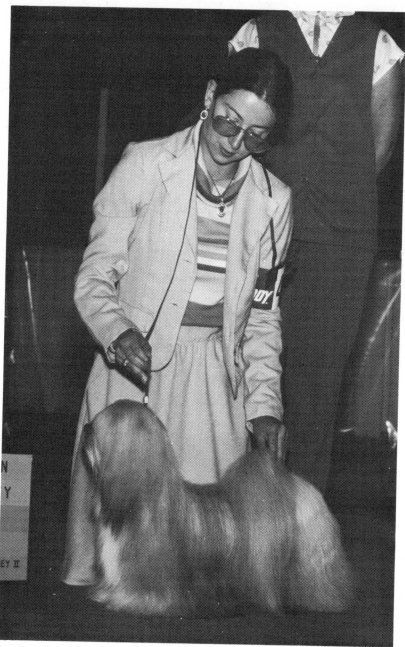

Ch. Chiz Ari Autumn, a Group-placing Lhasa by Ch. San Jo's Shenanigan, C.D., ROM, ex Ch. Chiz Ari Sehilot, ROM, bred by Lois H. and Paul S. Voight and Maddie Chizever Durholz. The Eastern Grand Futurity winner in 1980.

A.L.A.C. 1984

Ch. Wyndwood's Honeysuckle Rose, winner of a 5-point major, age seven months, at the Astrohall Series of Dog Shows. Finished at 13 months, owner-handled. Owned by Bobby and Kay Hales, Wyndwood Lhasas.

meet all of these criteria in so far as they are able. They are looking forward to the next generation with anticipation and pride.

WYNDWOOD

Wyndwood Lhasas, owned by Kay and Bobby Hales at Manvel, Texas, came into existence in 1976 with the purchase of Lhasa Apsos of Orlane linebreeding. In 1977, Kay Hales made her first purchase of the breed from Dorothy Kendall of Orlane. Her purchase, a bitch, Orlane's Sweet Finale, ROM, became the foundation producer at Wyndwood.

In her first litter, Sweet Finale produced a male who went on to become a Best in Show winner, Champion Wyndwood's Here Comes D Tank, as well as a well-known bitch, Champion Orlane's Solarie.

In 1979, Kay divorced and relocated in Texas where she now lives. Her husband, Bobby, and she really got going with the Lhasas in 1980. Their kennel is truly a team effort with both of them sharing the responsibility of breeding and showing Lhasas, with a little help from their youngest son when possible. Wyndwood is one of three Lhasa kennels in Texas eligible for the ROM rating, as it has bred ten or more Lhasa champions.

The original Wyndwood Lhasas were all of Orlane breeding. In 1983, a young male was purchased from Marianne Nixon whom the Hales finished that year, Champion San Jo's Wingtips. "Winger" has been bred to the Haleses' Orlane bitches, and that blending has proved a beautiful combination for them. So far, Winger has four champion offspring with several more major pointed. Kay and Bobby feel very pleased with the Orlane-San Jo outcrossing they have done, and are now beginning to see the second and third generation results from this breeding.

In August of 1985, the Hales experienced the thrill of a lifetime for breeders when one of their puppies, Wyndwood's Sundance of Mai-Li, shown by their son, was Best Puppy in Futurity from the 6-9 months class at the Eastern Futurity, and their 13-month-old bitch, Champion Wyndwood's Stormy Weather, handled by Kay, was Best Adult and Grand Futurity winner the same day. The Eastern Futurity was held in conjunction with the American Lhasa Apso Club National Specialty and had over 70 entries.

The Hales believe in showing their own dogs, and they encour-

Ch. Hamilton Shim-Tru, by Ch. Hamilton Snadupa ex Hamilton Saung, is the foundation of Zijuh Kennels. This representative of the pure Hamilton breeding is the background of the American Lhasa world. Owned by Mildred B. Loeb, Zujuh Lhasa Apsos.

age people purchasing puppies from them to do the same. They offer any help needed with handling and grooming instructions, and most of their patrons have been extremely successful. One of them in whom the Hales take pride is Mrs. Alan (Leslie) Bean, who purchased her first dog from them, a bitch whom she successfully finished in approximately three months of showing, and with whom she now has won a Group First, all owner-handled.

ZIJUH

Zijuh Lhasa Apsos, owned by Mildred B. Loeb, Napa, California, are founded on the pure Hamilton lines represented by their first bitch, Champion Hamilton Shim Tru. Later, another bitch was added, and between the two of them and their puppies, the Lhasa population at Zijuh, to quote their owner, "grew like the Nutcracker tree."

The second bitch was Donna Cardella's Tsng Shim-Tru, who among her puppies had four who became champions and a fifth who pointed but never finished.

During the early years, Mildred Loeb always went out for stud service on her bitches. Later she decided that she would like to have a stud dog of her own, which led to the purchase of Champion Everglo Zijuh Tomba.

Tsng was bred to Champion Zijuh Tsam (one of Shim Tru's puppies), producing a litter of four puppies. One of these was a bitch who became Champion Zijuh Jinda. She, in her turn, was bred to Tomba, producing the Best in Show winner Champion Sharbo Zijuh Zer Khan, Group winner Champion Sharbo Zijuh Kamara, and Champion Sharbo Zijuh Cha-La.

Shim-Tru's offspring were Champion Zijuh Tsam (dog), Champion Zijuh Kata (bitch, no offspring), Champion Zijuh Seng-Tru (dog), and Champion Zijuh El Toro (dog).

Best in Show winning Japanese Ch. Marlo Madame, by Ch. San Jo Soshome Up, ROM, ex Ch. Marlo's I Love Lucy (ROM eligible) was born in July 1982. Sold to Mr. Maehara in Japan, Madame has won two Bests in Show there and was that country's Top Winning Lhasa for 1984. Pictured at six months of age taking Reserve Winners Bitch at North California Lhasa Apso Club Specialty while a puppy. Bred by Lynn Lowy, Marlo, Beverly Hills, California.

Chapter 4

Lhasa Apsos Around the World

LHASA APSOS IN GREAT BRITAIN

It was the custom of the Dalai Lama of Tibet to present Lhasa Apsos to esteemed friends and dignitaries who visited him from other countries. British friends were among those so honored, and so it was that these little dogs found their way to England during the 1930s. As the breed was then new to Great Britain, fanciers there were not quite sure of the differences between Lhasas and other breeds from Tibet which were also being seen. Confusion arose, as there is a similarity in type between several of the Tibetan breeds. The logical solution seemed to be a club which could separate the breeds and publicize the conformation and characteristics of each. Thus, the Tibetan Breeds Association was established in 1934.

The breeding of Lhasa Apsos in England rolled along on a fairly even keel from that year until the late 1970s, when it was arranged for Dorothy Kendall's fantastic dog, Champion Orlane's Intrepid, to visit England for championship competition and do some stud work there.

When Intrepid returned to the United States, he left behind a legacy of greatness among his British friends which will benefit the breed over years and generations to come, for his achievements as a sire have been remarkable indeed.

For example there is the celebrated young dog Champion Saxonwoods Hackensack, bred by Mrs. A. Matthews and owned by Mrs. Blyth, who achieved the notable success of being the *first* Lhasa Apso to go Best in Show at the prestigious Cruft's event. What a day and occasion for the Lhasa! Jubilation was high and Hackensack's admirers were plentiful.

Hackensack, whose dam is Champion Saxonsprings Chussekuankuan, was born May 22, 1979, which made him four and one half years old at the time of his great achievement.

As a sire, Hackensack's progeny includes the well-known winner Champion Hardacres Hunters Moon (from Hardacres Midnight Rambler), born in December 1981, bred by Mrs. Matthews but owned by Mrs. Ewers. Hackensack also sired Champion Ragoosa Mitoyah (ex Saxonsprings Amarillo), born in 1981 and bred and owned by Mrs. T. Lewis.

Mrs. Blyth, as a breeder, has a record of many exciting accomplishments. It is certain that none is more valued than that of having bred the superb bitch Champion Saxonwoods Fresno, who has become the Top Winning Lhasa Apso of all time in Great Britain.

Owned by Goeff Corish of Ormskirk, Lancs, Fresno's victories include the winning of at least 38 Challenge Certificates, Best of Breed at Crufts in 1981 and 1985, and Dog of the Year for 1982. She is a half sister to Hackensack, being by English and American Champion Orlane's Intrepid ex Champion Hardacre Not So Dandy at Saxonsprings.

At Crufts in 1987, the winner of the Dog Challenge Certificate went on to Best of Breed. He is Champion Lingston Midas, born October 24, 1982, by Lingston The Jester ex Dewell Hannah. A homebred, he belongs to Mrs. S. Linge. The Bitch Challenge Certificate and Best of Opposite Sex were awarded to Champion Timazinti Clemenciae of Sudek (by Timazinti Teddy ex Clarween Lindy Lu), who was bred by Mrs. J. Scarll and born in October 1982.

Reserve C.C.s at Crufts in 1987 went to Champion Monkspath Golden Boy, a homebred dog belonging to Mrs. S. A. Wilkes, and Domensa's Only You, a bitch bred and owned by Mrs. Poole.

Other breeders doing well in the British Lhasa Apso world in-

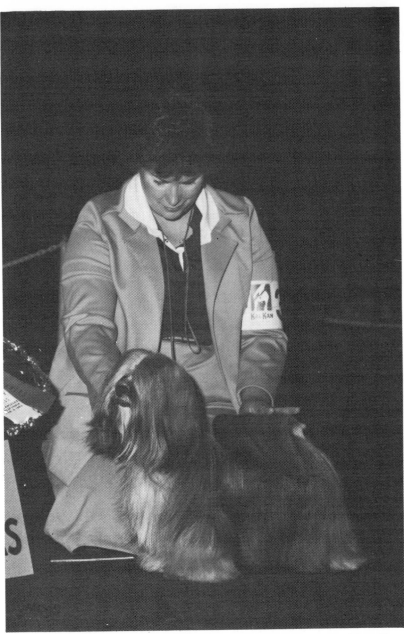

Am. and Ger. Ch. Marlo Dolsa Jazzercize, by Ch. Jampo's Tis Himself ex Marlo Dolsa Brimfield Parfay. Sold as a puppy, this dog was returned, after which he completed title in three months, then was sold to Gitta Haberle in West Germany. Bred by Lynn Lowy, Beverly Hills, California.

clude Mrs. P. T. C. Luiz, who has English and American Champion Kinderland's Ta Sen Nito of Parlu. Bred by Ellen Lonigro in the United States, he was born in 1978 and is a son of Champion Windsong's Gusto of Innsbrook.

LHASA APSOS IN CANADA

The Lhasa Apso enjoys fine popularity in Canada, where there are a number of breeders producing really top quality dogs. Canadian Lhasas are now competing on a level with United States dogs, making it very exciting when all of these beautiful dogs come together at specialty and other important shows.

At least two Canadian specialty clubs are busy promoting the best interests of their breed with specialty shows and other programs beneficial to fanciers. One is the Lhasa Apso Club of Canada. The other, for those folks in the eastern part of the country is the Lhasa Apso Club of Ontario. I am sure that Canadian Lhasa fanciers are welcome to contact either club if they are interested in joining. Specialty club membership is extremely beneficial to anyone either new or established in a particular breed.

The Standard for the Lhasa Apso is quite similar between Canada and the United States, with one major exception: in Canada a Lhasa Apso measuring more than 11 1/2 inches in height at the withers shall be disqualified from competition at Canadian Kennel Club dog shows. This action, in this writer's (and judge's) opinion is a giant step forward toward correcting the obvious oversize in many Lhasa rings. We understand that during 1985 several Lhasas were measured out for oversize. As much as we who judge dislike having to do so, it should be remembered that disqualifications in a breed Standard exist for purpose, and that no judge should ever overlook this fact. I have often been aghast at the huge size of many otherwise gorgeous Lhasas at shows in the United States and feel that Canada has set a sterling example by taking positive steps to prevent or correct this problem.

Canadian breeders must have literally floated on air after the 1985 American Lhasa Apso Club (ALAC) Specialty Show. Just think of the triumph in the fact that the Best in Specialty Show (or Best of Breed), Winners Dog, and Winners Bitch at this most important of all U.S. Lhasa events were awarded to three different entries from Canada. I am quite certain this was the first time this occurred with ALAC, and I can only comment that Canadian breeders must be doing a great deal that is right.

Its 1985 specialty show was the largest specialty held by the American Lhasa Apso Club. When Canadian and American Champion Nexus Lam Can Chin won, he thereby became the only Canadian-bred Lhasa Apso ever to have gained both an all-breed American Best in Show and the American Lhasa Apso Club Specialty. "Casper," as this dog is called, was bred by Gerri and Tony Viklicky and is owned by Lilliam Woods and Rebecca Kraus.

Irlees

Irlees (pronounced earlys) Lhasa Apsos are situated in Toronto, Ontario, and were established in 1974. Cathy (nee Freedman) Groulx and her husband Jim have become the breeders and/or owners of more than 35 champions in Canada, the United States, and Bermuda since that time. They have always worked together as a family, with Jim's son, Paul, doing much of the handling now. Having a small kennel, Cathy and Jim seldom have more than five adult dogs in the house and raise one or two litters annually.

The foundation stud dog at Irlees, multiple Group-winning Canadian, American, and Bermudian Champion Ja-ma's Rennegade, ROM, as of 1985, is the sire of more than 23 champions, some having C.D. and U.D. obedience titles. He was bred by Janet and Marv Whitman (Ja-Ma Lhasas) and Dr. and Mrs. Kornfeld.

Another Group-winning stud dog at this kennel is Canadian and American Champion Ma Lee's Finagle, ROM, who to date has sired six champions. He was bred by Marilyn Lisciandro (Ma Lee's Lhasas).

The goal of Cathy and Jim Groulx is to breed producers. Champion Irlees Llenroc Steppen Stone, owned by Margaret Northey, is the sire of four champions. American and Canadian Champion Irlees Matter of Choice is at stud in Holland with Mrs. Beryl Hickman O'Donnell. Several of the Irlees girls are ROM producers. These include Cajim's Black Nava for Irlees (ROM eligible), dam of three champions; her daughter, Champion Irlees Golden Opportunity, ROM, dam of four champions; and Champion Irlees Tremar By Golly By Gosh, ROM, dam of four champions, whose mom, American, Canadian, and Bermudian Champion Shangrelu Rainy Days O'Irlees, ROM, is the dam of three champions.

Ch. Tru Blu's Huoai Tahna (by Best in Show winning Am. and Can. Ch. San Jo's Soshome, ROM, ex Hudai Meiti Nijin) is another Lhasa from Tahna Kennels, Barbara E. Hamon, Keswick, Ontario.

Then there are Champion Irlees Cajim Razzle Dazzle and Champion Irlees Reina Marie Zolee, owned by Carlos and Valerie Diaz. Both girls are producing outstanding progeny who are destined for the show ring.

Never to be forgotten by those at Irlees is their very first female, Utsu Kushi Yuvo, who produced four champions in her only litter (consisting of five puppies). Utsu certainly put her owners off to an excellent start as successful breeders.

With intensive study in genetics and pedigree, the owners of Irlees are working for good temperament, correct size, and breed type.

Tahna

Tahna Lhasa Apsos, a well-established Canadian kennel over a number of years, is located at Keswick, Ontario, where it is owned by Barbara Hamon.

This kennel has been associated with many an important Lhasa, either by breeder or by owner. Among the former, multiple Best in Show and Group-winning Champion Tahna's Tarbaby of Tebar, born in October 1974, blazed quite a trail of glory. Bred by Barbara, he was owned by Pam Bruce and is a son of Champion Potala Keke's Tumba Tu ex Champion Tarah Shan of Zaralingka.

Also bred by Barbara, Champion Tahna's Caroling Caroline, born in 1979, is a lovely daughter of Champion Tahna's Storm'N Norman ex Champion Tahna's Afternoon Delight.

Caroline is the foundation bitch of a Mr. and Mrs. Cunningham, for whom, with limited breeding, she has produced five champions. Additionally, she is a Best of Breed winner with Group placements to her credit.

Multiple Group-placing Champion Tahna's Storm'N Norman was born in July 1976. Bred and owned by Barbara, he has been a tremendous asset at Tahna, particularly as a sire. He is a son of American Champion Tabu's Fame and Fortune ex Champion Tarah Shan of Zaralina.

Champion Cameo's Austin Healey was bred by Dr. Janine J. Charboneau but is owned by Barbara Hamon. He is a son of American and Canadian Champion Hell's A Blazen Billy The Kid ex American and Canadian Champion Cameo's Porsche, and at his first show, at age eleven months, he took a five-point major. Austin is now a multiple Group placer and the sire of numerous champions.

Champion Tahna's Spanish Coffee is a Group-placing dog who completed his championship at eight months of age undefeated. He also won Best Bred by Exhibitor for the Non-Sporting Group in a sweepstakes judged by Dr. Richard Meen.

Champion Cookies N' Cream of Tahna, by Champion Tru Blu's Hudai Tahna ex Pekoe, was bred by S. Stark and is owned by Barbara Hamon. This exciting parti-color bitch won Best of Winners at the American Lhasa Apso Club National Specialty in Lockport, New York (September 1985) over the largest entry of Lhasas ever assembled to date.

She went on from the National to win Best of Opposite Sex at the Ontario Lhasa Apso Specialty the following month. Then in December 1985, she won the National Canadian Lhasa Apso Specialty under Mrs. Keke Blumberg. During very limited showing, this gorgeous bitch also gained multiple Group placements.

Talsma

Talsma Lhasa Apsos are at Lisle, Ontario, where Alan and Mary Capko are doing a super job with the breed.

The moment Mary Capko first saw a Lhasa, she was gone on the breed, even though she had never been a dog owner. Her heart literally stood still upon her first sight of a little girl Lhasa, belonging to a neighbor, at the Capkos' summer cottage. Mary was thoroughly convinced that this was the most beautiful and mysterious breed she had ever seen.

Obviously, Mary was yearning for a Lhasa of her own, as she immediately started doing research on not only the breed but on Tibet and its culture as well. Prompted by much coaxing at home, Alan discovered a newspaper advertisement which led to the Capko's acquaintance with Audrey Carpenter of Tree Point Kennels. A visit there led to the Capkos returning home with a Lhasa who became Tree Point Else, ROM, named for the lioness in the story *Born Free.*

Mary and Alan started out with the intention of just having a pet, but when the time came, it was decided that Elsa should be bred, even if just for one litter. Elsa did not possess the most abundant of coats, but she was a pretty girl with gorgeous color. Mary, to quote her own words, "Knew nothing about conformation, nor was thinking about conformation yet—that was to follow later."

The Capkos had heard of Sheila Pike, who breeds Lhasas in the London, Ontario, area so Mary made arrangements to breed Elsa to the Pike's Potala Ching-tu of Zaralinga. However, the choice of stud was changed at the last moment to a young son of this dog, Lord Raffles by name. This was in 1976, and the breeding produced a litter of eight.

By the time the puppies were to be registered and thought given to select a kennel prefix to add to their names and to those of future Lhasas owned or bred by the Capkos, the Lhasas had become a family project. So it seemed appropriate that the name be a combination of the first initial of each family member's name which is how Talsma was coined.

It was Sheila Pike, a most helpful friend as the puppies grew, who started the Capkos competing in the show ring. Out of that very first litter, five became Canadian Champions: Talsma's Oh So Sau-Ceih, Talsma's Sergeant Pepper, Talsma-Zara Zaralinga's Shining Star, Talsma's W. C. Muggins, and Talsma's Kara Mia Myne. Thus it was that Elsa was on her way to ROM eligibility! Although never shown, this lovely bitch made a notable contribution to her breed as a quality producer.

Lord Raffles, not long after this litter, was sold to a Lhasa fan-

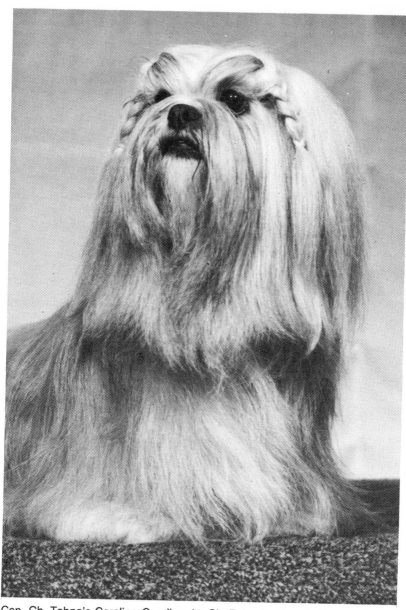

Can. Ch. Tahna's Caroling Caroline, by Ch. Tahna's Storm'n Norman ex Ch. Tahna's Afternoon Delight, owned by Mr. and Mrs. William Butterworth. Bred by Barbara Hamon, Tahna Lhasas, Keswick, Ontario.

Can. and Am. Ch. Talsma's E'Nuff Said (Talsma's Eight is Enough—Can. Ch. Talsma's Emprise) finishing his American title as Winners Dog at the American Lhasa Apso Club National Specialty in 1985. Handled by Wendy Paquette for owners Alan and Mary Capko, Lisle, Ontario.

cier in Brazil and thus became unavailable for Mary to use again as a stud dog. He made a name for himself (in Brazil) in short order as the winner of six or so Bests in Show, but considering the puppies he and Elsa had produced, it is a pity that this was his only litter in either Canada or the United States.

For the next litter at Talsma, the Raffles-Elsa daughter, Talsma's Oh So Sau-Ceih, was chosen. A Specialty winner by then, she was bred to Champion Sakya Hallelujah, a son of Windsong Gusto of Innsbrook. Following in her mom's pawprints, she too produced a litter of eight, these being seven boys and one girl. As was their usual custom, the Capkos kept the girl from the litter for show and breeding, but this time they saw their way clear to keeping a male as well. They named him Talsma Eight Is Enough as he had been the last puppy born. "Nuffers" was sent to the United States in due time to be prepared for showing and did very well as a youngster. However, due to unfortunate circumstances, his show career ended early, and Nuffers returned home to become the Capkos' "main man" around the house.

Nuffers made a very great contribution to the Lhasa world through his son, Champion Talsma's E'Nuff Said, from Talsma's Emprise, who has proved no less than a sensation in the keenest show competition.

"Mikey" (E'Nuff Said) became Canada's No. 2 Lhasa, *Dogs in Canada*, All-Breed System, in 1984 as well as No. 10 Non-Sporting Dog. Also, he was No. 1 Lhasa under the Lhasa Apso Club of Canada Breed System. He is a multiple Specialty winner in both the United States and Canada who completed his championship under Dorothy Nickles with a five-point major at the 1985 American Lhasa Apso Club Specialty Show. As he is a young dog, a continued highly exciting future is anticipated for him, as is considerable success as a sire.

Two Orlane bitches have recently joined the Lhasas at Talsma. They are Orlane Impact A'Talsma, who combines Orlane and English bloodlines, and Orlane Fortunate Cookie, who is an Intrepid daughter. These bitches, bred to E'Nuff Said, have given the Capko youngsters what should become marvelous additions to the kennel. They are Canadian Champion Talsma's Infinite Legend, who completed his title at age nine months, and a lovely bitch, Talsma's Golden Tee Bisket.

Am. and Can. Ch. Marlo Kaam Whistling Dixie was whelped in May 1982, by Ch. Marlo's Icecream Man O'Rimmon ex Kim Leng De Colour, bred and owned by Lynn Lowy, Marlo, Beverly Hills, California.

Family portrait: *Right,* Am. and Can. Ch. Tob Ci of Shukti Lingka, by Ch. Ling-khor Bhu of Norbulingka ex Yum Yum VII, with *left,* her daughter, Ka-Ra of Shukti Lingka, sired by Ch. Reiniet's Roial Chanticleer. Photographed at Vactionaland Dog Club with their owner, Harriet A. Silverman. Tob Ci won first in the Non-Sporting Group at this show.

Even though the Capkos breed on a small scale, all puppies are raised as show prospects, including those of pet quality. All are raised, trained, and housebroken; all receive equal love and attention. Talsma puppies have gone to super homes and have led to many valued new friendships for Alan and Mary Capko.

LHASAS IN AUSTRALIA

Australia is a country of great progress where purebred dogs are concerned. One can look there today and find outstanding kennels in most of the popular breeds.

To this Lhasa Apsos are no exception, and although I have not yet visited Australia, I do keep abreast of what is taking place there through friends and colleagues who have seen the dogs personally.

We note that there is considerable Saxonsprings breeding (from the United Kingdom) in Australia, represented by such dogs as Australian Champion Saxonsprings Flashback, a dog born in 1983 by English Champion Saxonsprings Hackensack (U.K.) ex English Champion Saxonsprings Fresno (U.K.). Flashback belongs to Mrs. H. J. Gillett at Bangor in New South Wales, who also owns a promising youngster, born in 1984, Sisakyi Fast Lane, a son of Flashback from another importation, Australian Champion Peni Pet Stop. (Ramornie Kennels have a littermate of Peni's, Sisakyi First Class.)

Another Saxonsprings import belongs to Ms. L. C. Christie, Double Bay, N.S.W., this one being Australian Champion Saxonsprings Flair. She is a litter sister to Mrs. Gillett's Flashback.

Miss A. D. Michaelis has the Singtuk Lhasas at Terry Hills, N.S.W., where she has several interesting representatives now in competition, sired by Australian Champion Everglo Carol of California (imported from the United States). Miss Michaelis also owns Australian Champion Singtuk Lhakyi, born in 1977, by a U.K. import, Australian Champion Hardacre Morning Shine ex Australian Champion Singtuk Syncopate; and Syncopate herself, born in 1975, by Singtul Flying Circus ex Champion Belazieths Birdsong, U.K. import.

An extremely dominant exhibitor in New South Wales is Ramornie Kennels which, at the 1985 Royal Easter Show, had no less than six champions among the entries with about an equal number of young hopefuls. They have two Australian-bred Australian Champion dogs, Ameson Autumn Frost and Ramornie Kula La, their parentage being Australian Champion Gyalwa Horris—Australian Champion Amesen Opal Moon for Autumn Frost; and Australian Champion Ranneks Halma—Australian Champion Delderland Kyitchu for Kula La.

Ramornie seems to be particularly strong in bitches. From Queensbury, they have Australian Champion Delderland Kala La, born in 1983, by Australian Champion Ramornie Kulu La—Delderland Sally Ann; and Delderland Misty Lara (Australian Champion Ramornie Pied Piper—Australian Champion Gyalwa Lavender).

Another at Ramornie is a son of Queensbury Australian Champion Delderland Yule Snow from Australian Champion Shelaurie Heatwave. He is Ramornie Shor Tesan, born in 1984. Plus there are two bitch puppies, Ramornie Kiri Tekanawa and Ramornie Spring Melody, littermated by Queensland Australian Champion Delderland Yule Snow ex Australian Champion Ramornie Trishna.

Mrs. P. F. Davis, N.S.W., owns a young imported dog from the United States, American Champion Hale Alii G Wata Grouch, sired by another U.S. import, Australian Champion Hale Alii Bit of Gusto, whom she also owns. Wata Grouch was from American Champion Hale Alii Sweet Okole. Sweet Okole is by American Champion Windsong's Gusto of Innsbrook from American Champion Hale Alii Kupono.

Mrs. D. Herbe has a Gusto son too, imported from Canada. He is Australian Champion Absosengky Cheng (ex Udelar Bidgy), born in 1983. Mrs. Herbe is a resident of Kambah.

Brackenbury Tong of Cheska, imported from the United Kingdom, is the sire of at least two Australian champions. They are Ladakh Pandora, owned by T. J. and Mrs. J. A. Thomas, and Udelewar Tonge Kia, owned by P. L. Warby.

LHASAS IN SOUTH AFRICA

Probably the most exciting Lhasa event of 1985 took place in South Africa, where a member of the breed scored a sensational victory in winning Best in Show at the famed Goldfields event, over an entry exceeding 2,300 dogs. Excitement was high as was

South African Ch. Tabu's Heart to Heart Gramar of Penash, by C. Tabu's Stars and Stripes ex Ch. Tabu's Queen of Hearts, bred by Carolyn Herbel and Grace Vanden Heuvel.

the approval of the crowds who witnessed the thrilling win by Champion Lady W's Boy Boy, owned by Mrs. Ian Bell.

The Bells, we understand, have a sizable Lhasa kennel and have bred many good Lhasa dogs. Winning was by no means a new experience for Boy Boy who, at age six years, had a good number of breed and Group successes on his record. His 1985 victory, however, was his first Best in Show.

Boy Boy is an American export to South Africa, carrying with him the bloodlines of multiple Best in Show winner Champion Potala Keke's Candy Bar and Lady W's Sweet Georgia Brown. Thus he represents the breeding programs of Mrs. Keke Blumberg and his own breeder, Barbara Chevalier.

Boy Boy's wins at Goldfields were made under Dr. Samuel Draper from Monroe, New York, in the Non-Sporting Group; and under Mrs. Dorothea Daniell-Jenkins, from Ontario, Canada, for Best in Show.

Ian Bell completely shares his wife's enthusiasm for Lhasas, participating in activities of the kennel as well as being a popular judge.

Ch. Marlo's Icecream Cone, by Ch. Marlo's Icecream Man O'Rimmon ex Bevalynn Maija of Marlo, was born February 1975. Bred by Lynn Lowy, this dog was sold to Maria Aspuru whose Tsung Lhasa Apsos were so very important and well known in the Florida area until Mrs. Aspuru's death a few years back.

Chapter 5

Standard of the Breed

AKC STANDARD FOR THE LHASA APSO

CHARACTER—Gay and assertive, but chary of strangers.

SIZE—Variable, but about 10 inches or 11 inches at shoulder for dogs, bitches slightly smaller.

COLOR—All colors equally acceptable with or without dark tips to ears and beard.

BODY SHAPE—The length from point of shoulders to point of buttocks longer than height at withers, well ribbed up, strong loin, well-developed quarters and thighs.

COAT—Heavy, straight, hard, not woolly nor silky, of good length, and very dense.

MOUTH AND MUZZLE—The preferred bite is either level or slightly undershot. Muzzle of medium length; a square muzzle is objectionable.

HEAD—Heavy head furnishings with good fall over eyes, good whiskers and beard; skull narrow, falling away behind the eyes in a marked degree, not quite flat, but not domed or apple-shaped; straight foreface of fair length. Nose black, the length from tip of nose to eye to be roughly about one-third of the total length from nose to back of skull.

EYES—Dark brown, neither very large and full, nor very small and sunk.

EARS—Pendant, heavily feathered.

LEGS—Forelegs straight, both forelegs and hind legs heavily furnished with hair.

FEET—Well feathered, should be round and catlike, with good pads.

TAIL AND CARRIAGE—Well feathered, should be carried well over back in a screw; there may be a kink at the end. A low carriage of stern is a serious fault.

Approved July 11, 1978

THE BRITISH STANDARD

The Kennel Club of Great Britain Standard for the Lhasa Apso is similar to that of the AKC, an exception being in the measurement of height. In Great Britain, the size, ideally, should be ten inches at shoulder for dogs; bitches slightly smaller.

LHASA APSOS THROUGH A JUDGE'S EYE

What do we look for in judging Lhasa Apsos? What are to be considered the breed's most valued attributes and most unsettling faults? How are decisions reached when comparison between dogs takes place? All are questions which I am sure arise frequently in the minds of the newcomer to a breed or a spectator at the average dog show.

The Lhasa Apso was developed to be a strong, sturdy, indoor guard dog. For that he must be capable of moving with strength and lasting power, covering ground with a minimum of effort. This is achieved through coordination between the forequarters

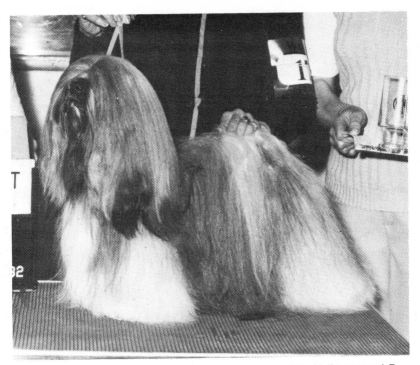

Ch. Anbara-Rimar Grin N'Bear It, co-owned by Mrs. Rita Holloway and Barbara Wood, shown at one of his many Group Firsts; this occasion under the author at North Country in 1982. "Grinner" is in residence with the Holloways at Newark, Delaware.

and the hindquarters. The shoulders and forelegs must be placed in a way to enable a long reaching out of the forepaws, which is created by correct placement and angulation of the shoulders. To keep things operating smoothly, the hindquarters must at the same time be sturdy and well muscled, with good bend at stifle and hocks placed low, the bone of the hind leg straight from hock joint to the ground. A dog built in this manner can cover ground with a minimum of effort, thus it has lasting power and does not tire at the slightest exertion.

The Lhasa should look strong and well proportioned, with everything in correct ratio. The neck should be nicely arched and of fair length to carry the head correctly. An overly short neck leads to the very ugly condition in which the dog forges along with its head seeming to stick straight out forward from the shoulders—a decidedly clumsy and unattractive appearance!

At the American Lhasa Apso Club Specialty in 1972. Ch. Chen Korum-T, on the *right* with Bob Sharp handling, Best of Breed. His daughter, on *left,* Best of Opposite Sex. Photo courtesy of Robert D. Sharp.

The head is of particular importance to Lhasa breed type. During the early 1930s a tremendous amount of speculation started over whether or not some breeders were crossing Shih Tzu blood with that of the pure Tibetan Lhasa Apso. The roar of protest from those who felt this to be true was understandably loud and clear. Whether or not such actions did take place, only the people involved could know, but it all led to very careful scrutiny of Lhasa heads, mouths, and muzzles for quite a period of time thereafter.

The true Lhasa Apso head is narrow, the muzzle slender and about equal to one third of the total head length. Any tendency toward a blunt muzzle is to be penalized. By *slender* it is not intended that the muzzle should be "snipey" or too pointed, just that it should look slender in correct balance to the skull. The bite finishes off the picture, correctly either level or slightly undershot.

126

The modern Lhasa Apso is a gorgeous picture of beauty. Coats, truly glorious, are long, thick, correctly textured, and, generally speaking, well put down.

The problem area in the breed, as far as conformation, is the number of truly huge dogs we are seeing. Perhaps it would be wise for the American Lhasa Apso Club to consider a height disqualification along the lines of that just under way in Canada.

Some hindquarters are very poorly assembled when one gets one's hands on the dog—this covered, at least to some extent, by the "full speed ahead" technique of racing one's charge around the ring. Dogs gaited in this manner always make me suspicious, as many a poor rear gets camouflaged in this manner. I like to see a Lhasa move out, but only as fast as he can do so smoothly. Bouncing along is decidedly unattractive and atypical of the breed.

Group winning Am. and Can. Ch. Marlo Rocky Road, July 19,1982, bred and owned by Lynn Lowy, Marlo, Beverly Hills, California.

Ch. Jolee's Spike Jones moves along with the good reach and drive so essential to correct action in a Lhasa. Elizabeth Faust, owner, New Braunfels, Texas. Photographed at Westminster 1985.

A poorly carried tail (which we do not see too frequently) is an important fault, since one of the type characteristics of the Tibetan breeds is the tight kink in the tail.

The body should feel solid and well muscled, with well-developed ribs and a strong loin. The back should be muscular, solid, and of correct porportion.

In judging, one must compare the dogs and select those who are closest to the standard's words as the winners. There is no such thing as a perfect, fault-free dog, but we must not lose sight of the assets of that dog. I would rather have a typical, well-balanced dog with a single fault than a common dog who is just mediocre all over—no great faults, but no particular assets. In looking at a dog, we must seek the beauty of the *total* dog, and not just hunt for faults. Positive judging is the most constructive type of judging and the most helpful to a breed.

1↑   2↓

← **Overleaf:**

1. Two winning sisters, a year apart in age, sired by Ch. Tn Hi Lammi Po Kah. Ch. Tn Hi I've got Pizazz, *left;* and Ch. Tn Hi Pixi Minx *right.* Joyce Hadden, Tn Hi Lhasa Apsos, Standfordville, New York.

2. *Right,* Keke Blumberg owner-handling Ch. Potala Keke's Tambu-Tu. *Left,* Jeanne Hope with Tomba's half brother, Ch. Potala Japalan Camelot. *Center;* Mrs. Anne Warner, judge.

Overleaf: →

1. Ch. Marlo Dolsa Coming Out Parti, by Ch. Suntory Four on the Floor ex Ch. Marlo's One Of A Kind, ROM, is a littermate of Ch. Marlo Somethin Else and Ch. Marlo Ultrabrite. Bred and owned by Lynn Lowy, Marlo, Beverly Hills, California.

2. Ch. Tabu's Very Short Tale, a young dog by Ch. Tabu's Rags to Riches ex Goldmere Dharma. Owned by Norman and Carolyn Herbel, Lucas, Kansas.

3. Can. and Am. Ch. Talsma's E'Nuff Said by Talsma's Eight is Enough ex Talsma's Emprise. Owned by Alan and Mary Capko, Lisle, Ontario, Canada.

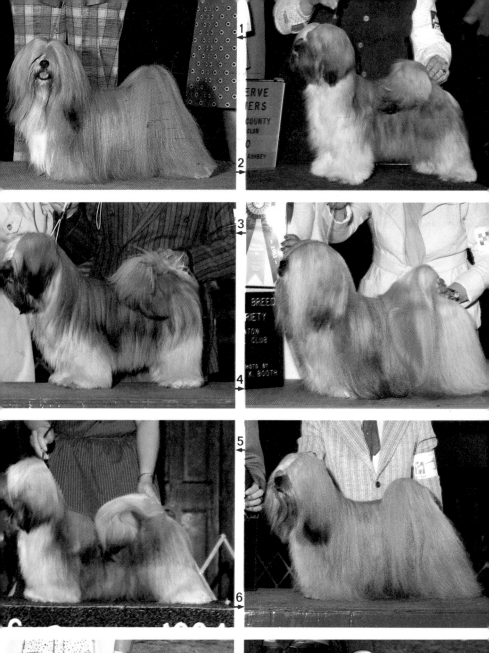
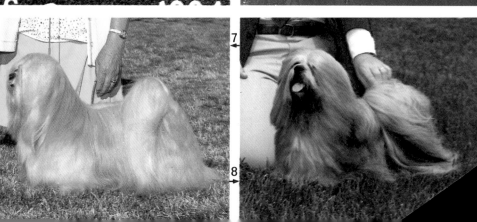

← **Overleaf:**

1. Am. and Can. Best in Show winning Ch. Orlane's Be-Sparky of Al-Mar, owner-handled by Marjorie Lewis, Independence, Missouri, winning one of his Bests in Show, at Southeastern Iowa K.C. in February 1985. "Sparky" won three all-breed Bests in Show in the U.S. and three in Canada along with 43 Groups during his distinguished career.

2. Ch. Anbara-Rimar's Footloose Fox ROM, at her first show at age six months, by Ch. Anbara's Hobgoblin ex Ch. Rimar's The Frivolous Fox, ROM, she was bred by Barbara Wood and Stephen Campbell. Best Puppy in Futurity at the 1980 ALAC National Specialty.

3. Ch. Gene's Victor of Art-Est, by Ch. Tabu's King of Hearts, ROM, ex Ch. Art-Est She-Ma, ROM, was born February 1981. Here winning the points and on to Best of Breed over specials from the Puppy Class at eight months age. Handled here by the late Gene Foss winning under judge Dr. Sam Draper. Art and Esther DeFalcis, owners, Lawrenceville, Georgia.

4. Ch. Brandy's Singtuk of Gold, multiple Best of Breed and Group placing Lhasa, the sire of three champions with numerous pointed progeny in the ring as well, was one of 1983's Top Ten Lhasa Apsos for 1983. Bred, owned, and handled by Barbara Jo Lipsky, Schaumburg, Illinois.

5. Ch. Anbara-Rimar Raisin' A Ruckus, by Best in Show winning Ch. San Jo's Rusty Nail ex Ch. Anbara-Rimar's Footloose Fox, ROM, bred by Barbara Wood and Stephen Campbell here is winning a 5-point major at American Lhasa Apso Club's 1984 National Specialty from the 9–12 Month Puppy Class. Barbara Wood, owner, handling, Anbara Lhasa Apsos, Cranford, New Jersey.

6. Ch. Gene's Han-Som of Art-Est, born February 1981, son of Ch. Tabu's King of Hearts, ROM, ex Ch. Art-Est She-Ma, ROM, breeder-owned by Esther DeFalcis. Finished with three majors handled by his former owner, the late Gene Foss on most occasions. Han-som is the sire of Ch. Knolwood's Orianna. Art-Est Lhasa Apsos, Art and Esther DeFalcis, Lawrenceville, Georgia.

7. Ch. Golden Rules Char-Lee Brown in November 1975. Owned by Richard Brown and Darrell Smith, Las Cruces, New Mexico, for whom he was handled by Marjorie Lewis. He was a grandson of "Red Boy," sired by Ch. Al-Mar's Ala Kazam.

8. Multi-Group winning Am. and Can. Ch. Joymarc's Terra Cotta was the first show quality bitch at Arkay Lhasa Apsos, Bill and Becki Kraus, Detroit, Michigan. Handled by Bill Kraus, Terra Cotta was bred by Winifred Graya.

4

1. Ch. Barjo's Chin Te of Max-Min, a multiple Best of Breed winning bitch in keenest competition. Completely breeder/owner/handled by Barbara Jo Lipsky, Barjo Lhasa Apsos, Schaumberg, Illinois.

2. Ch. Bel-Air's El Toro Romeo, by Ch. Zijun El Toro ex Beck's Parti Doll. This, the foundation stud dog at Lorraine Cole's Bel-Air Lhasas, is the sire of six champions including the 1981 Westminster Best of Breed, Ch. Cameo's Khor-Kee San O'Honey Dew. Owner-handled here by Lorraine Cole.

3. Am. and Can. Ch. Lai-Dieh-Jane at age 10 months, taking first in the Puppy Class at Sarnia, Ontario, Canada. Bred, owned, and handled by Bill and Becki Krauss, Arkay Lhasa Apsos, Detroit, Michigan.

4. Ch. Barker's Sugar Coated at age 12 months. Sired by Saxonspring's Earle ex Ch. Barker's Sugar Lace, ROM. This multiple breed winner from the classes and winner of 12–18 Month Class at 1985 National Futurity was bred by Drs. Randolph and Sandra Barker and Sherri Andrews. Owned by the Barkers.

5. Morgas Honey Lee of Bhe-Jei's, sired by Ch. Orlane's Just About Right ex Na-Tasha-Ling III, was bred by Barbara Ling. Brook and Diane Morgas owners, Union City, California.

6. Ch. Barker's Capital Offense is a champion producer, who was 1st in the 12–18 month bitch class at the 1983 American Lhasa Club Eastern Futurity. Sired by Eng. and Am. Ch. Orlane's Intrepid, ROM, ex Ch. Barker's Sugar Lace, ROM. Bred and owned by Drs. Randolph and Sandra Barker, Charleston, West Virginia.

7. Jolee's Phantom of Brynwood taking his third point from the puppy class owner-handled, May 1985. Owned by Denise and Anne Olejniczak, Loves Park, Illinois.

8. Multiple Group winning Ch. Bhe-Jei's Beau Jolais winning Best of Breed at Sacramento in April 1985, handled by Don Rodgers for Bobbie Ling, Bhe-Jei's Lhasas, Menlo Park, California. Sired by Best in Show winning Ch. Sho-Tru's The Main Event ex Na-Tasha Ling III.

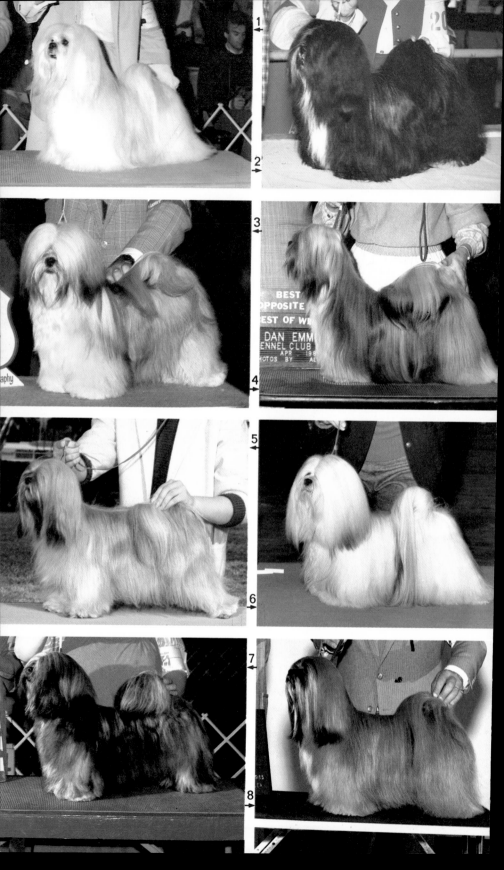

← **Overleaf:**

1. Talimer Danrew Gee Whiz, by Ch. Ja-Ma's Wen La Whiz, is co-owned by Andrew and Enid Londis, Danrew Kennels, Montgomery, New York.

2. Ch. Donicia's Tai-Suki Lu, ROM, by Ch. Mor-Knoll's Alex-A-Hente was bred by Janet Whitman and became the foundation bitch of Donicia's Lhasa Apsos. Four champions were produced by this bitch, all sired by Ch. Donicia's Chim Zu El Torro, ROM. Handled by owner, the late Pat Stewart, Donicia's Lhasas, Kansas City, Missouri.

3. Ch. Chiz Ari Sehilot, ROM, taking Winners Bitch and Best of Opposite Sex (4-point major) at Tuxedo Park K.C. in September 1976. Daryl Martin handled for owners Madeline P. Durholz and Joanne P. Baker. Sired by Group winning Ch. Pan Chen Tonka Sonan, ROM. Bred by Madeline P. Durholz and Ellen Lonigro, from Champion Kinderland's Winne of Chiz, ROM. Owned by Lois H. and Paul S. Voight and Madeline P. Durholz and Joanne Baker.

4. Ch. Chen Korum-Ti, one of the great winners of the Lhasa Apso breed, has a long list of important triumphs to his credit. Owned by Patricia Chenoweth of Saratoga, California. He was a dog with whom to reckon in the early 1970s, a National Specialty winner, a many times Best in Show winner, and a Group winner.

5. Ch. Jolee's Got To Be Lucky shown taking his first match placement at 10 months age. Owned by Denise and Anne Olejniczak, Brynwood Lhasa Apsos, Loves Park, Illinois.

6. Ch. **Mikado's** Tobias of Apku, by Best in Show winning Ch. Orlane's Be-Sparky of Al-Mar ex Tasha Gae Lady, handled here by Marjorie Lewis for owner, Lorraine R. Cole, Bel-Air Kennels, Grain Valley, Missouri.

7. Multiple Best in Show winning Ch. Billie's Follie Preakness, American Lhasa Apso Club, 1984. No.1 Lhasa Bitch, all systems, 1985. By Am. and Can. Ch. Sharbil Dolsa Fleetfoot Mac ex Chiz Ari Billie's Follie Belle, ROM. Bred and owned by Billie A. and Dr. Samuel L. Shaver, Charlotte, North Carolina. Pictured owner-handled to First in the Non-Sporting Group, Greater Clarksburg K.C. 1985.

8. Multiple Best in Show winning Ch. Billie's Follie Preakness taking one of those Bests in Show, at Southeast Alabama in February 1985. "The Group-winningest" bitch in the history of the breed, "P.K." is owned, bred, and handled by Billie A. Shaver and Dr. Samuel L. Shaver, Charlotte, Noth Carolina.

1. Ch. Taglha Dum Cho at age 11 years, one of the many beautiful Lhasas owned by Mrs. Wilson J. Browning, Jr., Norfolk, Virginia.

2. Ch. Wellington San Jo Tokyo Rose and littermate, Wellington's Bluberi Sauce. They were sired by San Jo's Out o' the Blue ex Ch. Wellington's Very Blackberi. Bred by Lois H. and Paul S. Voight, Burnsville, Minnesota. Owned by Leslie Engen and Lois H. Voight.

3. Group winning Ch. San Jo's Kian Kandi Kan, ROM, by Ch. Zoroshah Morific of San Jo ex Ch. San Jo's Tamata of Ron-Tell, ROM, has seven U.S.A. champion progeny. She was top Lhasa bitch in U.S.A. for 1979 and the mother of multiple Best in Show Ch. SJW Waffle Stumper. Bred by Ann and Kirk Lanterman and Marianne Nixon.Owned by Lois H. and Paul S. Voight (Wellington Lhasa, Burnsville, Minnesota) and Leslie Engen.

4. Ch. San Jo's Kian Black Jack, by Ch. San Jo Shenanigan, ROM, C.D., ex Ch. Kian's Hide N'Go Peep, ROM. Owned by Helen Engel, photo courtesy of Marianne Nixon, San Jo Lhasas, Bellevue, Washington.

5. Ch. Wyndwood's Honeysuckle Rose won a 5-point major at age seven months at Astro Hall Series of Dog Shows. Completed title at 13 months. Owned by Bobby and Kay Hales, Manvel, Texas. Handled by Kay. This bitch has proven an outstanding producer with her first litter by Ch. San Jo's Out-O'-The Blue.

1↑   2↓

← Overleaf:

1. Ch. Cameo's Khor-Ke-San O'Honey Dew, Best of Breed at Westminster in 1981, multiple Group winner, is Ch. Donicia's Chim Zu El Torro, ROM, ex Honey Dew Krissie Ku. Bred by Mary Ann Stafford, Honey Dew Lhasa. Owned by Joyce Hadden, Stanfordville, New York.

2. Multiple All-Breed and Specialty Best in Show winning Am. and Can. Ch. Anbara's Hobgoblin, by Ch. Tabu's King of Hearts, ROM, ex Am. and Can. Ch. Anbara's Abra-Ka-Dabra, ROM, was bred by owner Barbara Wood, Cranford, New Jersey. This Top Winning Lhasa Apso of 1980 and 1981 all systems, is handled as a special by Jean Lade and William and Betty Bowman.

1. The foundation bitch for Kar-Lee Lhasas, Am. and Can. Ch. Dee's Sagittarius Girl winning a Group 2nd at Canada's Belleville K.C. event in 1979. Wesley and Carol Rose, owners, Scotia, New York.

2. Ch. Mio's Shan-Tooz was Winners Bitch and Best of Winners at the American Lhasa Apso Club Specialty Show in 1984. Handled by co-owner Janet Whitman for herself and Joan and Burt Pettit.

3. Ch. Ja-Ma Orlane Peach of a Pearl pictured taking 1st place in Bred-by-Exhibitor Class at the National Capital Lhasa Apso Club Specialty under judge Carolyn Herbel in 1985. Bred by Janet Whitman and Linda Kendall Smith. Owned by Janet Whitman and Ronnie Ellen Fischler, Spring Valley, New York.

4. Kar-Lee's Tiger Lily, by Ch. Sharpette's Skeetzo ex Am. and Can. Ch. Dee's Sagittarius Girl was bred by Carol Rose and John Ioia and is owned by Carol and Wesley Rose, Kar-Lee Lhasa Apsos, Scotia, New York. Winning Best of Breed here from the author, Great Barrington K.C. 1984.

5. Am., Can., and Bda. Ch. Gold N Kismet on the way to her title in 1978. Handled by Bonnie Sellner for owner Virginia H. Snare, Gold N Lhasas, Voorheesville, New York.

6. Sharpette's Parti Gal in 1978, taking Best of Winners. Handled by Bonnie Sellner, Rensselaer, New York.

7. Am., Bda., and Can. Ch. Blahopolo's Norbulingka Ke-Ko, by Best in Show winning Ch. Everglo's Spark of Gold, ROM, ex Secunda Kye, taking Best in Show at Woodstock, Vermont, in July 1977. Handled by Bill Trainor for Joanne Pavlik, Joni's Lhasa Apsos, Newburgh, New York.

8. Ch. Donicia's Kha-Sha Kieh, by Ch. Donicia's Chim Zu El Torro, ROM, ex Ch. Donicia's Tai Suki Lu, ROM, one of four champions from this breeding. Handled here by the late Mrs. Pat Stewart. Now owned by Barbara Hack, Haltbar Lhasa Apsos.

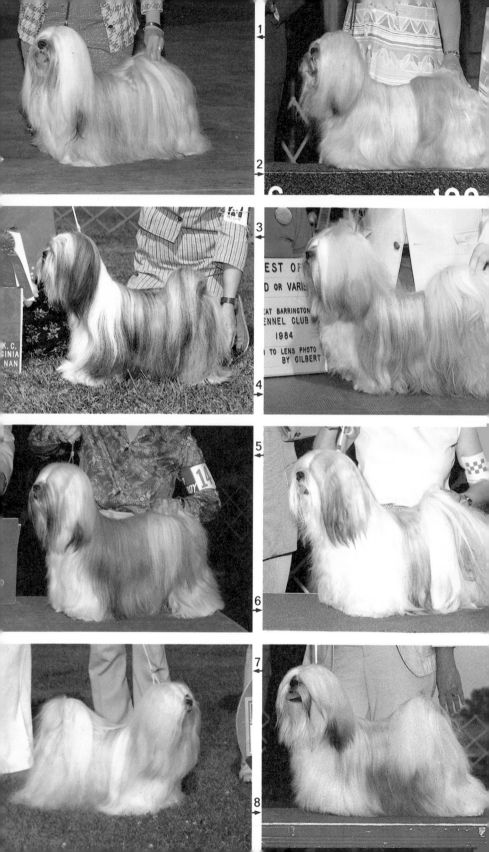

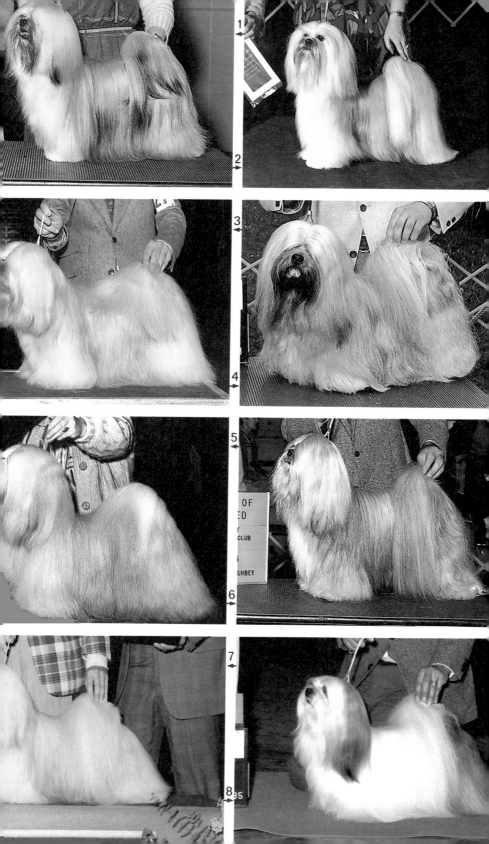

← **Overleaf:**

1. Ju-Ell's Vanity Fair, by World Champion Saxonsprings Alamo ex Group winning Ch. Orlane's Golden Girl, taking points toward the title in February 1985. Handled by breeder-owner Julie Elliott, Ju-Ell Lhasa Apsos, Janesville, Wisconsin.

2. Ch. Orlane's Golden Girl, by Best in Show English and Best in Show American Ch. Orlane's Intrepid, ROM, ex Ch. Orlane's Whimsey of Innsbrook, winning Group 1st from the classes at Minneapolis K.C., October 1985. Bred by Joan Kendall; owned and handled by Julie Elliott, Janesville, Wisconsin.

3. Ch. Joyslyn's Clown Prince at age two years winning points towards his title at Baltimore County in 1979. Owned by Joyce and Lynn Johanson, Joyslyn Lhasa Apsos, David City, Nebraska.

4. Am. and Can. Ch. Kachina R.D. Tauy-Jones, bred and owned by Sally Ann Helf, Kachina Lhasas, Clarkson, New York. By Am. and Can. Ch. Sharpette's Rumpie Dil-Dox ex Can. Ch. Sharpette's Munday's Dolly Lama. Here taking Best of Breed at Erie K.C. in 1983.

5. Ch. Innsbrook's Patrician O'Sulan, ROM, owned by Marion Knowlton, Knolwood Kennels, Dunwoody, Georgia. A son of Ch. Orlane's Inimitable ex Innsbrook's Scarlett Lady.

6. Ch. Ceala's Hustler, handled by John A. Mohr for owner Joanne Pavlik, Joni Lhasas, Newburgh, New York, taking Best of Breed, then on to a Group placement under the author at Troy K.C. in 1985. A son of Ch. Ceala's Fuzz Buster ex Ch. Syung's Shesa Lady, this handsome dog was bred by Larry and Ceata Iwen.

7. Multiple Best in Show winning Ch. Tom Lee Manchu of Knolwood, by Ch. Orlane's Inimitable ex Ch. Rulee's Peppermint Patti, here winning Best in Show. Handled by Michael Collins for owner, Marion Knowlton, Knolwood Lhasas, Dunwoody, Georgia. A multiple Best in Show winner and No. 2 Lhasa for 1983.

8. Am., Can., P.R. Ch. of the Americas (85) Kachina T.K.P. Jim Thorpe T.T., by Best in Show Ch. Taglha Kambu ex Can. Ch. Kachina Tu Rum-Pala Soya S.M., was bred and is owned by Sally Ann Helf, Clarkson. New York. Pictured taking a Group 2nd placement at Niagara Falls in 1985.

1. Magestic Damaru was sired by Am., Can., Mex. Ch. Magestic Gyad Po ex Magestic Tso Mo. Owned by Lois M. and Pamela Magette, Magestic Lhasa Apsos, Long Beach, California.

2. Ch. Marlo Kyi-Chu Artful Dodger, by Ch. San Jo's Soshome Up ex Marlo's Tara of Dolsa, ROM. Littermate to Ch. Marlo's Flim Flam Man, bred by Lynn Lowy, Marlo Kennels. Flim Flam Man is owned by Ruth Smith, Kyi-Chu Lhasa Apsos.

3. Ch. Misti Acres Strutter with breeder/owner/handler Beverly Drake, taking Best of Breed at Alamance K.C. in 1982. Misti Acres Lhasa, Glen Arm, Maryland.

4. Lamoc's Instant Mischief taking Best of Winners for a 4-point major in March 1985. Owned by Elizabeth Faust, New Braunfels, Texas.

5. Ch. Misti's I've Got Da Spirit produced two Grand Futurity winners, Ch. Misti Acres Strutter and Misti Acres Gin Jo's Bambi. Beverly Drake, owner, Glen Arm, Maryland.

6. Jolee's Windancer, taking Winners Bitch, Best of Winners, and Best of Opposite Sex for three points at Arkansas K.C. in June 1985. Elizabeth Faust. Owner, New Braunfels, Texas.

7. Ch. Magestic Dga Mo winning at the California Specialty, by Ch. Magestic Gro' Mo ex Ch. Karmo Rustimala. Owned by Magestic Lhasa Apsos, Lois M. and Pamela Magette, Long Beach, California.

8. Mohican Yankee Goldsmith, age 11 months, taking Best of Breed and Group 3rd from the Bred-by-Exhibitor Class, shown by Debbie Hartmann, Palisades K.C., October 1985. Mohican Lhasas owned by Thelma G. Hartmann, Fairfield, Connecticut.

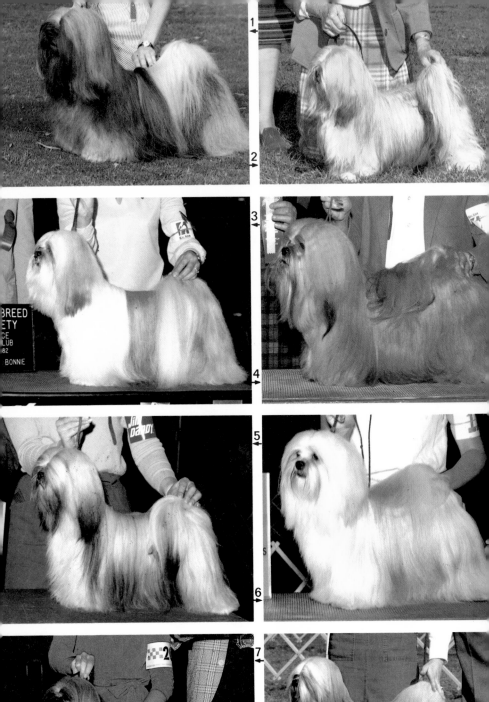
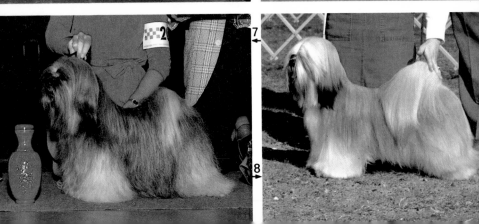

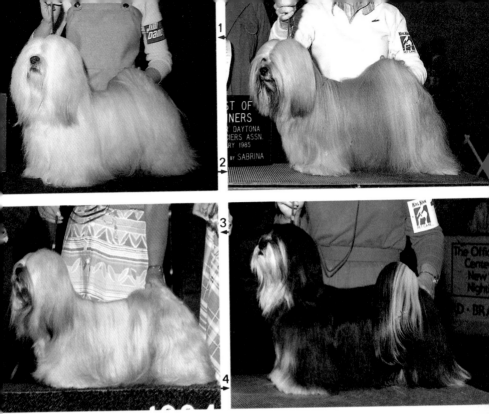

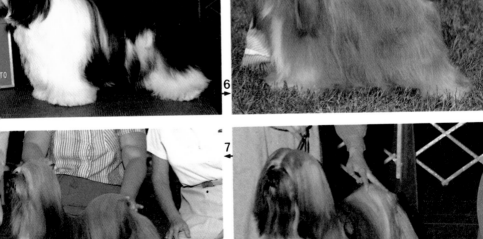

← **Overleaf:**

1. Ch. Mohican's Connecticut Yankee, by Ch. Bella Mu Go Get 'Em Tiger ex Ch. Baijai's Tara Ling of Mohican, at Springfield K.C. in 1976. Owned by Thelma G. Hartmann, Fairfield, Connecticut.

2. Ch. Gene's Victor of Art-Est, by Ch. Tabu's King of Hearts ex Ch. Art Est She Ma, was bred by Esther DeFalcis and is owned by Ruth M. Hatcher, Roanoke, Virginia. Took Best of Winners under noted Lhasa authority Mrs. Keke Blumberg at Greater Daytona, January 1985.

3. Ch. Mio's Shan-tooz, by Ch. Ocon Karba Seng ex Mio Fantasia was bred by Joan and Burt Pettit and is owned by Joan Pettit and Janet Whitman. Here taking Best of Winners at the American Lhasa Apso Club Specialty in Houston, Texas, 1984, Janet Whitman handling.

4. Ch. San Jo Hussel Mee, by Best in Show winning Ch. S.J.W. Waffle Stomper, ROM, ex Best in Show Ch. San Jo's Hussel Bussel, is co-owned by Liz Morgan and Marianne Nixon. Liz Morgan handling. Best of Breed at Elm City 1984.

5. Ch. Misti Acres Sindy Sue finished at 15 months. Bred, owned, and handled by Beverly Drake, Glen Arms, Maryland.

6. Ch. Mor-Knoll Chok's Farrah, by Best in Show Eng. and Am. Orlane's Intrepid ex Chok's Joppa Bu Mo, is one of three from an all-champion litter. Owned by Debbie Burke and Liz Morgan, the latter co-breeder with Carol Kuendel. Handled by Debbie Burke to Best of Winners at Schooley's Mountain in 1979.

7. Ch. Marlo's Flim Flam Man, by Ch. San Jo's Shenanigan ex Marlo's Tara of Dolsa, ROM, born December 1977. Sire of Ch. Marlo's I Love Lucy, this dog was in Hawaii as a puppy, then returned at age four years and gained championship at five years. Littermate to Ch. Kyi-Chu Artful Dodger. Bred and owned by Lynn Lowy, Marlo, Beverly Hills, California.

8. Best in Show Ch. Potala's Keke's Gandy Bar, outstanding Lhasa owned by Mrs. Keke Blumberg, Huntington Valley, Pennsylvania. Handled by Emily Gunnung to one of numerous Group 1st awards. Winner of four Bests in Show.

1. Summerhill's C. Robin of Sulan, by Ch. San Jo's O'The Blue ex Ch. Sulan's Victorian Sonnett. Bred by Jan and Doug Bernards, Sulan Lhasas, Suzette Michele; and Summerhill Lhasas, Jan Bernards, co-owners.

2. Ch. Torma of Shukti Lingka, by Ch. Shan Pa Ni-Khyim ex Dakini of Shukti Lingka, born 1980, finishing her championship from the Bred-by-Exhibitor Class. Bred and owned by Kenneth and Harriet Silverman, handled by Mrs. Silverman. Another outstanding Lhasa from Shukti Lingpa Kennels, Marblehead, Massachusetts.

3. Am. and Can. Ch.Tai Koo of Shukti Lingka winning points towards U.S. title under the late Mary Nelson Stephenson in 1981. Breeder/owner/handler, Harriet A. Silverman, Marblehead, Massachusetts. This handsome dog is the sire of winning progeny.

4. Summerhill's City Slicker at age eight months. Owned by Summerhill Lhasa Apsos, Valencia, California.

5. Am. and Can. Ch. Sharpette's Nip N' Tuck was bred by Robert Sharp and Dorothy Carpenter. Handled by Bonnie Sellner. Judge, the late Mary Nelson Stephenson. Owned by Arlene G. Dart, Ralda Lhasas, Stowe, Vermont.

6. Ch. Karma Ka-Sha, by Karma Kacho ex Ch. Karma Rus-TiLota, born September 1970, was bred by Dorothy Cohen, Karma Kennels. Owned and handled by Joan Pettit, Mio Lhasa Apsos, Woodmere, New York.

7. Best in Show Ch. Potala Keke's Yum Yum in 1976. Handled by Carolyn Herbel for owner, Mrs. Keke Blumberg, Potala Lhasas, Huntington Valley, Pennsylvania. Here winning a Non-Sporting Group.

8. Sunshine's Ch'in by Ch. Joyslyn's Piece of The Rock ex Ch. Tashi Sunshine's Gold Melody, owned and handled by Mary C. Soto, Sunshine Lhasas, Gary, Indiana.

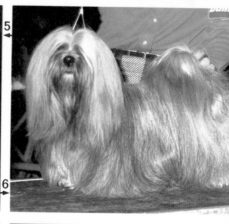

1 →

2 →

3 ↓

← Overleaf:

1. Such a pretty front view of Ch. Barker's Capital Offense. Owned by Drs. Randolph and Sandra Barker, Charleston, West Virginia.

2. Am. and Can. Ch. Joyslyn's Piece of the Rock, multiple Group winner, by Best in Show Am. and Can. Ch. Arborhill's Rah-Keih, ROM, ex Joyslyn's Miss Buffy Jo, retired in 1978 at three years of age after becoming one of the Top Ten Lhasas for 1976, 1977, and 1978.Pointed at seven months, finished at 13 months, began specials career two months later. This portrait appeared in the Hallmark and Ambassador calendars and was used as a model for artist G. Marlo Allen's ink drawing of a Lhasa Apso. Bred by Lynn and Joyce Johanson; owned by Joyce Johanson and Ethel Hines, David City, Nebraska.

3. Romeo's Carbon Copy, by Ch. Bel-Air's El Toro Romeo ex Ch. Che-She's Darling of Ming Toy, was bred by Lorraine R. Cole, Grain Valley, Missouri. Owned by Linda White, Mi-Lin Lhasas, Blue Springs, Missouri.

1. Ch. Ruffway Mashala Chu, ROM, by Ch. Ruffway Mashaka, ROM, ex Ruffway Doshala, is a Group winner and the sire of 20 champions. Owned by Georgia E. Palmer, Addison, Illinois.

2. Ch. Rimar's J.G. King Richard winning Best of Breed from the author at a mid-1970s show. Handled by Bob Sharpe for owner Stephen G.C. Campbell, Rimar Lhasa Apsos, Elizabeth, New Jersey. King Richard was also owned, at separate times, by Susan Lefferts and Mr. and Mrs. Thomas Weil.

3. Ch. Ruffway Tashi, ROM, by Ruffway Kadar ex Ch. Ruffway Byang-Kna, is the dam of 12 champions. Tashi is pictured finishing her own title in 1976 taking Winners Bitch at the American Lhasa Apso Club Specialty Show. Owned by Georgia E. Palmer and Patricia Boyd at the time of finishing and for most of her litters. Now owned solely by her breeder, Georgia E. Palmer, Ruffway Kennels, Addison, Illinois.

4. Group winning Ch. San Jo's Blew Em Away, a young son of Ch. San Jo's Out of the Blue, bred and owned by San Jo Lhasas, Marianne Nixon and Leslie Ann Engen, Bellevue, Washington.

5. Ch. Tabu's Hello Dolly, a daughter of Ch. Chen Korum Ti, at Elm City on 1976, handled by Robert D. Sharp, co-owner with Beth Munday. Sharpette Kennels, Albany, New York.

6. Ch. San Jo's Shindig, *Kennel Review's* No.1 Lhasa Apso in 1984, taking his first Best in Show at Walla Walla K.C. He is one of the 22 champions sired by Group winning Ch. San Jo Shenanigan, ROM. His dam is Group winning Ch. San Jo's Tabatha. Bred by San Jo Lhasas. Owned by Victor Cohen. Handled by Leslie Ann Engen.

7. Ch. Kyi-Chu Friar Tuck winning one of his Bests in Show, at Licking River K.C., Bob Sharpe handling. Tuck came out in 1967, quickly becoming the Top Winning Parti-Color Lhasa Apso of all time; with multiple all-breed Bests in Show, Group wins, and Specialty Shows to his credit. Bred by Ruth Smith, Kyi-Chu Lhasas, Tuck was handled by his owner Bob Sharpe throughout his exciting career, breaking many records over the years.

8. Ch. Rimar's Rumpelstiltskin winning the Non-Sporting Group at Westchester K.C. in 1978, after coming through an entry of over 100 Lhasas at the Lhasa Apso Club of Westchester Specialty Show that day. Jean Lade handled for owner Stephen G.C. Campbell, Elizabeth, New Jersey and for William and Betty Jo Bowman. Now retired with the Lades.

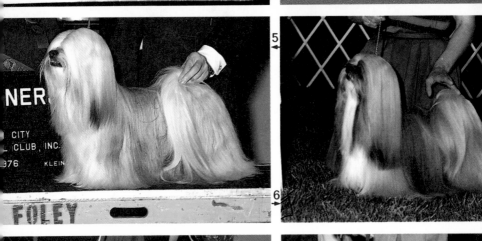

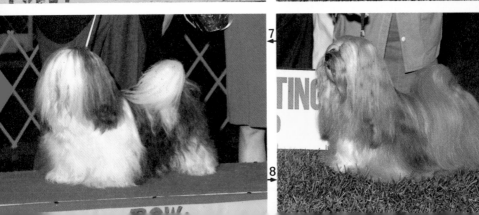

← Overleaf:

1. Ch. Wellington's Comeuppence, by Ch. San Jo's So Shome Up, ROM, ex Chiz Ari Sehilot, ROM, Best of Winners at the ALAC National Specialty in 1983. Bred by Lois H. and Paul S. Voight. Owned by Suzette Michelle and Marlene Kimbrel.

2. Ch. Sunshine's San Miquel, by Ch. Joysyln's Piece of The Rock ex Ch. Tashi Sunshine's Gold Melody, handled by Vic Cohen for owner Mary C. Soto, Sunshine Lhasas, Gary, Indiana.

3. Am. and Can. Ch. Ralda's Flowering Quince with handler Bonnie Sellner, Rensselaer, New York. Owner, Arlene Dartt.

4. Rhu-Ha's Regal Ruffles taking Winners and Best of Opposite Sex at Old Dominion K.C., handled by Jean Lade for Ruth M. Hatcher, Roanoke, Virginia.

5. Ch. Royal Cognac of San Lo II, littermate to Remy Martin of San Lo, taking Winners at Ravenna in August 1985, handled by Barbara Alderman for owners M. A. Santora and Alan J. Loso, San Jo Lhasas, Kendall, Florida.

6. Ch. Wyndwood's Poquita Mas finished championship in seven shows, owner-handled. This Best in Sweepstakes, Cascade Lhasa Apso Fanciers of Greater Seattle, in conjunction with the National Specialty in 1982 is the dam of Group winning Ch. Moonwalker's Fuzzerbear of Wyndwood and of Ch. Wyndwood's Summer Wine. Owned by Wyndwood Lhasas, Bobby and Kay Hales, Manvel, Texas.

1. Ch. Mi Taglha Tulip is the first Lhasa Apso to win Best in Show in Japan. Bred by Mrs. Wilson J. Browning, Jr., Taglha Lhasa Apsos, Norfolk, Virginia. Handled here by Dee Shepperd.

2. Sunshine's Black Velvet, by Tashi Sunshines High Society ex Tashi Sunshine Velvet Petal, taking her first point on her 6th month birthday at Sturgis K.C. in 1985. Bred, owned, and handled by Mary C. Soto, Sunshine Lhasas, Gary Indiana.

3. Ch. Cameo's Khor-Ke-San O'Honeydew, outstanding Group winner and a Westminster Best of Breed owned by Mrs. Joyce Hadden, TN HI Lhasas, Stanfordville, New York.

4. Ch. Tabu's Music Man, by Ch. Tabu's Jazz Man, ROM, ex Maru's Julie of Laran, ROM, is owned by Mr. and Mrs. Norman L. Herbel, Tabu, Lucas, Kansas. Handler, Nancy Clarke.

5. Tabu's Very Much A Lady, ROM, by Ch. Tabu's Rags to Riches ex Goldmere Dharma, owned by Carolyn and Norman Herbel, Tabu, Lucas, Kansas.

6. Am. and Can. Ch. Ja Ma's Kris-Tal Lea O'Tammering completing Canadian title, owner-handled by Elaine Scharf, Santa Barbara, California.

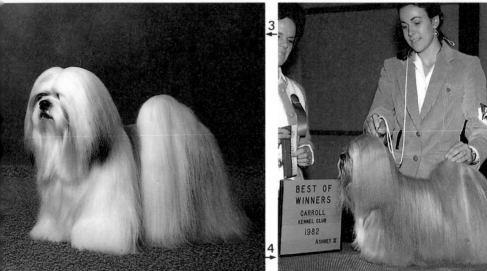

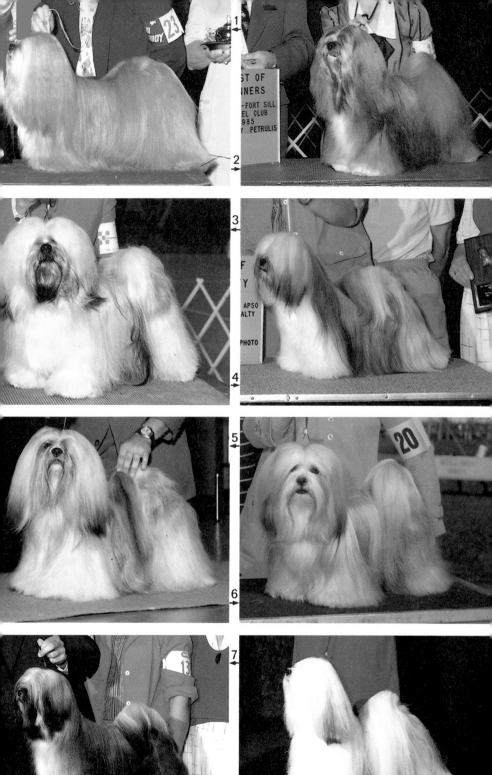

NON SPORTING

← Overleaf:

1. Ch. Taghlha Kambu winning Best in Show at Livonia K.C. in April 1978. Handled by Annette Lurton for breeder-owner Mrs. Wilson J. Browning, Jr., Norfolk, Virginia.

2. Ch. Tammering's Samara Lea on the way to the title in 1985. Owned by Elaine Scharf, Santa Barbara, California.

3. Takashi's El Capitan winning a 4-point major handled by Marjorie Lewis at Sioux Valley K.C. in 1981. By Bel-Air's Shazam ex Bel-Air's Branoi, this lovely dog needed just a major to finish for owners Linda White, Mi-Lin Lhasas, and Ronnie L. Crowder, Takashi Lhasa Apsos, Blue Springs, Missouri.

4. Ch. Wyndwoods Stormy Weather, a Grand Futurity Winner, taking this honor at the American Lhasa Apso Club National in 1985. Owned by Kay and Bobby Hales, Wynwood Lhasas, Manvel, Texas.

5. Ch. Sulan's Victorian Sonnett, first champion daughter of multi-Best in Show winning Ch. Sulan's Gregorian Chant, ROM, ex Jenifer Juniper of Sulan, ROM, is the dam of champions and the foundation bitch at Summerhill Kennels owned by Jan and Doug Bernards at Valencia, California.

6. Ch. ChezAri Sehilot, ROM, was sired by Ch. Pan Chen Tonka Sonan, ROM, ex Kinderlands Winnie of Chiz, ROM. Breeder, Maddie Chizever Durholz and Ellen Lonigro. Owner, Paul and Lois Voight, Wellington Lhasas, Burnsville, Minnesota. The producer of 16 U.S.A. champions, plus five more that are pointed.

7. Wynwood's Sundance of Mai-Li by Ch. San Jo's Out 'O The Blue ex Ch. Wyndwood's Honeysuckle Rose, was Best Puppy at Eastern Futurity, ALAC 1985. Bred by Bobby and Kay Hales, Manvel, Texas. Owned by Kay Hales and Anita Ponds.

8. Ch. Tn Hi Zeus the Dethroner is the result of eight generations of Tn Hi Lhasas. A multiple Group winner, pictured here winning one of them at Winnagamie K.C. in September, 1985. Mrs. Joyce Hadden, owner, Stanfordville, New York.

1. Multiple Best in Show winning Ch. San Jo's Shindig taking Best of Breed, pictured with two of his progeny, littermates, who were awarded Winners Dog and Winners Bitch on the same occasion. Winners Dog, *center,* Linsu Raider of the Stars. Winners Bitch and Best of Winners, *right,* Ch. San Jo's Thanks Vermillion. Shindig is owned by Victor Cohen.

2. Ch. Mor-Knoll's Victoria, ROM, 1969—84, by Pan Chen Tonka Sonan ex Hillside Acres Daffodil, was the foundation bitch of Mor-Knoll Lhasa Apsos. Owned by Liz Morgan, Florham Park, New Jersey.

← Overleaf:

1. Am., Can., and Bda. Ch. Shangrelu Rainy Days O' Irlees, ROM, by Best in Show winning American Ch. Shangrelu Sneak Preview, bred by Wendy Penn, owned by Catherine (Freedman) Groulx. The dam of three champions. Toronto, Canada.

2. Multiple Best in Show and Group winning Ch. Tahna's Tarbaby of Tebar, born October 1974, bred by Barbara E. Hamon. Pam Bruce, owner-handled, Ontario.

3. Group winning Am. and Can. Ch. Ma-Lee's Finagle, ROM, born Aug. 21st 1979, sired by Am. Ch. Bara's Wags to Witches out of Bara's Chautauqua. He is currently the sire of 6 champions. He was bred by Marilyn Lisciandro, Ma-Lees Lhasas. and is owned by Irlees Lhasas, Cathy and Jim Groulx, Toronto, Ontario.

1. Ch. Irlees Cajim Razzle Dazzle, born Nov. 9th 1983, by Am., Can., and Bda. Ch. Ja-ma's Rennegade, ROM, ex Can. Ch. Cajim Irlees Mischevious, dam of two champions. Irlees Lhasa Apsos, Jim and Cathy Groulx, Toronto, Ontario, Canada.

2. This is "Buttons," a small puppy making a big win! Owned by Ti Sendo, Betty Gilroy, London, Ontario. This pretty young bitch is pictured taking Winners at the Metropolitan.

3. Ch. Tahna's Spanish Coffee, multiple Group winner, owned by Tahna Lhasa Apsos, Barbara E. Hamon, Keswick, Ontario.

4. Am., Can., and Bda. Ch. Ja-Ma's Rennegade is one of the Top Producing Lhasas in Canada, and has also several champions in the United States. Bred by Ja-Ma Kennels. Owned by Catherine Freedman.

5. Ch. Ka-Ron's Bad Sam I Am with daughter Bala's Sugar Froster, both owned by Brenda Schmelzel, Bala Lhasa Apsos, Belleville, Ontario.

6. Can. and Am. Ch. Talsma's E'Nuff Said, by Talsma's Eight is Enough ex Can. Ch. Talsma's Emprise taking Group 1st at Caledon K.C. in 1985. Wendy Paquette handled for owners, Alan and Mary Capko, Lisle, Ontario.

7. Can. Ch. Talsma's Enuf Said at the Lhasa Apso Club of Ontario winning Best of Breed under judge Leslie Rogers. Wendy Paquette handled for owners, Alan and Mary Capko, Lisle, Ontario.

8. Int., Can., and Braz. Ch. Zaralinga's Lord Raffles, then owned by Mr. and Mrs. Bob Pike, London, Ontario, was the sire of the first litter born at Talsma Kennels, thus behind all of the current important winners from there over the years. This was Lord Raffles' only litter in North America before going to new owner Jaos Carlos Maximillian in Brazil, where he became a multiple Best in Show winner.

167

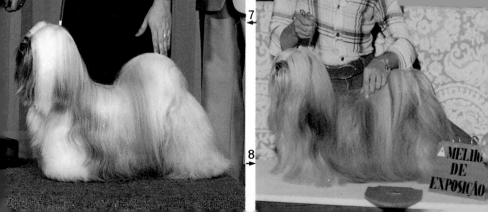

1

2

3

BEST OP
OPPOSITE
PUPPY

4

5

6

← **Overleaf:**

1. A magnificent South African-owned Lhasa Apso, Ch. Lady W's Boy Boy owned by Mrs. L. Bell, was Best in Show over close to 2,300 dogs at that country's prestigious Goldfield's Dog Show, in August 1985. Mrs. Daniel-Jenkins, Pickering, Ontario, Canada was the judge.

2. A "new young hopeful" at Alan and Mary Capko's kennels in Canada. This is Can. Ch. Talsma's Infinite Legend who completed title at age nine months and was sired by Am. and Can. Ch. Talsma's E'Nuff Said ex Orlane's Impact A'Talsma. Handled by Wendy Paquette, Belleville K.C. 1985, under judge Mrs. Daniel-Jenkins.

3. Dim Sum's Chami Leon, by Ch. Norbulingka's Robbie Gables ex Talsma's Masquarrah, bred and owned by Sharon Quan, Dim Sum Lhasas, Sterling, Ontario.

4. Talsma's Eight is Enough, handled here by Pat Keen, is the sire of the Sensational Am. and Can. Ch. Talsma's E'Nuff Said. Both are owned by Alan and Mary Capko, Talsma Lhasa Apsos.

5. Treepine Elsa, at age 12 years in 1986, is the foundation bitch at Talsma Kennels, Lisle, Ontario. Owned by Mary and Alan Capko.

6. Cathy Groulx's first Lhasa, Utsu Kushi Yuro, became the dam of four champions in her only litter consisting of five puppies. Irlees Lhasa Apsos, Catherine and Jim Groulx, Toronto, Ontario.

1. Ch. Cookies N' Cream of Tahna, by Can. Ch. Tru Blu's Hudai Tahna ex Pekoe, was bred by S. Stark and is owned by Barbara E. Hamon, Tahna Lhasa Apsos, Keswick, Ontario, Canada. Pictured taking Best of Winners at the National Lhasa Apso Club of America Specialty, Lockport, New York, September 1985.

2. Can. Ch. Talsma's Tibetian Echo, by Am. Ch. Sakya Hallelujah ex Can. Talsma's Oh-So Sau Ceih, here at eight months is taking a 5-point major at Woodstock, Ontario, Canada. Bred by Alan and Mary Capko, owned by Edna Bedard, Cambridge, Ontario. This is a litter brother to Talsma's Eight is Enough.

3. Can. Ch. Talsma's Seargent Pepper, by Int., Can. and Braz. Ch. Zaralinga's Lord Raffles ex Tree Pine Elsa, owned by Maureen Schuell, Burlington, Ontario. Bred by the Alan Capkos, Talsma Lhasa Apsos.

4. Can. Ch. Talsma's Emprise, by Ch. Sho Tru's Stardust Cow Boy ex Tree Pine Else, owned by Alan and Mary Capko, Talsma Lhasa Apsos, Lisle, Ontario.

5. Multiple Group winning Am., Can., and Bda. Ch. Ha-na's Rennegade, ROM, is the sire in January 1986 of a total 25 champions. He is a son of Am. Ch. Shyr-lyz Mieh Bah Bieh Tu ex Am. Ch. Lifelong's Stolen Hours, ROM. Born November 1976, he was bred by Marv and Janet Whitman and Dr. and Mrs. Kornfeld. Owned by Catherine (Freedman) Groulx, Irlees Lhasa Apsos, Toronto, Canada.

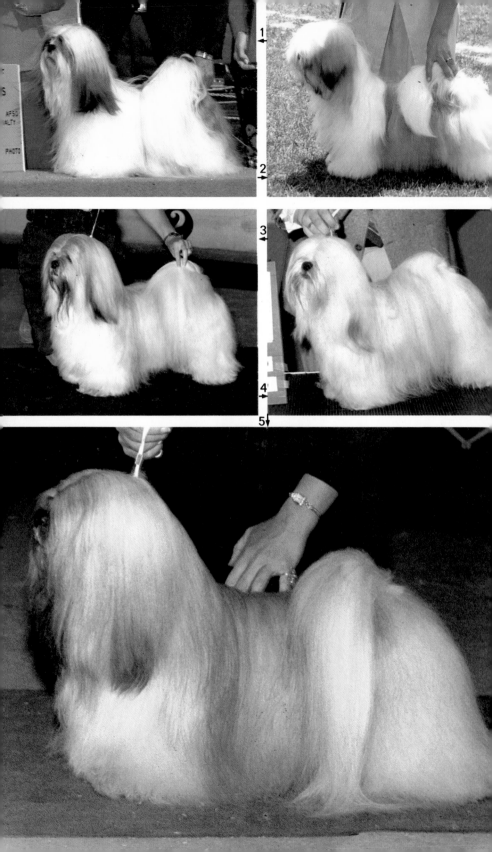

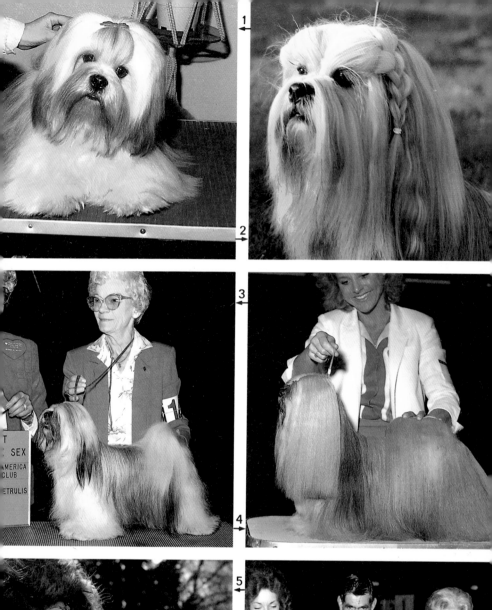

← Overleaf:

1. Jayslyn's Riunite is the *Dynasty* canine, the one who plays Joan Collins's dog in her role of Alexis in this popular television series. "Rio" is a son of Joyslyn's Rachmaninoff ex Ch. Joyslyn's Elfin Magic O' Jokang and is owned by Gary Gero, Bird and Animals Unlimited. Bred by Lynn and Joyce Johanson, David City, Nebraska.

2. Ch. Barker's Sugar Lace, ROM, was bred and is owned by Drs. Randolph and Sandra Barker, Charleston, West Virginia.

3. Bel-Air's Parade's Calliope, daughter of Bel-Air's Tomorrow ex Kizmet's Shenna Ten Su, is a homebred owned by Lorraine R. Cole, Grain Valley, Missouri. Marjorie Lewis handles her.

4. Multiple Best in Show winning Ch. San Jo's Rusty Nail, by Best in Show winning Ch. Anbara—Rimar's Grin N' Bear It ex Multiple Best in Show and Best in Specialty Show winning Ch. San Jo's Hussel Bussel, ROM. Breeder/owners Marianne L. Nixon and Leslie A. Engen, handled here by the latter. San Jo Kennels, Bellevue, Washington.

5. Monette Thiele, well-known Junior Showman, with Ju-Ell's Vanity Fair, by World Ch. Saxonsprings Alamo ex Ch. Orlane's Golden Girl, bred by her mother, Julie K. Elliott, Janesville, Wisconsin.

6. Two gorgeous Lhasas, "sweeping the boards" under judge Ed Bracy in 1975. *Left,* the bitch Ch. Apku's Empress Acapulco completing title at 13½ months after only seven weeks showing, handled by owner Nancy Magee. *Right,* Am. and Can. Ch. Orlane's Be-Sparky of Al-Man handled, as always, by Marjorie Lewis, Independence, Missouri. Taking Best of Breed, then going on to Best in Non-Sporting Group.

1. Ch. Light Up's Golden Graffitti, by Eng. Best in Show Ch. and Am. Best in Show Ch. Orlane's Intrepid ex Light Up's Soda's My Pop, is owned by Julie K. Elliott, Janesville, Wisconsin.

2. Note the lovely heads and expression of Marlo's Miranda and Ch. Marlo's Flim Flam Man in Hawaii in February 1980. Bred and owned by Lynn Lowy, Marlo Lhasa Apsos, Beverly Hills, California.

3. All-Breed and multiple Specialty Best in Show winner, Ch. Anbara–Rimar Mary Puppins is by Best in Show winning Ch. S.J.W. Waffle Stomper, ROM, ex Ch. Anbara–Rimar's Footloose Fox, ROM. Bred by Barbara Wood and Stephen Campbell, owner-handled by Barbara Wood, Mary Puppins became the breed's top winning breeder/owner/handled Lhasa campaigned in 1984. Barbara Wood, Anbara Kennels, Cranford, New Jersey.

4. Ch. Sulan's Minstral O' Summerhill was bred by S. Michele and M. Kimbrel, Sulan Lhasa Apsos, and is owned by Jan and Doug Bernards, Summerhill Lhasa Apsos, Valencia, California. Sired by the multi-Best in Show winner Ch. Sulan's Gregorial Chant ex Sulan's Stargazer.

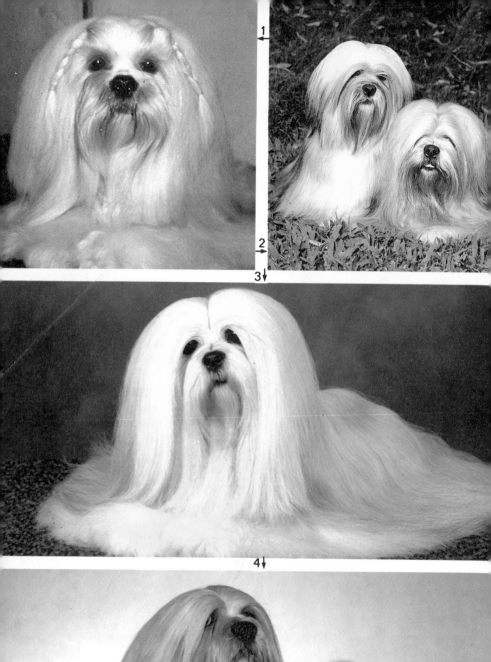

1 →

2 →

3 ↓

4 ↓

← Overleaf:

1. Ch. Potala Keke's Zintora, son of Ch. Chen Korun Ti, was bred by Keke Blumberg and handled by Robert D. Sharp for Dorothy Shottgen.

2. Ch. Kinderland's Kisnri Ruff, famous winning Lhasa bred and owned by Faith Kirie and Ellen Lonigro, handled by Annette Lurton to one of many important Group victories.

3. Ch. Kinderland's Tonka taking Best in Show at Ononadaga in 1972. Bob Sharpe showed this Lhasa for Carolyn and Norman Herbel.

4. Multiple Best in Show winning Ch. Yojimbo Orion was Ken-L-Ration's Top Non-Sporting Dog of the Year in 1977, having won more Group awards among Non-Sporting Dogs than any other. Owned by Elaine Spaeth of Van Nuys, California, and handled by John Thyssen, Orion, Van Nuys, was Best Non-Sporting Dog on 48 occasions during that year. Photo courtesy of Irlees Lhasa Apsos, Toronto, Ontario, Canada.

5. Cinders Tibetan Puzzle, by Ch. Quory Prince Pepe ex Rjay Lucianna of Cinder, owned by Helen E. Bailey, Albany, New York, taking Winners Dog under the author at Troy K.C. in 1985.

6. Ch. Corky's San O'Honeydew was No. 5 Lhasa in the Nation for 1982. Handled here to one of his many Group 1sts, at Carroll K.C., by Susan Heckman Buckel for owner Mrs. Joyce Hadden, Stanfordville, New York.

7. Ch. Kinderlands Tonka, owned by Norman and Carolyn Herbel, handled here by Robert D. Sharp to Best in Show at Union County K.C in 1972.

8. Best of Breed on the way to Group 1st that same day, Ch. Anbara-Rimar Mary Puppins, bred and owned by Barbara Wood and Stephen Campbell, handled by Barbara at Newton K.C. in 1985.

Overleaf: →

1. Am., Bda., and Can. Ch. Karnes Kee-O of Korky, a Best in Show winner in Bermuda and in Canada with numerous Group awards including some half dozen 1st prizes in the United States. Handled by Robert D. Sharp for interior designer Susan B. Hutchings of New York. Korky was one of about twenty Lhasas, included several noted winners, owned by Mrs. Hutchings during the 1970's.

2. Ch. Norbulingka's Crazy Daisy, daughter of Ch. Minda's Tsong of Bhu, taking Best of Winners for breeder/owner/handler Phyllis Marcy at Ladies Dog Club 1979.

3. Ch. Mi-Lin's Oriental Spice taking Winners and Best of Opposite Sex at Tri State K.C. in 1985 under judge Lorraine Heichel Masley. Bred by Linda White, My-Line Kennels, who is also the owner. Spice was handled in this event by Ronnie L. Crowder of Takashi Lhasa Apsos. This lovely bitch finished with back-to-back 4-point majors. My-Lin Lhasas are at Blue Springs, Missouri.

4. Golden Rules Mel-O-Ne O'Everglo, daughter of Ch. Licos Chulung La ex Everglo Buttercup, owned by Ken Shappton, Cameo Acres. She is the dam of Ch. Donicia's Chim Zu El Torro. Photo courtesy of Lorraine Cole.

5. Ch. Xanadu's Antares, co-owned by David Goldfarb and Fred Terman, bred by Mr. Goldfarb, handled by Mr. Terman, Staten Island, New York. Here winning Best of Breed, Saw Mill K.C. 1977.

6. Ch. Ruffway Patra Chuntse is by Ch. Ruffway Mashala Chu, ROM, ex Ch. Ruffway Tashi, ROM. Bred by Georgia E. Palmer and Patricia Boyd. Owned by Georgia E. Palmer, Addison Illinois.

7. Anbara-San Jo Scal-A-Wag, by Ch. Anbara-Rimar Grin 'N Bear It ex Ch. San Jo-Anbara 'N All That Jazz, was bred by Barbara Wood and Marianne Nixon, co-owned by Barbara with Rita Holloway. Grand Futurity Winner at 1983 Western Fururity, presenting his breeders with the American Lhasa Apso Club's Robert F. Griffing Memorial Trophy.

8. Ch. Cameo's Flash 'Em A Smile, by Bel-Air's Tomorrow ex Bel-Air's Dee Dee Kee, pictured finishing on the West Coast with Group placements. Bred by Lorraine R. Cole, handled by Mitch Wooten for owners Ken Sharpton and Bill Dawson, Cameo Lhasas. Photo courtesy of Lorraine Cole.

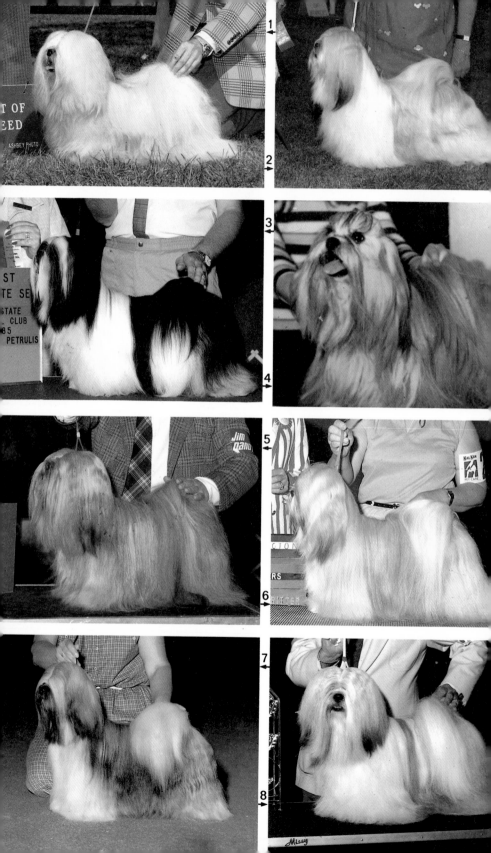

1

2

3

4

1. Magestic Kesar at age five months. This Lhasa by Ch. Magestic Gro Mo ex Magestic Tso Mo is owned by Magestic Lhasa Apsos, Lois and Pamela Magette, Long Beach, California.

2. Anbara Bo-Jangles C.D., one of Barbara Wood's earliest Lhasas, by Ch. Chig Rgyal-Po ex Gus-Po Shamen Da-Ra, is making a personal appearance here with Big Bird, Susan (Loretta Long) and the Mail Lady (Charlotte Rae). Bo had a modeling career that included, in addition to *Sesame Street,* appearances in movies and in such magazines as *Harper's Bazaar* plus being a treasured friend and companion to owner Barbara Wood, who does the sound effects for *Sesame Street.*

3. Ch.Orlane's Golden Girl finishing with Best of Breed from the classes over three specials. Bred by Joan Kendall; owned and handled by Julie K. El-liott, Ju-Ell Lhasa Apsos, Janesville, Wisconsin.

4. Kinderland's Sonan taking Best of Winners at James River in 1976, at age 15 months. Owned by Ellen Lonigro and Joanne P. Baker, Columbia, Maryland.

1. Ch. Rimar's J.G. King Richard handled by Robert D. Sharp for co-owners Stephen Campbell (breeder) and Mrs. Susan C. Hutchings, a noted interior designer who was very active with her Lhasas in the 1970s.

2. Group winning Ch. Anbara-Rimar's Cobble Cuddler, a Waffle Stumper daughter and litter sister to multi-Group winning Ch. Anbara-Rimar's Mary Puppins. Bred by Barbara Wood, Anbara; owned by M. L. Nixon, San Jo; handled by L. A. Engen.

3. Ch. Tashi Sunshine's Gold Melody, by Best in Show Ch. Yojimoa Orion ex Ch. Kyber Rum Poppy, was the first champion to be finished by Mary C. Soto, Sunshine Lhasa Apsos, Gary , Indiana.

4. Summerhill's Dream Weaver, by San Jo's Out O' The Blue ex Ch. Sulan's Victorian Sonnet, is owned by Summerhill Lhasa Apsos, Valencia, California.

5. Ch. Mohican Sammche Express, by Ch. Jawin's Shadow Image ex Ch. Mohican's Pony Express, handled by Debbie Hartmann for Thelma G. Hartmann, Mohican Lhasa, Fairfield, Connecticut. This bitch is a great-grandmother of Ch. Baijai's Tara Ling of Mohican. Both are splendid examples of perfectly marked parti-colors. Here taking Best of Breed at Ox Ridge K.C. in 1982.

6. Ch. Sankor Marlo's Good Fortune, by Marlo's Beau Brummel, was born in October 1977 and was a Group winner at 19 months of age. Bred by Gene and Vivian Sanford, owned by Lynn Lowy. Marlo Lhasas, Beverly Hills, California.

7. Best in Show Champion Chiz-Ari Wellington Shofar, ROM, (by multi-Best in Show winning Little Fir's Shel Ari of Chiz, ROM, ex Chiz Ari Sehilot, ROM) was bred by Lois and Paul S. Voight and Maddie Chizener Durholz. Owned by Emily Svendsen and Elnore Slette.

8. Multi-Best in Show winning Ch. San Jo's Shindig winning under breeder judge Norman Herbel, October 1985. Owned by Victor Cohen; bred by San Jo Kennels; handled by L. Ann. Engen.

← Overleaf:

1. Winner of the Stud Dog Class at Beverly Hills in 1971, Ch. Chen Nyun Ti, here with his kids; Ch. Chen Korum Ti and Ch. Chen Krisna Nor. Owned by Pat Chenoweth. Photo courtesy of Robert D. Sharp.

2. The first Anbara Lhasa Apso, on the *right,* was Buttons, C.D. pictured here with her son, *left,* Anbara Bo-Jangles, C.D. Both owned by Barbara Wood, Cranford, New Jersey.

3. Ch. Yeri Rimar's Ginger Snaps, age eight months, doing her famous act. Finished at Westminster K.C. and won universal appeal with her begging tactics. Ginger is the dam of two champions. Owned by Barbara Wood and Stephen Campbell.

4. Ch. Donicia's Rhe-Ghe San, by Ch. Donicia's Chim Zu El Torro, ROM, ex Ch. Donicia's Tai Suki Lu, ROM. Bred by the late Patricia Stewart, Donicia's Lhaso Apsos, now owned by Jerec Kennels.

5. Ch. San-Jo's Wingtips, foundation stud at Wynwood Lhasas, is the sire of four champions. Owners, Bobby and Kay Hales, Manvel, Texas.

Overleaf: →

1. Best in Show winning Ch. Anbara-Rimar Grin 'N Bear It, ROM, by Am. and Ger. Int. Ch. Anbara Justa Teddy Bear ex Ch. Rimar's The Frivolous Fox, ROM, was bred by Barbara Wood and Stephen Campbell. Owned by Barbara Wood and Rita Holloway, Newark, Delaware.

2. Multiple Best in Show winning Am. and Can. Ch. Arborhill's Rapso-Dieh is the sire of more than 20 champions, including Best in Show and Group winners. Bred by Sharon Binkowski (Arborhill). Owned by Janet and Marv Whitman (Ja-Ma), Spring Valley, New York.

1↑ 2↓

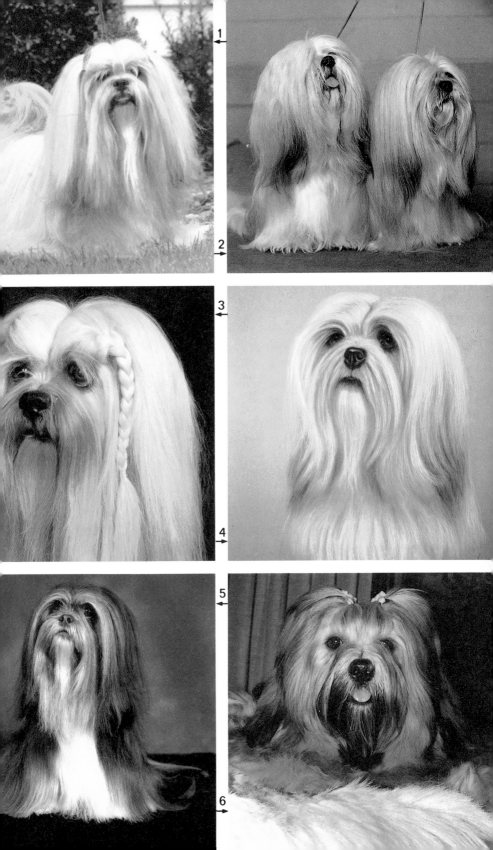

← **Overleaf:**

1. Am. and Can. Ch. Sharpette's Skeetzo, the foundation stud dog at Kar-Lee. Owned by Carol and Wes Rose, bred by Robert D. Sharp.

2. *Left,* Can. Ch. Ralda's Cinnamon Shrub; right, Can. Ch. Ralda's Squash Blossom. This Multi-Group winning Brace in the United States and Canada is owned by Arlene G. Dartt, Ralda Lhasas, Stowe, Vermont.

3. Handsome head-study of multiple-Group winning Am. and Can. Ch. Joyslyn's Piece of the Rock. Owned by Joyslyn's Lhasa Apsos, Lynn and Joyce Johanson, David City, Nebraska.

4. Best in Show winning Ch. Tibet of Cornwallis, ROM; from a portrait by Robert Hickey. Owned by Tabu Lhasa Apsos, Carolyn and Norman Herbel, Lucas, Kansas.

5. Ch. Wellington's Veri Blackberri, by Ch. San Jo's Shenanigan, C.D., ROM, ex Ch. Chiz Ari Sehi Lot, ROM, is the dam of Ch. Wellington San Jo Tokyo Rose. Bred and owned by Paul and Lois Voight, Wellington Lhasa Apsos, Burnsville, Minnesota.

6. Panamanian Ch. Art-Est Takashi King, eight months old here, grew up to become a South American Best in Show dog. Bred by Art-Est Kennels, Art and Esther DeFalcis, Lawrenceville, Georgia.

1. Ch. Barker's Capital Offense pictured at age four months. This gorgeous show puppy is from Barker's Lhasa Apsos, Charleston, West Virginia.

2. "Ying Su" at five months. This young Lhasa is by Ch. Joyslyn's Piece of the Rock ex Hatchers Mai Ling Poppi.

3. The look of a future multiple Best in Show winner. Ch. Anbara's Hobgoblin at age six months. Owned by Barbara Wood, Anbara Lhasa Apsos, Cranford, New Jersey.

4. This handsome youngster is Marlo Tinker Bell, born May 15, 1985 by Ch. Marlo Rocky Road ex Ch. Yojimbo Feather, shown here at seven months. A star of the future? We think so. Tinker was bred and is owned by Lynn Lowy and Marilyn Campbell, Beverly Hills, California.

5. Puppies by Ch. Sharpette' s Nip N' Tuck and Ch. Gold N Elegance. Photo courtesy of Bonnie Sellner, Rensselaer, New York.

6. Bhe-Jei's Samson of Dundee, by Ch. Bhe-Jei's Beau Jolais ex Na-Tasha Ling III, as a 4-month-old puppy handled by breeder and co-owner Bobbie Ling, Menlo Park, California.

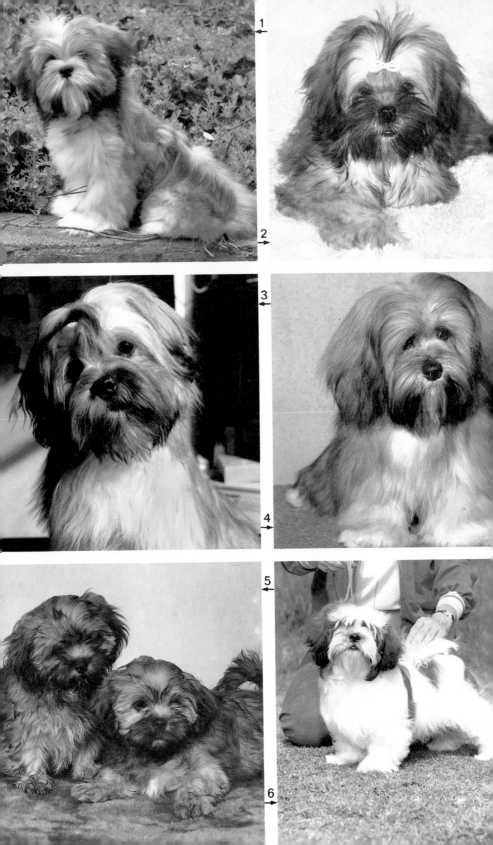

1

2

3

4

5

6

Chapter 6

The Purchase of Your Lhasa Apso

Careful consideration should be given to what breed of dog you wish to own prior to your purchase of one. If several breeds are attractive to you, and you are undecided as to which you prefer, learn all you can about the characteristics of each before making your decision. As you do so, you are thus preparing yourself to make an intelligent choice; and this is very important when buying a dog who will be, with reasonable luck, a member of your household for at least a dozen years or more. Obviously, since you are reading this book, you have decided on the breed—so now all that remains is to make a good choice.

It is never wise to just rush out and buy the first cute puppy who catches your eye. Whether you wish a dog to show, one with whom to compete in obedience, or one as a family dog purely for his (or her) companionship, the more time and thought you invest as you plan the purchase, the more likely you are to meet with complete satisfaction. The background and early care behind your pet will reflect in the dog's future health and temperament. Even if you are planning the purchase purely as a pet, with no thoughts of showing or breeding in the dog's or puppy's future, it is essential that, if the dog is to enjoy a trouble-free future, you assure yourself of a healthy, properly raised puppy or adult from sturdy, well-bred stock.

Throughout the pages of this book you will find the names and locations of many well-known and well-established kennels in various areas. Another source of information is the American Kennel Club (51 Madison Avenue, New York, New York 10010), from whom you can obtain a list of recognized breeders in the vicinity of your home. If you plan to have your dog campaigned by a professional handler, by all means let the handler help you locate and select a good dog. Through their numerous clients, handlers have access to a variety of interesting show prospects; and the usual arrangement is that the handler re-sells the dog to you for what his cost has been, with the agreement that the dog be campaigned for you by him throughout the dog's career. It is most strongly recommended that prospective purchasers follow these suggestions, as you thus will be better able to locate and select a satisfactory puppy or dog.

Your first step in searching for your puppy is to make appointments at kennels specializing in your breed, where you can visit and inspect the dogs, both those available for sale and the kennel's basic breeding stock. You are looking for an active, sturdy puppy with bright eyes and intelligent expression and who is friendly and alert; avoid puppies who are hyperactive, dull, or listless. The coat should be clean and thick, with no sign of parasites. The premises on which he was raised should look (and smell) clean and be tidy, making it obvious that the puppies and their surroundings are in capable hands. Should the kennels featuring the breed you intend to own be sparse in your area or not have what you consider attractive, do not hesitate to contact others at a distance and purchase from them if they seem better able to supply a puppy or dog who will please you—*so long as it is a recognized breeding kennel of that breed.* Shipping dogs is a regular practice nowadays, with comparatively few problems when one considers the number of dogs shipped each year. A reputable, well-known breeder wants the customer to be satisfied; thus, he will represent the puppy fairly. Should you not be pleased with the puppy upon arrival, a breeder, such as described, will almost certainly permit its return. A conscientious breeder takes real interest and concern in the welfare of the dogs he or she causes to be brought into the world.

Such a breeder also is proud of a reputation for integrity. Thus on two counts, for the sake of the dog's future and the breeder's reputation, to such a person a *satisfied* customer takes precedence over a sale at any cost.

If your puppy is to be a pet or "family dog," the earlier the age at which it joins your household the better. Puppies are weaned and ready to start out on their own, under the care of a sensible new owner, at about six weeks old; and if you take a young one, it is often easier to train it to the routine of your household and to your requirements of it than is the case with an older dog which, even though still technically a puppy, may have already started habits you will find difficult to change. The younger puppy is usually less costly, too, as it stands to reason the breeder will not have as much expense invested in it. Obviously, a puppy that has been raised to five or six months old represents more in care and cash expenditure on the breeder's part than one sold earlier; therefore he should be, and generally is, priced accordingly.

There is an enormous amount of truth in the statement that "bargain" puppies seldom turn out to be that. A "cheap" puppy, raised purely for sale and profit, can and often does lead to great heartbreak, including problems and veterinarian's bills which can add up to many times the initial cost of a properly reared dog. On the other hand, just because a puppy is expensive does not assure one that is healthy and well reared. There have been numerous cases where unscrupulous dealers have sold, for several hundred dollars, puppies that were sickly, in poor condition, and such poor specimens that the breed of which they were supposedly members was barely recognizable. So one cannot always judge a puppy by price alone. Common sense must guide a prospective purchaser, plus the selection of a *reliable,* well-recommended dealer whom you know to have well-satisfied customers or, best of all, a specialized breeder. You will probably find the fairest pricing at the kennel of a breeder. Such a person, experienced with the breed in general and with his or her own stock in particular, through extensive association with these dogs, has watched enough of them mature to have obviously learned to assess quite accurately each puppy's potential—something impossible where such background is non-existent.

One more word on the subject of pets. Bitches make a fine

choice for this purpose as they are usually quieter and more gentle than the males, easier to house train, more affectionate, and less inclined to roam. If you do select a bitch and have no intention of breeding or showing her, by all means have her spayed, for your sake and for hers. The advantages to the owner of a spayed bitch include avoiding the nuisance of "in season" periods which normally occur twice yearly—with the accompanying eager canine swains haunting your premises in an effort to get close to your female—plus the unavoidable messiness and spotting of furniture and rugs at this time, which can be annoying if she is a household companion in the habit of sharing your sofa or bed. As for the spayed bitch, she benefits as she grows older because this simple operation almost entirely eliminates the possibility of breast cancer ever occurring. It is recommended that all bitches eventually be spayed—even those used for show or breeding when their careers have ended—in order that they may enjoy a happier, healthier old age. Please take note, however, that a bitch who has been spayed (or an altered dog) *cannot be shown at American Kennel Club dog shows once this operation has been performed.* Be certain that you are *not* interested in showing her before taking this step.

Also, in selecting a pet, never underestimate the advantages of an older dog, perhaps a retired show dog or a bitch no longer needed for breeding, who may be available and quite reasonably priced by a breeder anxious to place such a dog in a loving home. These dogs are settled and can be a delight to own, as they make wonderful companions, especially in a household of adults where raising a puppy can sometimes be a trial.

Everything that has been said about careful selection of your pet puppy and its place of purchase applies, but with many further considerations, when you plan to buy a show dog or foundation stock for a future breeding program. Now is the time for an in-depth study of the breed, starting with every word and every illustration in this book and all others you can find written on the subject. The Standard of the breed has now become your guide, and you must learn not only the words but also how to interpret them and how to apply them to actual dogs before you are ready to make an intelligent selection of a show dog.

If you are thinking in terms of a dog to show, obviously you must have learned about dog shows and must be in the habit of attending them. This is fine, but now your activity in this direction should be increased, with your attending every single dog show within a reasonable distance from your home. Much can be learned about a breed at ringside at these events. Talk with the breeders who are exhibiting. Study the dogs they are showing. Watch the judging with concentration, noting each decision made, and attempt to follow the reasoning by which the judge has reached it. Note carefully the attributes of the dogs who win and, for your later use, the manner in which each is presented. Close your ears to the ringside know-it-alls, usually novice owners of a dog or two and very new to the Fancy, who have only derogatory remarks to make about all that is taking place unless they happen to win. This is the type of exhibitor who "comes and goes" through the Fancy and whose interest is usually of very short duration, owing to lack of knowledge and dissatisfaction caused by the failure to recognize the need to learn. You, as a fancier whom we hope will last and enjoy our sport over many future years, should develop independent thinking at this stage; you should learn to draw your own conclusions about the merits, or lack of them, seen before you in the ring and, thus, sharpen your own judgement in preparation for choosing wisely and well.

Note carefully which breeders campaign winning dogs—not just an occasional isolated good one, but consistent, homebred winners. It is from one of these people that you should select your own future "star."

If you are located in an area where dog shows take place only occasionally or where there are long travel distances involved, you will need to find another testing ground for your ability to select a worthy show dog. Possibly, there are some representative kennels raising this breed within a reasonable distance. If so, by all means ask permission of the owners to visit the kennels and do so when permission is granted. You may not necessarily buy then and there, as they may not have available what you are seeking that very day, but you will be able to see the type of dog being raised there and to discuss the dogs with the breeder. Every time you do this, you add to your knowledge. Should one of these kennels have dogs which especially appeal to you, perhaps you could reserve a show-prospect puppy from a coming litter. This is frequently done, and it is often worth waiting for a puppy, unless you have seen a dog with which you truly are greatly impressed and which is immediately available.

Best in Show winning Ch. Taglha Kambu at home. This 12-year-old Lhasa was bred and is owned by Mrs. Wilson J. Browning, Jr., Taglha Lhasa Apsos, Norfolk, Virginia.

Ch. Anbara-Rimar Raisin' A Ruckus completed title undefeated at three Specialty events including the National from the Puppy Dog Class. Owner-handled by Barbara Woods, Anbara Lhasa Apsos, Cranford, New Jersey.

The purchase of a puppy has already been discussed. Obviously this same approach applies in a far greater degree when the purchase involved is a future show dog. The only place from which to purchase a show prospect is a breeder who raises show-type stock; otherwise, you are almost certainly doomed to disappointment as the puppy matures. Show and breeding kennels obviously cannot keep all of their fine young stock. An active breeder-exhibitor is, therefore, happy to place promising youngsters in the hands of people also interested in showing and winning with them, doing so at a fair price according to the quality and prospects of the dog involved. Here again, if no kennel in your immediate area has what you are seeking, do not hesitate to contact top breeders in other areas and to buy at long distance. Ask for pictures, pedigrees, and a complete description. Heed the breeder's advice and recommendations, after truthfully telling exactly what your expectations are for the dog you purchase. Do you want something with which to win just a few ribbons now and then? Do you want a dog who can complete his championship? Are you thinking of the real "big time" (i.e., seriously campaigning with Best of Breed, Group wins, and possibly even Best in Show as your eventual goal)? Consider it all carefully in advance; then honestly discuss your plans with the breeder. You will be better satisfied with the results if you do this, as the breeder is then in the best position to help you choose the dog who is most likely to come through for you. A breeder selling a show dog is just as anxious as the buyer for the dog to succeed, and the breeder will represent the dog to you with truth and honesty. Also, this type of breeder does not lose interest the moment the sale has been made but, when necessary, will be right there to assist you with beneficial advice and suggestions based on years of experience.

As you make inquiries of at least several kennels, keep in mind that show-prospect puppies are less expensive than mature show dogs, the latter often costing close to four figures, and sometimes more. The reason for this is that, with a puppy, there is always an element of chance, the possibility of it's developing unexpected faults as it matures or failing to develop the excellence and quality that earlier had seemed probable. There definitely is a risk factor in buying a show-prospect puppy. Sometimes all goes well, but occasionally the swan becomes an ugly duckling. Reflect on this as you consider available puppies and young adults. It just might be a good idea to go with a more mature, though more costly, dog if one you like is available.

When you buy a mature show dog, "what you see is what you get," and it is not likely to change beyond coat and condition, which are dependent on your care. Also advantageous for a novice owner is the fact that a mature dog of show quality almost certainly will have received show-ring training and probably match-show experience, which will make your earliest handling ventures much easier.

Frequently it is possible to purchase a beautiful dog who has completed championship but who, owing to similarity in bloodlines, is not needed for the breeder's future program. Here you have the opportunity of owning a champion, usually in the two-to-five-year-old range, which you can enjoy campaigning as a special (for Best of Breed competition) and which will be a settled, handsome dog for you and your family to enjoy with pride.

If you are planning foundation for a future kennel, concentrate on acquiring one or two really superior bitches. These need not be top show-quality, but they should represent your breed's finest producing bloodlines from a strain noted for producing quality, generation after generation. A proven matron who is already the dam of show-type puppies is, of course, the ideal selection; but these are usually difficult to obtain, no one being anxious to part with so valuable an asset. You just might strike it lucky, though, in which case you are off to a flying start. If you cannot find such a matron available, select a young bitch of finest background from top-producing lines who is herself of decent type, free of obvious faults, and of good quality.

Great attention should be paid to the pedigree of the bitch from whom you intend to breed. If not already known to you, try to see the sire and dam. It is generally agreed that someone starting with a breed should concentrate on a fine collection of topflight bitches and raise a few litters from these before considering keeping one's own stud dog. The practice of buying a stud and then breeding everything you own or acquire to that dog does not always work out well. It is better to take advantage of the many noted sires who are available to be used at stud, who represent all of the leading strains, and, in each case, to carefully select the one who in type and pedigree seems most compatible to each of your bitches, at least for your first several litters.

O Beau's Kaszwell, by Can. and Am. Ch. Mio's Clean Sweep ex Ch. Llenroc Tasha Belle, taking Best in Sweepstakes at the Lhasa Apso Club of Greater New York Specialty in 1984. Bred and handled by Olivia Feldman, co-owner with Joan Pettit, Woodmere, New York.

To summarize, if you want a "family dog" as a companion, it is best to buy it young and raise it according to the habits of your household. If you are buying a show dog, the more mature it is, the more certain you can be of its future beauty. If you are buying foundation stock for a kennel, then bitches are better, but they must be from the finest *producing* bloodlines.

When you buy a pure-bred dog that you are told is eligible for registration with the American Kennel Club, you are entitled to receive from the seller an application form which will enable you to register your dog. If the seller cannot give you the application form, you should demand and receive an identification of your dog, consisting of the name of the breed, the registered names and numbers of the sire and dam, the name of the breeder, and your dog's date of birth. If the litter of which your dog is a part is already recorded with the American Kennel Club, then the litter number is sufficient identification.

Do not be misled by promises of papers at some later date. Demand a registration application form or proper identification as described above. If neither is supplied, do not buy the dog. So warns the American Kennel Club, and this is especially important in the purchase of show or breeding stock.

THE LHASA APSO AS A FAMILY DOG

What a marvelous family companion one gets in a Lhasa Apso! Here is a dog of intelligence, sturdiness, and loyalty who is small enough in size to fit in anywhere yet has all the attributes of a big dog.

Remember that the Lhasa was used as an indoor guard dog in Tibet. Thus, the instinct to protect has been in the breed over hundreds of years. Remember also that he comes from a land known for its harsh climate and rugged terrain. Yet he survived. The Lhasa is a dog of little trouble since he is so hardy a breed and one who will guard you and your home (and other family members) with his life.

Where could you possibly find a more beautiful, eye appealing animal? The personal pride in having one of these dogs adorn your home is considerable. Also, they have interesting personalities owing to their great deal of intelligence. The more I learn about

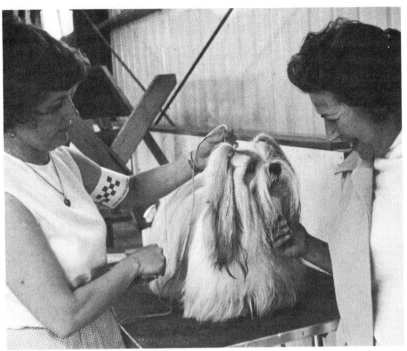

"Mutual admiration" seems quite evident between the judge and Sharpette's Parti Girl, so nicely handled by Bonnie Sellner.

them, the more I realize that they are a very long-lived breed. Many reach sixteen years or more, which certainly is worth considering when one has experienced the sadness of losing a loved pet and that in many breeds the normal life span is far shorter.

Lhasas are good travelers and good "doers." Their coats are a care, but doesn't everything have its price? If you follow the basics of grooming recommended for the breed, you will find that coat care is very simple.

Youngsters and Lhasas seem to get on extra well together and are great companions. Some of our most successful Junior Showmanship handlers are working with this breed of dog.

If you are considering a Lhasa Apso as a family companion, you couldn't make a better choice. Try it—you'll like it, I promise.

Multiple Best in Show Ch. San Jo's Torgi by Ch. Gyal Kham-nag of San Jo ROM ex Am. and Can. Ch. Kyi Chu Kissami, ROM, was the first Lhasa Apso in the Northwest to win Best in Show All Breeds. Bred and shown by Marianne L. Nixon, San Jo, Bellevue, Washington.

Chapter 7

The Care of Your Lhasa Apso

The moment you decide to be the new owner of a puppy is not one second too soon to start planning for the puppy's arrival in your home. Both the new family member and you will find the transition period easier if your home is geared in advance of the arrival.

The first things to be prepared are a bed for the puppy and a place where you can pen him up for rest periods. Every dog should have a crate of its own from the very beginning, so that he will come to know and love it as his special place where he is safe and happy. It is an ideal arrangement, for when you want him to be free, the crate stays open. At other times you can securely latch it and know that the pup is safely out of mischief. If you travel with him, his crate comes along in the car; and, of course, in traveling by plane there is no alternative but to have a carrier for the dog. If you show your dog, you will want him upon occasion to be in a crate a good deal of the day. So from every consideration, a crate is a very sensible and sound investment in your puppy's future safety and happiness and for your own peace of mind.

The crates most desirable are the wooden ones with removable side panels, which are ideal for cold weather (with the panels in place to keep out drafts) and in hot weather (with the panels removed to allow better air circulation). Wire crates are all right in the summer, but they give no protection from cold or drafts. Aluminum crates, due to the manner in which the metal reflects surrounding temperatures, are not recommended. If it is cold, so is the metal of the crate; if it is hot, the crate becomes burning hot.

When you choose the puppy's crate, be certain that it is roomy enough not to become outgrown. The crate should have sufficient height so the dog can stand up in it as a mature dog and sufficient area so that he can stretch out full length when relaxed. When the puppy is young, first give him shredded newspaper as a bed; the papers can be replaced with a mat or turkish towels when the dog is older. Carpet remnants are great for the bottom of the crate, as they are inexpensive and in case of accidents can be quite easily replaced. As the dog matures and is past the chewing age, a pillow or blanket in the crate is an appreciated comfort.

Sharing importance with the crate is a safe area in which the puppy can exercise and play. If you are an apartment dweller, a baby's playpen works out well for a young dog; for an older puppy use a portable exercise pen which you can use later when travelling with your dog or for dog shows. If you have a yard, an area where he can be outside in safety should be fenced in prior to the dog's arrival at your home. This area does not need to be huge, but it does need to be made safe and secure. If you are in a suburban area where there are close neighbors, stockade fencing works out best, as then the neighbors are less aware of the dog and the dog cannot see and bark at everything passing by. If you are out in the country where no problems with neighbors are likely to occur, then regular chain-link fencing is fine. For added precaution in both cases, use a row of concrete blocks or railroad ties inside against the entire bottom of the fence; this precludes or at least considerably lessens the chances of your dog digging his way out.

Be advised that if yours is a single dog, it is very unlikely that it will get sufficient exercise just sitting in the fenced area, which is what most of them do when they are there alone. Two or more dogs will play and move themselves around, but one by itself does little more than make a leisurely tour once around the area to check things over and then lie down. You must include a daily walk or two in your plans if your puppy is to be rugged and well. Exercise is extremely important to a puppy's muscular development and to keep a mature dog fit and trim. So make sure that those exercise periods, or walks, a game of ball, and other such activities, are part of your daily program as a dog owner.

If your fenced area has an outside gate, provide a padlock and key and a strong fastening for it, and use them, so that the gate cannot be opened by others and the dog taken or turned free. The ultimate convenience in this regard is, of course, a door (unused for other purposes) from the house around which the fenced area can be enclosed, so that all you have to do is open the door and out into his area he goes. This arrangement is safest of all, as then you need not be using a gate, and it is easier in bad weather since then you can send the dog out without taking him and becoming soaked yourself at the same time. This is not always possible to manage, but if your house is arranged so that you could do it this way, you would never regret it due to the convenience and added safety thus provided. Fencing in the entire yard, with gates to be opened and closed whenever a caller, deliveryman, postman, or some other person comes on your property, really is not safe at all because people not used to gates are frequently careless about closing and latching them *securely*. Many heartbreaking incidents have been brought about by someone carelessly half closing a gate (which the owner had thought to be firmly latched) and the dog wandering out. For greatest security a fenced *area* definitely takes precedence over a fenced *yard*.

The puppy will need a collar (one that fits now, not one to be grown into) and a lead from the moment you bring him home. Both should be an appropriate weight and type for his size. Also needed are a feeding dish and a water dish, both made preferably of unbreakable material. Your pet supply shop should have an interesting assortment of these and other accessories from which you can choose. Then you will need grooming tools of the type the breeder recommends and some toys. Equally satisfactory is Nylabone®, a nylon bone that does not chip or splinter and that "frizzles" as the puppy chews, providing healthful gum massage. Avoid plastics and any sort of rubber toys, *particularly those with squeakers* which the puppy may remove and swallow. If you want a ball for the puppy to use when playing with him, select one of very hard construction made for this purpose and do not leave it alone with him because he may chew off and swallow bits of the rubber. Take the ball with you when the game is over. This also applies to some of those "tug of war" type rubber toys which are fun when used with the two of you for that purpose but again should *not* be left behind for the dog to work on with his teeth. Bits of swallowed rubber, squeakers, and other such foreign articles can wreak great havoc in the intestinal tract—do all you can to guard against them.

Too many changes all at once can be difficult for a puppy. For at least the first few days he is with you, keep him on the food and feeding schedule to which he is accustomed. Find out ahead of time from the breeder what he feeds his puppies, how frequently, and at what times of the day. Also find out what, if any, food supplements the breeder has been using and recommends. Then be prepared by getting in a supply of the same food so that you will have it there when you bring the puppy home. Once the puppy is accustomed to his new surroundings, then you can switch the type of food and schedule to fit your convenience, but for the first several days do it as the puppy expects.

Your selection of a veterinarian should also be attended to before the puppy comes home, because you should stop at the vet's office for the puppy to be checked over as soon as you leave the breeder's premises. If the breeder is from your area, ask him for recommendations. Ask you dog-owning friends for their opinions of the local veterinarians, and see what their experiences with those available have been. Choose someone whom several of your friends recommend highly, then contact him about your puppy, perhaps making an appointment to stop in at his office. If the premises are clean, modern, and well equipped, and if you like the veterinarian, make an appointment to bring the puppy in on the day of purchase. Be sure to obtain the puppy's health record from the breeder, including information on such things as shots and worming that the puppy has had.

JOINING THE FAMILY

Remember that, exciting and happy an occasion as it is for you, the puppy's move from his place of birth to your home can be, for him, a traumatic experience. His mother and littermates will be missed. He quite likely will be awed or frightened by the change of surroundings. The person on whom he depended will

In addition to Nylabones illustrated here, Gumabones and Gumadiscs are now available. These new devices are made of polyurethane, a synthetic substance that is safe, non-toxic, very tough and yet flexible. Like Nylabones, Gumabones and Gumadiscs are produced in a variety of sizes, shapes and flavors, too.

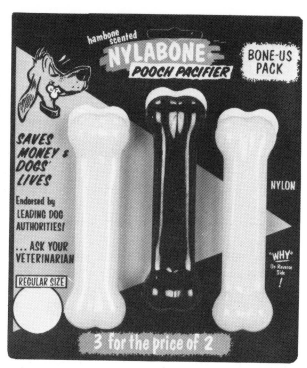

Am. and Can. Ch. Mio's Clean Sweep *(left)* and Ch. Mio's Shar-tooz. Litter-mates born in May 1980 bred by Joan and Burt Pettit, Mio Lhasa Apsos, Woodmere, New York.

be gone. Everything should be planned to make his arrival at your home pleasant—to give him confidence and to help him realize that yours is a pretty nice place to be after all.

Never bring a puppy home on a holiday. There is just too much going on with people and gifts and excitement. If he is in honor of an "occasion," work it out so that his arrival will be a few days earlier, or perhaps even better, a few days later than the "occasion." Then your home will be back to its normal routine and the puppy can enjoy your undivided attention. Try not to bring the puppy home in the evening. Early morning is the ideal time, as then he has the opportunity of getting acquainted and the initial strangeness should wear off before bedtime. You will find it a more peaceful night that way. Allow the puppy to investigate as he likes, under your watchful eye. If you already have a pet in the household, keep a careful watch that the relationship between the two gets off to a friendly start or you may quickly find yourself with a lasting problem. Much of the future attitude of each toward the other will depend on what takes place that first day, so keep your mind on what they are doing and let your other activities slide for the moment. Be careful not to let your older pet become jealous by paying more attention to the puppy than to him, as that will start a bad situation immediately.

If you have a child, here again it is important that the relationship start out well. Before the puppy is brought home, you should have a talk with the youngster. He must clearly understand that puppies are fragile and can easily be injured; therefore, they should not be teased, hurt, mauled, or overly rough-housed. A puppy is not an inanimate toy; it is a living thing with a right to be loved and handled respectfully, treatment which will reflect in the dog's attitude toward your child as both mature together. Never permit your children's playmates to mishandle the puppy, tormenting the puppy until it turns on the children in self-defense. Children often do not realize how rough is too rough. You, as a responsible adult, are obligated to assure that your puppy's relationship with children is a pleasant one.

Do not start out by spoiling your puppy. A puppy is usually pretty smart and can be quite demanding. What you had considered to be "just for tonight" may be accepted by the puppy as "for keeps." Be firm with him, strike a routine, and stick to it. The puppy will learn more quickly this way, and everyone will be happier as a result. A radio playing softly or a dim night light are often comforting to a puppy as it gets accustomed to new surroundings and should be provided in preference to bringing the puppy to bed with you—unless, of course, you intend him to share the bed as a permanent arrangement.

SOCIALIZING AND TRAINING

Socialization and training of your puppy should start the very day of his arrival in your home. Never address him without calling him by name. A short, simple name is the easiest to teach as it catches the dog's attention quickly; avoid elaborate call names. Always address the dog by the same name, not a whole series of pet names; the latter will only confuse the puppy.

Use his name clearly, and call the puppy over to you when you see him awake and wandering about. When he comes, make a big fuss over him for being such a good dog. He thus will quickly associate the sound of his name with coming to you and a pleasant happening.

Several hours after the puppy's arrival is not too soon to start accustoming him to the feel of a light collar. He may hardly notice it; or he may struggle, roll over, and try to rub it off his neck with his paws. Divert his attention when this occurs by offering a tasty snack or a toy (starting a game with him) or by petting him. Before long he will have accepted the strange feeling around his neck and no longer appear aware of it. Next comes the lead. Attach it and then immediately take the puppy outside or otherwise try to divert his attention with things to see and sniff. He may struggle against the lead at first, biting at it and trying to free himself. Do not pull him with it at this point; just hold the end loosely and try to follow him if he starts off in any direction. Normally his attention will soon turn to investigating his surroundings if he is outside or you have taken him into an unfamiliar room in your house; curiosity will take over and he will become interested in sniffing around the surroundings. Follow him with the lead slackly held until he seems to have completely forgotten about it; then try with gentle urging to get him to follow you. Don't be rough or jerk at him; just tug gently on the lead in short quick motions (steady pulling can become a battle of wills), repeating his name or trying to get him to follow your hand which is holding a bite of food or an interesting toy. If you have an older lead-trained dog, then it should be a cinch to get the puppy to follow along after *him*. In any event the average puppy learns quite quickly and will soon be trotting along nicely on the lead. Once that point has been reached, the next step is to teach him to follow on your left side, or heel. This will not likely be accomplished all in one day; it should be done with short training periods over the course of several days until you are satisfied with the result.

During the course of house training your puppy, you will need to take him out frequently and at regular intervals: first thing in the morning directly from the crate, immediately after meals, after the puppy has been napping, or when you notice that the puppy is looking for a spot. Choose more or less the same place to take the puppy each time so that a pattern will be established. If he does not go immediately, do not return him to the house as he will probably relieve himself the moment he is inside. Stay out with him until he has finished; then be lavish with your praise for his good behavior. If you catch the puppy having an accident indoors, grab him firmly and rush him outside, sharply saying "No!" as you pick him up. If you do not see the accident occur, there is little point in doing anything except cleaning it up, as once it has happened and been forgotten, the puppy will most likely not even realize why you are scolding him.

If you live in a big city or are away many hours at a time, having a dog that is trained to go on paper has some very definite advantages. To do this, one proceeds pretty much the same way as taking the puppy outdoors, except now you place the puppy on the newspaper at the proper time. The paper should always be kept in the same spot. An easy way to paper train a puppy if you have a playpen for it or an exercise pen is to line the area with newspapers; then gradually, every day or so, remove a section of newspaper until you are down to just one or two. The puppy acquires the habit of using the paper; and as the prepared area grows smaller, in the majority of cases the dog will continue to use whatever paper is still available. It is pleasant, if the dog is alone for an excessive length of time, to be able to feel that if he needs it the paper is there and will be used.

The puppy should form the habit of spending a certain amount of time in his crate, even when you are home. Sometimes the puppy will do this voluntarily, but if not, he should be taught to do so, which is accomplished by leading the puppy over by his collar, gently pushing him inside, and saying firmly, "Down" or "Stay." Whatever expression you use to give a command, stick to the very same one each time for each act. Repetition is the big thing in training—and so is association with what the dog is expected to do. When you mean "Sit," always say exactly that. "Stay" should mean *only* that the dog should remain where he receives the command. "Down" means something else again. Do not confuse the dog by shuffling the commands, as this will create training problems for you.

As soon as he had had his immunization shots, take your puppy with you whenever and wherever possible. There is nothing that will build a self-confident, stable dog like socialization, and it is extremely important that you plan and give the time and energy necessary for this, whether your dog is to be a show dog or a pleasant, well-adjusted family member. Take your puppy in the car so that he will learn to enjoy riding and not become carsick, as dogs may do if they are infrequent travelers. Take him anywhere you are going where you are certain he will be welcome: visiting friends and relatives (if they do not have housepets who may resent the visit), busy shopping centers (keeping him always on lead), or just walking around the streets of your town. If someone admires him (as always seems to happen when one is out with puppies), encourage the stranger to pet and talk with him. Socialization of this type brings out the best in your puppy and helps him to grow up with a friendly outlook, liking the world and its inhabitants. The worst thing that can be done to a puppy's personality is to shelter him. By always keeping him at home away from things and people unfamiliar to him, you may be creating a personality problem for the mature dog that will be a cross for you to bear later on.

FEEDING YOUR DOG

Time was when providing nourishing food for dogs involved a far more complicated procedure than people now feel is necessary. The old school of thought was that the daily ration must consist of fresh beef, vegetables, cereal, egg yolks, and cottage cheese as basics with such additions as brewer's yeast and vitamin tablets on a daily basis.

During recent years, however, many minds have changed regarding this procedure. Eggs, cottage cheese, and supplements to the diet are still given, but the basic method of feeding dogs has changed; and the change has been, in the opinion of many authorities, definitely for the better. The school of thought now is that you are doing your dogs a favor when you feed them some of the fine commercially prepared dog foods in preference to your own home-cooked concoctions.

The reason behind this new outlook is easily understandable. The dog food industry has grown to be a major one, participated in by some of the best known and most respected names in America. These trusted firms, it is agreed, turn out excellent products, so people are feeding their dog food preparations with confidence and the dogs are thriving, living longer, happier, and healthier lives than ever before. What more could one want?

There are at least half a dozen absolutely top-grade dry foods to be mixed with broth or water and served to your dog according to directions. There are all sorts of canned meats, and there are several kinds of "convenience foods," those in a packet which you open and dump out into the dog's dish. It is just that simple. The convenience foods are neat and easy to use when you are away from home, but generally speaking a dry food mixed with hot water (or soup) and meat is preferred. It is the opinion of many that the canned meat, with its added fortifiers, is more beneficial to the dogs than the fresh meat. However, the two can be alternated or, if you prefer and your dog does well on it, by all means use fresh ground beef. A dog enjoys changes in the meat part of his diet, which is easy with the canned food since all sorts of beef are available (chunk, ground, stewed, and so on), plus lamb, chicken, and even such concoctions as liver and egg, plain liver flavor, and a blend of five meats.

There is also prepared food geared to every age bracket of your dog's life, from puppyhood on through old age, with special additions or modifications to make it particularly nourishing and beneficial. Previous generations never had it so good where the canine dinner is concerned, because these commercially prepared foods are tasty and geared to meeting the dog's gastronomic approval.

Additionally, contents and nutrients are clearly listed on the labels, as are careful instructions for feeding just the right amount for the size, weight, and age of each dog.

With these foods the addition of extra vitamins is not necessary, but if you prefer there are several kinds of those, too, that serve as taste treats as well as being beneficial. Your pet supplier has a full array of them.

Of course there is no reason not to cook up something for your dog if you would feel happier doing so. But it seems unnecessary when such truly satisfactory rations are available with so much less trouble and expense.

How often you feed your dog is a matter of how it works out best for you. Many owners prefer to do it once a day. It is generally agreed that two meals, each of smaller quantity, are better for the digestion and more satisfying to the dog, particularly if yours is a household member who stands around and watches preparations for the family meals. Do not overfeed. This is the shortest route to all sorts of problems. Follow directions and note carefully how your dog is looking. If your dog is overweight, cut back the quantity of food a bit. If the dog looks thin, then increase the amount. Each dog is an individual and the food intake should be adjusted to his requirements to keep him feeling and looking trim and in top condition.

From the time puppies are fully weaned until they are about twelve weeks old, they should be fed four times daily. From three months to six months of age, three meals should suffice. At six months of age the puppies can be fed two meals, and the twice daily feedings can be continued until the puppies are close to one year old, at which time feeding can be changed to once daily if desired. If you do feed just once a day, do so by early afternoon at the latest and give the dog a snack, a biscuit or two, at bedtime.

Remember that plenty of fresh water should always be available to your puppy or dog for drinking. This is of utmost importance to his health.

Charbet's Red Baron taking Winners Dog at Baytown K.C., April 1980, on a windy Texas afternoon under the author.

Chapter 8

Grooming Your Lhasa Apso

Being appreciative of the importance of the Lhasa Apso coat and its correct maintenance, which involves basic knowledge, experience, and artistry, I decided to consult someone experienced in the fine points of beautifully grooming a Lhasa. The first person who came to mind was Robert D. Sharp, who has won many individual honors and great records with Lhasas, either as a professional handler or owner. Who could better tell us how the unforgettable beauty of a well-groomed Lhasa is created? So I asked Bob if he would be willing to share his expertise and technique with our readers, and shall ever be grateful that his answer was yes.

One word from the author as we start—be sure to accustom your puppy to being brushed just as soon as you possibly can! Formal grooming may not be possible, but a five-to six-week-old Lhasa puppy is not too young to be taken on your lap and gently brushed with a natural bristle brush. First brush his back, then turn him over to do the stomach and underarms. Make this a fun event for the puppy with lots of petting and sweet talk, so that he will associate the brush and grooming with pleasure rather than dread. This will make a great difference in his outlook about the whole matter.

A.K. Nicholas

There are many different grooming techniques, as each breeder has a favorite routine which works out best for him. However, some rules are basic and need to be observed by all.

Never brush or comb the Lhasa's coat when it is dry. Doing so will lead to splitting and broken ends. It is important to spray the coat as you work, using a good coat dressing or distilled water.

Never use a nylon brush on your dog's coat as it will tend to break off the ends. Only a good quality natural bristle brush or an equally good quality pin brush will do the job properly for you. This also applies to combs. Those made of rough (cheap) metal tear at the coat, doing more harm than good. Think of your grooming tools as an investment, and buy top quality. They will last longer and work better.

Never brush vigorously or tear at your dog's coat with long, sweeping strokes to the very ends of the hair. The coat should be handled gently and parted in sections as you carefully brush from the skin to the tips, watching for mats which may be starting.

Whether your Lhasa is a show dog or a pet, his eyes should be cleaned out daily as a part of grooming. Matter that is left to collect in the corner of the eye is unsightly, becomes smelly, and leads to staining and matting of the facial hair. A Lhasa Apso is not adequately groomed unless his eyes are attended to each and every day. An old toothbrush, small and easy to work with, can be used around the face.

Toenails should be kept short. Cut them back to the quick at least monthly, or more frequently if they are growing too fast. Nails which are allowed to become too long throw the dog back on his feet, giving him an awkward gait. Eventually, if the nails are permitted to remain overly long, they can cause the dog to throw out his shoulders or toe out with his hind feet.

Keep the hair between the pads on the bottom of the feet trimmed short, especially in wet, sandy, or muddy areas. Do not trim between the toes.

Eye falls (the long hair covering the eyes) should be held up in barrettes to prevent staining and to make seeing easier for the dog. Use foam rubber-backed types of barrettes with two prongs rather than a single bar, and alternate between two barrettes (Maltese style) and one barrette (ponytail style) to prevent sore spots or irritation from developing.

Every bath should be preceded by a very thorough brushing to remove dead hair and mats. A mat becomes almost impossible to separate once it has been washed in.

Last on this part of the list, but far from least, your most important part of Lhasa coat care is to prevent mats from forming. For a long, luxuriant coat, it is far easier to groom your dog regularly (and keep problems from arising) than to disentangle the hair once it has been neglected and has started to mat.

Basic equipment for grooming includes a number of essentials starting, as already pointed out, with a good quality natural bristle brush and a good quality pin brush. You will also need the following: lanolin spray (either a preparation for dogs or one for humans); RX-7, to be used in the ears at least twice weekly or as needed; a wide-tooth comb such as a Resco 80C or an Oliver mat and tangle comb; a Resco professional fine comb or other metal comb with similar toothing; either a prepared coat oil (available at pet shops) or a home-prepared mixture of lanolin and mineral oil; and a detangler, which also is available at pet shops.

Finally, you should purchase what will become one of your most useful pieces of equipment, both at home and at dog shows: a rubber-topped grooming table of the size suitable for a Lhasa, equipped with an arm and a noose which are used to steady the dog as you work on him.

Now to how it's done! Nearly every healthy Lhasa Apso grows hair, although the rate of this growth may differ with the individual dog. The problem is principally a matter of preventing the hairs from breaking off and the regular removal of dead hair to keep mats from forming.

Train your Lhasa to lie on his side on the grooming table. Groom him frequently enough so that mats have no chance to get started. A good grooming does not mean once over lightly. It means a complete grooming job from nose to tail.

First brush the coat out, separating with your fingers any little mats that may have formed and carefully brushing to remove dead hair. Part and divide the coat in layers, and brush every hair on the dog, from the skin out, in short, quick strokes. As you go along, dampen him with coat dressing or water, using a spray dispenser. Brush the dog first on one side and then the other, using the same method of dampening, parting, and brushing. Then comb carefully behind the ears, on the stomach, and beneath the armpits with a wide-tooth comb. Use a fine tooth comb only on the face and paws. The less combing and the more brushing that is done, the more coat your dog will have. If the dog has not been thoroughly brushed out, a comb will remove live as well as dead hair.

Next, stand the dog up, part him, comb his face, brush his tail (backcomb for fullness), spray the part lightly with either coat dressing or lanolin-based coat spray, and stand back to admire the finished product.

If you are then going to put the fall into a hair clasp, make sure that the dog's eyebrows and eyelashes are not caught in the clasp. You can easily see them on a short-haired dog; but on one who is long coated with head furnishings, they look like part of the fall. Brows and lashes are coarse, and if they are caught up with the rest of the fall, the dog will not be able to blink its eyes and will try to rub the clasp off. When being shown, the dog does not wear a clasp. Instead, the fall is parted so that the hair falls on either side of the nose. For everyday wear, however, a clasp means a cleaner face, no chewed-off fall, and a happier dog.

If you are starting to train a puppy to be groomed, brush him on a grooming table (a rubber top prevents slipping) and train him to lie on his side so you can get at his stomach and underarms. Never yank on his coat or yank a comb through a mat. The result will be a skittish dog and a wrestling match on your hands at future groomings. Do not let your puppy bite or snap at the comb or brush, as this not only interferes with your grooming, but can result in the dog losing teeth. When you have completed grooming your puppy, play with him for a few minutes and give him a treat. Make it a pleasant experience and he soon will be coming to you and asking for another session.

Lhasa puppies frequently "blow their coats" at some point between six months and a year of age. The easiest way to remove the dead hair from a young dog in the process of shedding out his puppy coat is by daily combing. This is the one time when combing is preferable to brushing, as you have less chance of breaking off the new adult coat with a comb than with a brush. A No. 80 Resco comb is invaluable. Its teeth are long and strong, and the comb is easy to use. A comb with more fine teeth may also be helpful, but a comb that is too fine will split and break off hair. If the dog has become so matted close to the skin that you cannot comb out the mats, even after breaking them up with your finger-

Left: Mio's To Ka, litter brother to Clean Sweep and Shan-tooz, says "please" from atop the grooming table. Joan Pettit, owner, Mio Lhasa Apsos, Woodmere, New York. *Right:* Under the dryer, Rhu-Ha's Dragon Lhadi, obviously thinking of the price of being beautiful as she endures the rigors of grooming. Owned by Ruth M. Hatcher, Roanoke, Virginia. Dragon Lhadi is by Ch. Thmilos Magic Dragon ex Hatcher's Mai-Ling Poppi.

tips and a disentangler, naturally you will have to go to a wire pin brush or a slicker brush. In this case, a Werner's slicker brush is ideally constructed for a Lhasa coat. Be sure to use short, quick strokes, keeping in mind that long, sweeping strokes down to the tips merely break off the hair. Start in the near-center of the mat, clear a spot down to the skin, and gradually work out the matted hair to the tips, where you then can remove it with a comb or slicker.

GROOMING FOR SHOW

So much for the regular care of your Lhasa's coat. Now to the heart of the matter—preparing your Lhasa Apso for the show ring. The night before clip his nails; trim pads; give a good run, even if you are exhausted. Bathe the dog. If he is dark in color, you can bathe him ahead of time, then just go over his face with Johnson's No More Tears shampoo.

Bring an exercise pen if clean grass is not readily available. Also bring a plastic drop cloth to put under the pen if the grass is wet or dusty. Crates are desirable as dogs can sleep comfortably in them and be protected from patting hands. Inexpensive, collapsible crates are available.

Have your dog brushed, sprayed, parted, and ready about 30 minutes before your scheduled time of judging. You usually will need about half an hour per dog to accomplish this. Also, have someone check the progress of the judging preceding yours to ascertain whether it is on time, ahead of time, or late. Leave barrettes or hair clips in place. Brush chest coat down. Brush beard forward.

Now you can take a deep breath and have a moment's relaxation, but only briefly, as then the dog returns to the grooming table and out comes your spray net. Using a knitting needle, make certain that the part is meticulous, every hair exactly in place, centered exactly from nose to tail. Liberally spray along the part from the top of the rump and along the sides. With your hands, gently smooth the coat as flat and as long as possible. Allow the spray to dry, then repeat if necessary. Take out the barrettes and comb the eyefall forward, over the eyes to each side of the nose. Fluff up the leg furnishings. Comb part of the hind leg furnishings forward to make the groin coat appear longer, as this is usually an inch shorter than the rest of the coat. Hold the tail straight up in the air, then brush the lower third down to give a nice plume over the rear. If you can, part the upper two-thirds so that the plume will fall evenly to either side.

Put your coarse comb in your pocket, pick up the dog carefully, and take him to ringside. Hold him until you enter the ring to keep him immaculately clean. Once in the ring, run the coarse comb through his coat gently before the judge gets to him. Never touch his coat while he is moving, and do not have your mind on anything except moving him at that time. There will be plenty of opportunity to arrange stray hairs and check the eyefall when you are standing still again.

Never leave your dog unattended at a show. Dogs have been stolen, poisoned, and tranquilized in the owner's absence. Children often like to pet and handle the dogs, which should be discouraged for a variety of reasons.

PUTTING YOUR LHASA IN OIL

In the beginning, it is best to put your Lhasa in oil only about three days before bathing. If you are showing every weekend, then usually it will work well to simply spray the ends with lanolin diluted with water, rather than using the oil treatment.

When oil is most needed, actually, is during the dry winter months when central heating takes its toll by drying out the coat's natural oils. Wintertime is when an adult dog will need to spend much of his time oiled down and have his coat brushed thoroughly each day as a preventative against breaking ends and dryness. Normally the coat absorbs the oil in about three days.

To apply oil to the Lhasa's coat, spray or pour it on your hands then stroke it on the coat starting about one quarter inch away from the skin. Taking the oil right to the skin surface tends to make the coat mat, preventing the insulation against cold which is important.

Lately, many people have been treating their dogs' coats with cream rinse diluted with water rather than using the oil. This method is less messy and cream rinse washes out far more easily. You may have to experiment a bit in making up the mixture. For some coats, exactly half cream rinse and half water will be ideal; for some it will work out well to go more heavily on one than the other. For example, with puppies usually a higher proportion of water than cream rinse does the trick.

In applying either oil or the cream rinse mixture, brush into the coat, using a bristle brush. When the dog is "in oil," never permit him to remain for any length of time in the direct sunshine. Fresh air is as good for dogs as it is for humans, but the sun's rays will burn the coat, which obviously should be avoided. Additionally, too much sun tends to cause a brittle condition of the coat.

Conditioning dry or brittle hair, and preventing the hair from being dried out by wind, sun, and central heating are tremendously important factors in caring for long-coated breeds.

LHASA COAT PROBLEMS

Should you own a dog who does not seem able to grow coat regardless of your best care and efforts, seriously consider his background, and whether or not he comes from a line which produces correct coat. Look to his parents for what may be the cause of your problem, then work from there. It is very logical that poorly coated parents may produce poorly coated offspring; there is just no "coat grower" that can be externally applied or used internally that will bring about any great improvement if your dog is bred from a poorly coated line.

Let's assume that you started out with a heavily coated puppy whom you have raised on a well-balanced diet (adequate amounts of protein and fat) and supplied with sufficient exercise. If the coat does not come on well despite your good efforts, take the dog to be checked by your veterinarian for worms. Parasites are among the world's most efficient coat devastators; sometimes worm infestation causes the coat to "blow" practically overnight.

A poor coat, slight appetite, lack of animation, and bloated belly on a puppy should make you suspicious of worms. Roundworms are white when passed and will almost immediately roll into little balls. Hookworms cannot be detected in the stool without the aid of a microscope, but a dog suffering from them will eventually become anemic and develop pale, grayish gums. Tapeworms are difficult to catch, but check the dog's stool periodically. (Tapeworms often look like grains of rice.)

If your dog has tapeworms, check for fleas and vice versa. The tapeworm must pass part of its life cycle in a flea.

Naturally you must keep your dog free of external parasites. A single flea can start a chain reaction of itching and scratching that can reduce your dog to a mess of broken off coat and sore, red skin.

Fleas, lice, ticks, and nits (louse eggs) usually are picked up from neighborhood four-legged friends if the dog is permitted to run loose, or sometimes from the pets of visiting friends who bring their dogs along to visit.

The most gorgeous show coat in the world can be chewed or scratched out in large patches in only two or three days when under the attack of external parasites—a heartbreaking state of affairs when one considers the months involved in restoring a coat's full beauty!

Keep your dog away from strays and from other people's pets. At dog shows, do not let your dog mingle freely. You have to take enough risk when you exercise your dogs on the grass, or when going into the rings during breed and Group judging where many other dogs have preceded yours. A dip in a good flea killer should be used immediately following your return home in an effort to kill off any unwanted traveling companions collected while away from home. Fleas are a particular problem since they can so quickly infest your home, as well as your dog. They lay eggs in the woodwork, necessitating fumigation of the house and spraying of the yard and the dog quarters if they are to be entirely eliminated. Obviously, it is far simpler to just be watchful and not let fleas get started in the first place.

Moist eczema, more prevelant in males, is easily controlled by Variton Ointment, obtainable without prescription at any drug store. A dog with this malady will chew and rub the afflicted area, making it red, raw, and wet looking. Just rub in the Variton frequently. Don't cut the fur, but do not let it mat. Wash the Variton out with soap and water when the skin has healed.

Sometimes a dog who constantly itches for no obvious reason needs to have his anal glands expressed. These glands, located at the base of the tail on either side of the anus, can become filled with fluid and eventually abcess if the pressure is not relieved. Have your veterinarian show you how to check the anal glands. It's a messy procedure, but one which you should know, although many dog owners prefer to have the veterinarian attend to it for them.

Climate often plays a part in your dog's coat development. A cool, humid climate will produce glorious coats with half the effort required in a high, hot, and dry area.

If all else fails, have your veterinarian thoroughly check your dog. He may have a sluggish thyroid which can be retarding the coat growth.

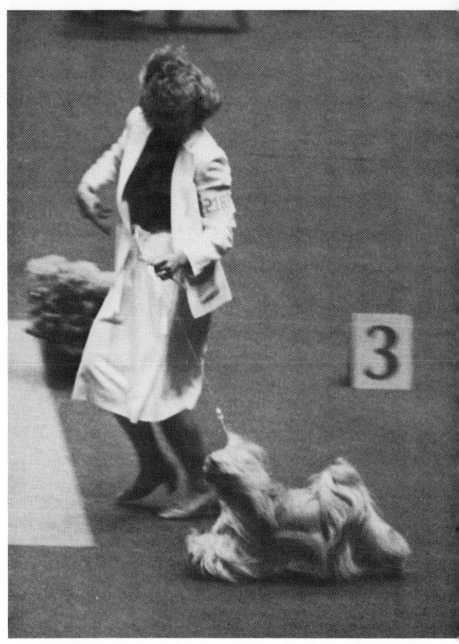

Multiple Best in Show winning Ch. San Jo's Shindig making a good showing in the Westminster Group, Madison Square Garden 1985. Owned by Victor Cohen, bred by San Jo Lhasas, handled by Lesley Ann Engen, co-breeder.

Chapter 9

The Making of a Show Dog

If you have decided to become a show dog exhibitor, you have accepted a very real and very exciting challenge. The groundwork has been accomplished with the selection of your future show prospect. If you have purchased a puppy, it is assumed that you have gone through all the proper preliminaries concerning good care, which should be the same if the puppy is a pet or future show dog, with a few added precautions for the latter.

GENERAL CONSIDERATIONS

Remember the importance of keeping your future winner in trim, top condition. Since you want him neither too fat nor too thin, his appetite for his proper diet should be guarded, and children and guests should not be permitted to constantly feed him "goodies." The best treat of all is a small wad of raw ground beef or a packaged dog treat. To be avoided are ice cream, cake, cookies, potato chips, and other fattening items which will cause the dog to put on weight and may additionally spoil his appetite for the proper, nourishing, well-balanced diet so essential to good health and condition.

The importance of temperament and showmanship cannot possibly be overestimated. They have put many a mediocre dog across, while lack of them can ruin the career of an otherwise outstanding specimen. From the day your dog joins your family, socialize him. Keep him accustomed to being with people and to being handled by people. Encourage your friends and relatives to "go over" him as the judges will in the ring so this will not seem a strange and upsetting experience. Practice showing his "bite" (the manner in which his teeth meet) quickly and deftly. It is quite simple to slip the lips apart with your fingers, and the puppy should be willing to accept this from you or the judge without struggle.

Some judges prefer that the exhibitors display the dog's bite and other mouth features themselves. These are the considerate ones, who do not wish to chance the spreading of possible infection from dog to dog with their hands on each one's mouth—a courtesy particularly appreciated in these days of virus epidemics. But the old-fashioned judges still persist in doing it themselves, so the dog should be ready for either possibility.

Take your future show dog with you in the car, thus accustoming him to riding so that he will not become carsick on the day of a dog show. He should associate pleasure and attention with going in the car, van, or motor home. Take him where it is crowded: downtown, to the shops, everywhere you go that dogs are permitted. Make the expeditions fun for him by frequent petting and words of praise; do not just ignore him as you go about your errands.

Do not overly shelter your future show dog. Instinctively you may want to keep him at home where he is safe from germs or danger. This can be foolish on two counts. The first reason is that a puppy kept away from other dogs builds up no natural immunity against all the things with which he will come in contact at dog shows, so it is wiser to keep him up-to-date on all protective shots and then let him become accustomed to being among dogs and dog owners. Also, a dog who is never among strange people, in strange places, or among strange dogs may grow up with a shyness or timidity of spirit that will cause you real problems as his show career draws near.

Keep your show prospect's coat in immaculate condition with frequent grooming and daily brushing. When bathing is necessary, use a mild dog shampoo or whatever the breeder of your

Ch. Kyi-Chu Shara, handled by Jane Kay for Mrs. Keke Blumberg, Huntington Valley, Pennsylvania, was the second Lhasa bitch in history to become a Best in Show winner. Here winning a Non-Sporting Group at Tidewater K.C. in 1966.

puppy may suggest. Several of the brand-name products do an excellent job. Be sure to rinse thoroughly so as not to risk skin irritation by traces of soap left behind, and protect against soap entering the eyes by a drop of castor oil in each before you lather up. Use warm water (be sure it is not uncomfortably hot or chillingly cold) and a good spray. Make certain you allow your dog to dry thoroughly in a warm, draft-free area (or outdoors, if it is warm and sunny) so that he doesn't catch cold. Then proceed to groom him to perfection.

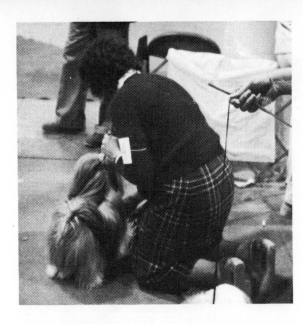

Dolsa Puf N Stuf Maple Leaf, "set up" properly awaiting the judge's attention. Photo courtesy of Julie K. Elliott.

A show dog's teeth must be kept clean and free of tartar. Hard dog biscuits can help toward this, but if tartar accumulates, see that it is removed promptly by your veterinarian. Bones for chewing are not suitable for show dogs as they tend to damage and wear down the tooth enamel.

Assuming that you will be handling the dog yourself, or even if he will be professionally handled, a few moments each day of dog show routine is important. Practice setting him up as you have seen the exhibitors do at the shows you've attended, and teach him to hold this position once you have him stacked to your satisfaction. Make the learning period pleasant by being firm but lavish in your praise when he responds correctly. Teach him to gait at your side at a moderate rate on a loose lead. When you have mastered the basic essentials at home, then hunt out and join a training class for future work. Training classes are sponsored by show-giving clubs in many areas, and their popularity is steadily increasing. If you have no other way of locating one, perhaps your veterinarian would know of one through some of his other clients; but if you are sufficiently aware of the dog show world to want a show dog, you will probably be personally acquainted with other people who will share information of this type with you.

Accustom your show dog to being in a crate (which you should be doing with a pet dog as well). He should relax in his crate at the shows "between times" for his own well being and safety.

MATCH SHOWS

Your show dog's initial experience in the ring should be in match show competition. This type of event is intended as a learning experience for both the dog and the exhibitor. You will not feel embarrassed or out of place no matter how poorly your puppy may behave or how inept your attempts at handling may be, as you will find others there with the same type of problems. The important thing is that you get the puppy out and into a show ring where the two of you can practice together and learn the ropes.

Only on rare occasions is it necessary to make match show entries in advance, and even those with a pre-entry policy will usually accept entries at the door as well. Thus you need not plan several weeks ahead, as is the case with point shows, but can go when the mood strikes you. Also there is a vast difference in the cost, as match show entries only cost a few dollars while entry fees for the point shows may be over ten dollars, an amount none of us needs to waste until we have some idea of how the puppy will behave or how much more pre-show training is needed.

Match shows are frequently judged by professional handlers who, in addition to making the awards, are happy to help new exhibitors with comments and advice on their puppies and their presentation of them. Avail yourself of all these opportunities before heading out to the sophisticated world of the point shows.

POINT SHOWS

As previously mentioned, entries for American Kennel Club point shows must be made in advance. This must be done on an official entry blank of the show-giving club. The entry must then be filed either personally or by mail with the show superintendent or the show secretary (if the event is being run by the club members alone and a superintendent has not been hired, this information will appear on the premium list) in time to reach its destination prior to the published closing date or filling of the quota. These entries must be made carefully, must be signed by the owner of the dog or the owner's agent (your professional handler), and must be accompanied by the entry fee; otherwise they will not be accepted. Remember that it is not when the entry leaves your hands that counts, but the date of arrival at its destination. If you are relying on the mails, which are not always dependable, get the entry off well before the deadline to avoid disappointment.

A dog must be entered at a dog show in the name of the actual owner at the time of the entry closing date of that specific show. If a registered dog has been acquired by a new owner, it must be entered in the name of the new owner in any show for which entries close after the date of acquirement, regardless of whether the new owner has or has not actually received the registration certificate indicating that the dog is recorded in his name. State on the entry form whether or not transfer application has been mailed to the American Kennel Club, and it goes without saying that the latter should be attended to promptly when you purchase a registered dog.

In filling out your entry blank, type, print, or write clearly, paying particular attention to the spelling of names, correct registration numbers, and so on. Also, if there is more than one variety in your breed, be sure to indicate into which category your dog is being entered.

The **Puppy Class** is for dogs or bitches who are six months of age and under twelve months and who are not champions. The age of a dog shall be calculated up to and inclusive of the first day of a show. For example, the first day a dog whelped on January 1st is eligible to compete in a Puppy Class at a show is July 1st of the same year; and he may continue to compete in Puppy Classes up to and including a show on December 31 of the same year, but he is *not* eligible to compete in a Puppy Class at a show held on or after January 1 of the following year.

The Puppy Class is the first one in which you should enter your puppy. In it a certain allowance will be made for the fact that they *are* puppies, thus an immature dog or one displaying less than perfect showmanship will be less severely penalized than, for instance, would be the case in Open. It is also quite likely that others in the class will be suffering from these problems, too. When you enter a puppy, be sure to check the classification with care, as some shows divide their Puppy Class into a 6-9 months old section and a 9-12 months old section.

The **Novice Class** is for dogs six months of age and over, whelped in the United States or Canada, who *prior to the official closing date for entries* have *not* won three first prizes in the Novice Class, any first prize at all in the Bred-by-Exhibitor, American-bred, or Open Classes, or one or more points toward championship. The provisions for this class are confusing to many people, which is probably the reason exhibitors do not enter in it more frequently. A dog may win any number of first prizes in the Puppy Class and still retain his eligibility for Novice. He may place second, third, or fourth not only in Novice on an unlimited number of occasions, but also in Bred-by-Exhibitor, American-bred and Open and still remain eligible for Novice. But he may no longer be shown in Novice when he has won three blue ribbons in that class, when he has won even one blue ribbon in either Bred-by-Exhibitor, American-bred, or Open, or when he has won a single championship point.

In determining whether or not a dog is eligible for the Novice Class, keep in mind the fact that previous wins are calculated according to the official published date for closing of entries, not by the date on which you may actually have made the entry. So if in the interim, between the time you made the entry and the official closing date, your dog makes a win causing him to become ineligible for Novice, change your class *immediately* to another for which he will be eligible, preferably either Bred-by-Exhibitor or American-bred. To do this, you must contact the show's superintendent or secretary, at first by telephone to save time and then in writing to confirm it. The Novice Class always seems to have the fewest entries of any class, and therefore it is a splendid "practice ground" for you and your young dog while you are getting the "feel" of being in the ring.

Bred-by-Exhibitor Class is for dogs whelped in the United States or, if individually registered in the American Kennel Club Stud Book, for dogs whelped in Canada who are six months of age or older, are not champions, and are owned wholly or in part by the person or by the spouse of the person who was the breeder or one of the breeders of record. Dogs entered in this class must be handled in the class by an owner or by a member of the immediate family of the owner. Members of an immediate family for this purpose are husband, wife, father, mother, son, daughter, brother, or sister. This is the class which is really the "breeders' showcase," and the one which breeders should enter with particular pride to show off their achievements.

The **American-bred Class** is for all dogs excepting champions, six months of age or older, who were whelped in the United States by reason of a mating which took place in the United States.

The **Open Class** is for any dog six months of age or older (this is the only restriction for this class). Dogs with championship points compete in it, dogs who are already champions are eligible to do so, dogs who are imported can be entered, and, of course, American-bred dogs compete in it. This class is, for some strange reason, the favorite of exhibitors who are "out to win." They rush to enter their pointed dogs in it, under the false impression that by doing so they assure themselves of greater attention from the judges. This really is not so, and some people feel that to enter in one of the less competitive classes, with a better chance of winning it and thus earning a second opportunity of gaining the judge's approval by returning to the ring in the Winners Class, can often be a more effective strategy.

One does not enter the **Winners Class.** One earns the right to compete in it by winning first prize in Puppy, Novice, Bred-by-Exhibitor, American-bred, or Open. No dog who has been defeated on the same day in one of these classes is eligible to compete for Winners, and every dog who has been a blue-ribbon winner in one of them and not defeated in another, should he have been entered in more than one class (as occasionally happens), *must* do so. Following the selection of the Winners Dog or the Winners Bitch, the dog or bitch receiving that award leaves the ring. Then the dog or bitch who placed second in that class, unless previously beaten by another dog or bitch in another class at the same show, re-enters the ring to compete against the remaining first-prize winners for Reserve. The latter award indicates that the dog or bitch selected for it is standing "in reserve" should the one who received Winners be disqualified or declared ineligible through any technicality when the awards are checked at the American Kennel Club. In that case, the one who placed Reserve is moved up to Winners, at the same time receiving the appropriate championship points.

Winners Dog and Winners Bitch are the awards which carry points toward championship with them. The points are based on the number of dogs or bitches actually in competition, and the points are scaled one through five, the latter being the greatest number available to any one dog or bitch at any one show. Three-, four-, or five-point wins are considered majors. In order to become a champion, a dog or bitch must have won two majors under two different judges, plus at least one point from a third judge, and the additional points necessary to bring the total to fifteen.

The Top Winning Brace in Lhasa Apso history, Group winning Am. and Can. Ch. Anbara's Abra-Ka-Dabra ROM *(right)* and Ch. Anbara's Ruffian *(left)*, bred by Barbara Wood and Stephen Campbell, owner-handled by Barbara Wood. Abby was 1976 ALAC Grand Futurity Winner and the dam of Best in Show Ch. Anbara's Hobgoblin.

Left: Best of Breed, Am. and Bda. Ch. Kinderlands Tonka, ROM (by Best in Show Ch. Tibet of Cornwallis, ROM-Ch. Kinderland's Sang Po, ROM), handled by Barbara Alderman. *Right:* Best of Opposite Sex, Ch. Daktazl Tsung (by Best in Show winning Ch. Karma Frosty Knight O'Everglo, ROM-Everglo Mai Ling Tsung, ROM), handled by Carolyn Herbel. Both owned by Mrs. Herbel at Tabu when this photo was made.

When your dog has gained fifteen points as described above, a championship certificate will be issued to you, and your dog's name will be published in the champions of record list in the *Pure-Bred Dogs/American Kennel Gazette*, the official publication of the American Kennel Club.

The scale of championship points for each breed is worked out by the American Kennel Club and reviewed annually, at which time the number required in competition may be either changed (raised or lowered) or remain the same. The scale of championship points for all breeds is published annually in the May issue of the *Gazette*, and the current ratings for each breed within that area are published in every show catalog.

When a dog or bitch is adjudged Best of Winners, its championship points are, for that show, compiled on the basis of which sex had the greater number of points. If there are two points in dogs and four in bitches and the dog goes Best of Winners, then *both* the dog and the bitch are awarded an equal number of points, in this case four. Should the Winners Dog or the Winners Bitch go on to win Best of Breed or Best of Variety, additional points are accorded for the additional dogs and bitches defeated by so doing, provided, of course, that there were entries specifically for Best of Breed competition or Specials, as these specific entries are generally called.

If your dog or bitch takes Best of Opposite Sex after going Winners, points are credited according to the number of the same sex defeated in both the regular classes and Specials competition. If Best of Winners is also won, then whatever additional points for each of these awards are available will be credited. Many a one- or two-point win has grown into a major in this manner.

Moving further along, should your dog win its **Variety Group** from the classes (in other words, if it has taken either Winners Dog or Winners Bitch), you then receive points based on the greatest number of points awarded to any member of any breed included within that Group during that show's competition. Should the day's winning also include Best in Show, the same rule of thumb applies, and your dog or bitch receives the highest number of points awarded to any other dog of any breed at that event.

Best of Breed competition consists of the Winners Dog and the Winners Bitch, who automatically compete on the strength of those awards, in addition to whatever dogs and bitches have been entered specifically for this class for which champions of record are eligible. Since July 1980, dogs who, according to their owner's records, have completed the requirements for a championship after the closing of entries for the show (but whose championships are unconfirmed) may be transferred from one of the regular classes to the Best of Breed competition, provided this transfer is made by the show superintendent or show secretary *prior to the start of any judging at the show.*

This has proved an extremely popular new rule, as under it a dog can finish on Saturday and then be transferred and compete as a Special on Sunday. It must be emphasized that *the change must be made prior to the start of any part of the day's judging, not for just your individual breed.*

In the United States, Best of Breed winners are entitled to compete in the Variety Group which includes them. This is not mandatory; it is a privilege which exhibitors value. (In Canada, Best of Breed winners *must* compete in the Variety Group or they lose any points already won.) The dogs winning *first* in each of the seven Variety Groups *must* compete for Best in Show. Missing the opportunity of taking your dog in for competition in its Group is foolish, as it is there where the general public is most likely to notice your breed and become interested in learning about it.

Non-regular classes are sometimes included at the all-breed shows, and they are almost invariably included at Specialty shows. These include Stud Dog Class and Brood Bitch Class, which are judged on the basis of the quality of the two offspring accompanying the sire or dam. The quality of the latter two is beside the point and should not be considered by the judge; it is the youngsters who count, and the quality of *both* are to be averaged to decide which sire or dam is the best and most consistent producer. Then there is the Brace Class (which, at all-breed shows, moves up to Best Brace in each Variety Group and then Best Brace in Show) which is judged on the similarity and evenness of appearance of the two brace members. In other words, the two dogs should look like identical twins in size, color, and conformation and should move together almost as a single dog, one person handling with precision and ease. The same applies to the Team Class competition, except that four dogs are involved and, if necessary, two handlers.

The Veterans Class is for the older dog, the minimum age of

Ch. Marlo Somethin Else and Ch. Marlo Dolsa Coming Out Parti, littermates, taking Best of Breed and Best of Opposite Sex at a Lhasa Apso Club Match Show in July 1982. By Ch. Suntory Four on the Floor ex Ch. Marlo's One Of A Kind. Bred and owned by Lynn Lowy, Beverly Hills, California.

The Open Dog Class at a recent Topeka, Kansas, event. Pictured are Marjorie Lewis, the late Pat Stewart, Carolyn Herbel, and Ann Mann. Winners Dog, for a 3-point major, was Donicia's Rhe Ghan San owned by Pat Stewart.

whom is seven years. This class is judged on the quality of the dogs, as the winner competes in Best of Breed competition and has, on a respectable number of occasions, been known to take that top award. So the point is *not* to pick out the oldest dog, as some judges seem to believe, but the best specimen of the breed, exactly as in the regular classes.

Then there are Sweepstakes and Futurity Stakes sponsored by many Specialty clubs, sometimes as part of their regular Specialty shows and sometimes as separate events on an entirely different occasion. The difference between the two stakes is that Sweepstakes entries usually include dogs from six to eighteen months of age with entries made at the same time as the others for the show, while for a Futurity the entries are bitches nominated when bred and the individual puppies entered at or shortly following their birth.

JUNIOR SHOWMANSHIP COMPETITION

If there is a youngster in your family between the ages of ten and sixteen, there is no better or more rewarding hobby than becoming an active participant in Junior Showmanship. This is a marvelous activity for young people. It teaches responsibility, good sportsmanship, the fun of competition where one's own skills are the deciding factor of success, proper care of a pet, and how to socialize with other young folks. Any youngster may experience the thrill of emerging from the ring a winner and the satisfaction of a good job well done.

Entry in Junior Showmanship Classes is open to any boy or girl who is at least ten years old and under seventeen years old on the day of the show. The Novice Junior Showmanship Class is open to youngsters who have not already won, at the time the entries close, three firsts in this class. Youngsters who have won three firsts in Novice may compete in the Open Junior Showmanship Class. Any junior handler who wins his third first-place award in Novice may participate in the Open Class at the same show, provided that the Open Class has at least one other junior handler entered and competing in it that day. The Novice and Open Classes may be divided into Junior and Senior Classes. Youngsters between the ages of ten and twelve, inclusively, are eligible for the Junior division; and youngsters between thirteen and seventeen, inclusively, are eligible for the Senior division.

Any of the foregoing classes may be separated into individual classes for boys and for girls. If such a division is made, it must be so indicated on the premium list. The premium list also indicates the prize for Best Junior Handler, if such a prize is being offered at the show. Any youngster who wins a first in any of the regular classes may enter the competition for this prize, provided the youngster has been undefeated in any other Junior Showmanship Class at that show.

Junior Showmanship Classes, unlike regular conformation classes in which the quality of the dog is judged, are judged solely on the skill and ability of the junior handling the dog. Which dog is best is not the point—it is which youngster does the best job with the dog that is under consideration. Eligibility requirements for the dog being shown in Junior Showmanship, and other detailed information, can be found in *Regulations for Junior Showmanship*, available from the American Kennel Club.

A junior who has a dog that he or she can enter in both Junior Showmanship and conformation classes has twice the opportunity for success and twice the opportunity to get into the ring and work with the dog, a combination which can lead to not only awards for expert handling, but also, if the dog is of sufficient quality, for making a conformation champion.

LHASA APSOS IN JUNIOR SHOWMANSHIP

Lhasas seem to be a popular breed with junior handlers, despite the coat care necessary to keep members of this breed looking in top form. We have noted that a number of junior handlers are consistently highly successful with their dogs. Monette Thiele, who is Julie Elliott's daughter, has been active in Junior Showmanship since she first walked into a match ring at age ten years. She has been notably successful and held the No. 1 Junior Handler in Lhasas award several times, as well as having qualified and competed in the finals at Westminster on three occasions. She also competes in the conformation classes, helping with her mother's dogs as well as with her own, and she has shown several different Lhasas in the Junior Handling Classes.

At Westminster 1986, several youngsters qualified to compete with their Lhasas at this prestigious event. They included Stephanie Kodis, Dawn Miccile, and Anne Olejniczak.

12-year-old Joanne P. Baker winning First Prize in Junior Showmanship at Old Dominion K.C. in 1973. Lhasa pictured is the pointed Pongo's Tashi-ta owned by Madeline Durholz and Joanne; bred by Edmund and Carolyn Sledzig.

Anne has been competing in Junior Showmanship since early August 1984 when she turned 10 years of age. In her first year of open competition she accumulated 11 open first place wins, 8 of which qualified her to compete at Westminster, plus 1 Best Junior Handler win. In December 1985, she was rated in the *Lhasa Apso Reporter* as No. 1 for the placements she had gained during that year. Anne has worked mostly with Champion Jolee's Got To Be Lucky whom she co-owns with Denise Olejniczak.

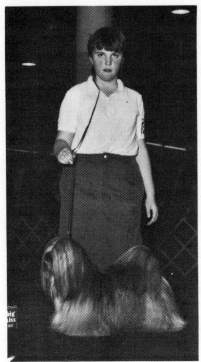

Left: Monette Thiele winning Best Junior Showman at Arkansas K.C. in 1985. Her Lhasa Apso is Amberwood's Alcheringa, by Ch. Shyr-Lyz Shan Mar ex Princess Jewel Chung Woo. Monette is the daughter of Julie Elliott, owner of Ju-Ell Lhasa Apsos. *Right:* Anne Olejniczak with Ch. Jolee's Got To Be Lucky taking First Place in Junior Handlers Class at Cudahy K.C. in March 1985. Owned by Denise and Anne Olejniczak, Brynwood Lhasa Apsos, Loves Park, Illinois.

PRE-SHOW PREPARATIONS

Preparation of the items you will need as a dog show exhibitor should not be left until the last moment. They should be planned and arranged several days in advance of the show in order for you to remain calm and relaxed as the countdown starts.

The importance of the crate has already been mentioned and should already be part of your equipment. Of equal importance is the grooming table, which very likely you have also already acquired for use at home. You should take it along with you to the shows, as your dog will need last minute touches before entering the ring. Should you have not yet made this purchase, folding tables with rubber tops are made specifically for this purpose and can be purchased at most dog shows, where concession booths with marvelous assortments of "doggy" necessities are to be found, or at your pet supplier. You will also need a sturdy tack box (also available at the dog show concessions) in which to carry your grooming tools and equipment. The latter should include: brushes; combs; scissors; nail clippers; whatever you use for last minute clean-up jobs; cotton swabs; first-aid equipment; and anything you are in the habit of using on the dog, including a leash or two of the type you prefer, some well-cooked and dried-out liver or any of the small packaged "dog treats" for use as bait in the ring, an atomizer in case you wish to dampen your dog's coat when you are preparing him for the ring, and so on. A large turkish towel to spread under the dog on the grooming table is also useful.

Take a large thermos or cooler of ice, the biggest one you can accommodate in your vehicle, for use by "man and beast." Take a jug of water (there are lightweight, inexpensive ones available at all sporting goods shops) and a water dish. If you plan to feed the dog at the show, or if you and the dog will be away from home more than one day, bring food for him from home so that he will have the type to which he is accustomed.

You may or may not have an exercise pen. While the shows do provide areas for exercise of the dogs, these are among the most likely places to have your dog come in contact with any illnesses which may be going around, and having a pen of your own for your dog's use is excellent protection. Such a pen comes in handy while you're travelling; since it is roomier than a crate, it becomes a comfortable place for your dog to relax and move around in, especially when you're at motels or rest stops. These pens are available at the show concession stands and come in a variety of heights and sizes. A set of "pooper scoopers" should also be part of your equipment, along with a package of plastic bags for cleaning up after your dog.

Bring along folding chairs for the members of your party, unless all of you are fond of standing, as these are almost never provided by the clubs. Have your name stamped on the chairs so that there will be no doubt as to whom the chairs belong. Bring whatever you and your family enjoy for drinks or snacks in a picnic basket or cooler, as show food, in general, is expensive and usually not great. You should always have a pair of boots, a raincoat, and a rain hat with you (they should remain permanently in your vehicle if you plan to attend shows regularly), as well as a sweater, a warm coat, and a change of shoes. A smock or big cover-up apron will assure that you remain tidy as you prepare the dog for the ring. Your overnight case should include a small sewing kit for emergency repairs, bandaids, headache and indigestion remedies, and any personal products or medications you normally use.

In your car, you should always carry maps of the area where you are headed and an assortment of motel directories. Generally speaking, Holiday Inns have been found to be the nicest about taking dogs. Ramadas and Howard Johnsons generally do so cheerfully (with a few exceptions). Best Western generally frowns on pets (not always, but often enough to make it necessary to find out which do). Some of the smaller chains welcome pets; the majority of privately-owned motels do not.

Have everything prepared the night before the show to expedite your departure. Be sure that the dog's identification and your judging program and other show information are in your purse or briefcase. If you are taking sandwiches, have them ready. Anything that goes into the car the night before the show will be one thing less to remember in the morning. Decide upon what you will wear and have it out and ready. If there is any question in your mind about what to wear, try on the possibilities before the day of the show; don't risk feeling you may want to change when you see yourself dressed a few moments prior to departure time!

In planning your outfit, make it something simple that will not detract from your dog. Remember that a dark dog silhouettes attractively against a light background and vice-versa. Sport clothes always seem to look best at dog shows, preferably conservative in type and not overly "loud" as you do not want to detract from your dog, who should be the focus of interest at this point. What you wear on your feet is important. Many types of flooring can be hazardously slippery, as can wet grass. Make it a habit to wear rubber soles and low or flat heels in the ring for your own safety, especially if you are showing a dog that likes to move out smartly.

Your final step in pre-show preparation is to leave yourself plenty of time to reach the show that morning. Traffic can get amazingly heavy as one nears the immediate area of the show, finding a parking place can be difficult, and other delays may occur. You'll be in better humor to enjoy the day if your trip to the show is not fraught with panic over fear of not arriving in time!

ENJOYING THE DOG SHOW

From the moment of your arrival at the show until after your dog has been judged, keep foremost in your mind the fact that he is your reason for being there and that he should therefore be the center of your attention. Arrive early enough to have time for those last-minute touches that can make a great difference when he enters the ring. Be sure that he has ample time to exercise and that he attends to personal matters. A dog arriving in the ring and immediately using it as an exercise pen hardly makes a favorable impression on the judge.

When you reach ringside, ask the steward for your arm-card and anchor it firmly into place on your arm. Make sure that you are where you should be when your class is called. The fact that you have picked up your arm-card does not guarantee, as some seem to think, that the judge will wait for you. The judge has a full schedule which he wishes to complete on time. Even though you may be nervous, assume an air of calm self-confidence. Remember that this is a hobby to be enjoyed, so approach it in that state of mind. The dog will do better, too, as he will be quick to reflect your attitude.

Always show your dog with an air of pride. If you make mistakes in presenting him, don't worry about it. Next time you will do better. Do not permit the presence of more experienced exhibitors to intimidate you. After all, they, too, were once newcomers.

The judging routine usually starts when the judge asks that the dogs be gaited in a circle around the ring. During this period the judge is watching each dog as it moves, noting style, topline, reach and drive, head and tail carriage, and general balance. Keep your mind and your eye on your dog, moving him at his most becoming gait and keeping your place in line without coming too close to the exhibitor ahead of you. Always keep your dog on the inside of the circle, between yourself and the judge, so that the judge's view of the dog is unobstructed.

Calmly pose the dog when requested to set up for examination. If you are at the head of the line and many dogs are in the class, go all the way to the end of the ring before starting to stack the dog, leaving sufficient space for those behind you to line theirs up as well, as requested by the judge. If you are not at the head of the line but between other exhibitors, leave sufficient space ahead of your dog for the judge to examine him. The dogs should be spaced so that the judge is able to move among them to see them from all angles. In practicing to "set up" or "stack" your dog for the judge's examination, bear in mind the importance of doing so quickly and with dexterity. The judge has a schedule to meet and only a few moments in which to evaluate each dog. You will immeasurably help yours to make a favorable impression if you are able to "get it all together" in a minimum amount of time. Practice at home before a mirror can be a great help toward bringing this about, facing the dog so that you see him from the same side that the judge will and working to make him look right in the shortest length of time.

Listen carefully as the judge describes the manner in which the dog is to be gaited, whether it is straight down and straight back; down the ring, across, and back; or in a triangle. The latter has become the most popular pattern with the majority of judges. "In a triangle" means the dog should move down the outer side of the ring to the first corner, across that end of the ring to the second corner, and then back to the judge from the second corner, using the center of the ring in a diagonal line. Please learn to do this pattern without breaking at each corner to twirl the dog around you, a senseless maneuver that has been noticed on occasion. Judges like to see the dog in an uninterrupted triangle, as they are thus able to get a better idea of the dog's gait.

It is impossible to overemphasize that the gait at which you move your dog is tremendously important and considerable study and thought should be given to the matter. At home, have someone move the dog for you at different speeds so that you can tell which shows him off to best advantage. The most becoming action almost invariably is seen at a moderate gait, head up and topline holding. Do not gallop your dog around the ring or hurry him into a speed atypical of his breed. Nothing being rushed appears at its best; give your dog a chance to move along at his (and the breed's) natural gait. For a dog's action to be judged accurately, that dog should move with strength and power, but not excessive speed, holding a straight line as he goes to and from the judge.

As you bring the dog back to the judge, stop him a few feet away and be sure that he is standing in a becoming position. Bait him to show the judge an alert expression, using whatever tasty morsel he has been trained to expect for this purpose or, if that works better for you, use a small squeak-toy in your hand. A reminder, please, to those using liver or treats: take them with you when you leave the ring. Do not just drop them on the ground where they will be found by another dog.

When the awards have been made, accept yours graciously, no matter how you actually may feel about it. What's done is done, and arguing with a judge or stomping out of the ring is useless and a reflection on your sportsmanship. Be courteous, congratulate the winner if your dog was defeated, and try not to show your disappointment. By the same token, please be a gracious winner; this, surprisingly, sometimes seems to be still more difficult.

Looking good in motion! Ch. Ja-Ma's Flor-Es-Cent owned by Janet and Marvin Whitman, Ja Ma Lhasa Apsos, Spring Valley, New York.

Mohican X-Tra Tempting, C.D., by Ch. Jawin's Shadow Image ex Ch. Mohican's Pony Express, was bred by Thelma G. Hartmann and Sandra Pond. Owned, trained and handled by Marilyn B. Kain, this is the youngest Lhasa, at one year and one day age, known to have attained a C.D. degree, which she did in three consecutive shows scoring 191½, 190 and 185.

Chapter 10

Your Lhasa and Obedience

For its own protection and safety, every dog should be taught, at the very least, to recognize and obey the commands "Come," "Heel," "Down," "Sit," and "Stay." Doing so at some time might save the dog's life and in less extreme circumstances will certainly make him a better behaved, more pleasant member of society. If you are patient and enjoy working with your dog, study some of the excellent books available on the subject of obedience and then teach your canine friend these basic manners. If you need the stimulus of working with a group, find out where obedience training classes are held (usually your veterinarian, your dog's breeder, or a dog-owning friend can tell you) and you and your dog can join. Alternatively, you could let someone else do the training by sending the dog to class, but this is not very rewarding because you lose the opportunity of working with your dog and the pleasure of the rapport thus established.

If you are going to do it yourself, there are some basic rules which you should follow. You must remain calm and confident in ʌttitude. Never lose your temper and frighten or punish your dog unjustly. Be quick and lavish with praise each time a command is correctly followed. Make it fun for the dog and he will be eager to please you by responding correctly. Repetition is the keynote, but it should not be continued without recess to the point of tedium. Limit the training sessions to ten- or fifteen-minute periods at a time.

Formal obedience training can be followed, and very frequently is, by entering the dog in obedience competition to work toward an obedience degree, or several of them, depending on the dog's aptitude and your own enjoyment. Obedience trials are held in conjunction with the majority of all-breed conformation dog shows, with Specialty shows, and frequently as separate Specialty events. If you are working alone with your dog, a list of trial dates might be obtained from your dog's veterinarian, your dog breeder, or a dog-owning friend; the AKC *Gazette* lists shows and trials to be scheduled in the coming months; and if you are a member of a training class, you will find the information readily available.

The goals for which one works in the formal AKC Member or Licensed Trials are the following titles: Companion Dog (C.D.), Companion Dog Excellent (C.D.X.), and Utility Dog (U.D.). These degrees are earned by receiving three "legs," or qualifying scores, at each level of competition. The degrees must be earned in order, with one completed prior to starting work on the next. For example, a dog must have earned C.D. prior to starting work on C.D.X.; then C.D.X. must be completed before U.D. work begins. The ultimate title attainable in obedience work is Obedience Trial Champion (O.T.Ch.)

When you see the letters C.D. following a dog's name, you will know that this dog has satisfactorily completed the following exercises: heel on leash and figure eight, heel free, stand for examination, recall, long sit, and long down. C.D.X. means that tests have been passed on all of those just mentioned plus heel free and figure eight, drop on recall, retrieve on flat, retrieve over high jump, broad jump, long sit, and long down. U.D. indicates that the dog has additionally passed tests in scent discrimination (leather article), scent discrimination (metal article), signal exercise, directed retrieve, directed jumping, and group stand for examination. The letters O.T.Ch. are the abbreviation for the only obedience title which precedes rather than follows a dog's name. To gain an obedience trial championship, a dog who already holds a Utility Dog degree must win a total of one hundred points and must win three firsts, under three different judges, in Utility and Open B Classes.

250

Tiger Ming, C.D.X., was High in Trial at the first American Lhasa Apso Club Obedience Trial, in conjunction with the National Specialty in 1983. Tiger was bred, trained, and is handled by Brenda Schmelzel, Bala Lhasa Apsos, Belleville, Illnois. Note the beautiful form of Tiger as he clears the jump.

There is also a Tracking Dog title (T.D.) which can be earned at tracking trials. In order to pass the tracking tests the dog must follow the trail of a stranger along a path on which the trail was laid between thirty minutes and two hours previously. Along this track there must be more than two right-angle turns, at least two of which are well out in the open where no fences or other boundaries exist for the guidance of the dog or the handler. The dog wears a harness and is connected to the handler by a lead twenty to forty feet in length. Inconspicuously dropped at the end of the track is an article to be retrieved, usually a glove or wallet, which the dog is expected to locate and the handler to pick up. The letters T.D.X. are the abbreviation for Tracking Dog Excellent, a more difficult version of the Tracking Dog test with a longer track and more turns to be worked through.

Honey Ming, C.D. bred, owned, trained and handled by Brenda Schmelzel Bala Lhasa Apsos, Belleville, Illnois. Another case of brains combined with beauty. Honey Ming and Tiger Ming C.D.X. are littermates.

TOP LHASA OBEDIENCE DOGS

The American Lhasa Apso Club National Specialty in 1983 held the first Obedience Trial in conjunction with its conformation show. We were pleased to receive a letter from Brenda Schmelzel of Belleville, Illinois, ALAC's Obedience Chairman, whose dog, Tiger Ming, C.D.X, won the High in Trial award.

Tiger received High in Trial from the Open A Class, his first time out in open. (He received his C.D. at 13 and one half months of age.)

Brenda also owns Honey Ming, C.D., who is Tiger's littermate. Both were trained and are handled by their owner.

At the 1985 American Lhasa Apso Club Awards Banquet, awards for Obedience were presented to Clyde's Black Berry, C.D., owned by Genevieve Moore; Kim-Ber's Tell a Friend, C.D., owned by Linette Edwards; Sir Prize Tu Suntory and Mee Tu, C.D., owned by June O'Brien; Tiger Ming III, C.D.X., owned by Brenda Schmelzel; Watcher Under Free Flyte Objex,

C.D.X., owned by Janine Grinta; and Champion San Jo Shenanigan, C.D., owned by Marianne Nixon and Leslie Engen.

A Register of Merit (ROM) Award was presented to Brenda Schmelzel, Bala Lhasa Apsos, as a breeder of outstanding Obedience Lhasas.

High Scoring Dog in Trial at the August 1985 National Specialty was Halcyon's Golden Kismet, U.D., with a score of 197. Kismet belongs to Betty Wathne. Halcyon completed his Utility Dog degree in 1985 with total scores exceeding 2,300 points. Also, he has several High in Trials to his credit.

Kublai Khan of St. James, C.D., and Green Ponds Jayhawk, C.D., are also among the top several Obedience Lhasas.

The American Lhasa Apso Club makes every effort to encourage fanciers to train and work their dogs in the obedience classes. For club members obtaining an Obedience degree, an award plaque is offered. A Registration of Merit is available to any club member who has trained one or more Lhasa Apsos for a minimum total of three Obedience degrees.

Since 1980, the following are among the Lhasas who have distinguished themselves with Obedience degrees.

For C.D.X. (in addition to Tiger Ming III and Watcher Under Free Flyte Objex), have been Copeland's Geraldine Jones, C.D.X., who completed title in 1981 for owner Yvonne Copeland, and Sunshine Rusty Boy, C.D.X., who, as did Tiger Ming and Watcher, gained the final leg in 1984.

Honey Ming and Chu Chu Smokey Bear, C.D., attained the C.D. degree in 1981 for keen enthusiasts Frank and Barb Trujillo. Honey Ming's sister, Honey Ming II, C.D., also earned her degree.

1984 was an especially big year for Obedience degrees, as in addition to the three who became C.D.X., there were also Sera Mar's Mi-Tu, C.D., Honey Bun's Abso Seng Kye, C.D., Nik-Ki's Singtuk, C.D., all owned by Florence Kantor; Little Dream's Tinkerbell, C.D., owned by Jane H. Kirby; Phoo's Tigger, C.D., owned by Steve Winchester; and Tawni Taps, C.D., owned by Ramona Hadenfeld.

For those who may assume that a dog as elegant as a Lhasa Apso cannot work well, these awards are proof that they *can* and *do,* if given the opportunity.

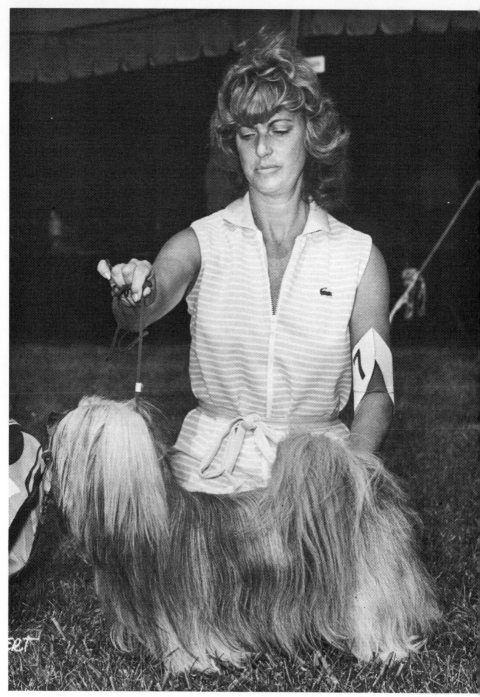

Ch. Karma San Po winning Best of Breed at Talbot K.C. in 1971. Owner-handled by Keke Blumberg, Potala Kennels, Huntington Valley, Pennsylvania.

Chapter 11

Breeding Your Lhasa Apso

The first responsibility of any person breeding dogs is to do so with care, forethought, and deliberation. It is inexcusable to breed more litters than you need to carry on your show program or to perpetuate your bloodlines. A responsible breeder should not cause a litter to be born without definite plans for the safe and happy disposition of the puppies.

A responsible dog breeder makes absolutely certain, so far as is humanly possible, that the home to which one of his puppies will go is a good home, one that offers proper care and an enthusiastic owner. To be admired are those breeders who insist on visiting (although doing so is not always feasible) the prospective owners of their puppies to see if they have suitable facilities for keeping a dog, to find out if they understand the responsibility involved, and to make certain if all members of the household are in accord regarding the desirability of owning one. All breeders should carefully check out the credentials of prospective purchasers to be sure that the puppy is being placed in responsible hands.

No breeder ever wants a puppy or grown dog he has raised to wind up in an animal shelter, in an experimental laboratory, or as a victim of a speeding car. While complete control of such a situation may be impossible, it is important to make every effort to turn over dogs to responsible people. When selling a puppy, it is a good idea to do so with the understanding that should it become necessary to place the dog in other hands, the purchaser will first contact you, the breeder. You may want to help in some way, possibly by buying or taking back the dog or placing it elsewhere. It is not fair to sell puppies and then never again give a thought to their welfare. Family problems arise, people may be forced to move where dogs are prohibited, or people just grow bored with a dog and its care. Thus the dog becomes a victim. You, as the dog's breeder, should concern yourself with the welfare of each of your dogs and see to it that the dog remains in good hands.

The final obligation every dog owner shares, be there just one dog or an entire kennel involved, is that of making detailed, explicit plans for the future of these dearly loved animals in the event of the owner's death. Far too many people are apt to procrastinate and leave this very important matter unattended to, feeling that everything will work out or that "someone will see to them." Neither is too likely, at least not to the benefit of the dogs, unless you have done some advance planning which will assure their future well-being.

Life is filled with the unexpected, and even the youngest, healthiest, most robust of us may be the victim of a fatal accident or sudden illness. The fate of your dogs, so entirely in your hands, should never be left to chance. If you have not already done so, please get together with your lawyer and set up a clause in your will specifying what you want done with each of your dogs, to whom they will be entrusted (after first making absolutely certain that the person selected is willing and able to assume the responsibility), and telling the locations of all registration papers, pedigrees, and kennel records. Just think of the possibilities which might happen otherwise! If there is another family member who shares your love of the dogs, that is good and you have less to worry about. But if your heirs are not dog-oriented, they will hardly know how to proceed or how to cope with the dogs themselves, and they may wind up disposing of or caring for your dogs in a manner that would break your heart were you around to know about it.

It is advisable to have in your will specific instructions concerning each of your dogs. A friend, also a dog person who regards his or her own dogs with the same concern and esteem as you do, may agree to take over their care until they can be placed accordingly and will make certain that all will work out as you have planned. This person's name and phone number can be prominently displayed in your van or car and in your wallet. Your lawyer can be made aware of this fact. This can be spelled out in your will. The friend can have a signed check of yours to be used in case of an emergency or accident when you are traveling with the dogs; this check can be used to cover his or her expense to come and take over the care of your dogs should anything happen to make it impossible for you to do so. This is the least any dog owner should do in preparation for the time their dogs suddenly find themselves alone. There have been so many sad cases of dogs unprovided for by their loving owners, left to heirs who couldn't care less and who disposed of them in any way at all to get rid of them, or left to heirs who kept and neglected them under the misguided idea that they were providing them "a fine home with lots of freedom." These misfortunes must be prevented from befalling your own dogs who have meant so much you!

Conscientious breeders feel quite strongly that the only possible reason for producing puppies is the ambition to improve and uphold quality and temperament within the breed—definitely *not* because one hopes to make a quick cash profit on a mediocre litter, which never seems to work out that way in the long run and which accomplishes little beyond perhaps adding to the nation's heartbreaking number of unwanted canines. The only reason ever for breeding a litter is, with conscientious people, a desire to improve the quality of dogs in their own kennel or, as pet owners, to add to the number of dogs they themselves own with a puppy or two from their present favorites. In either case, breeding should not take place unless one definitely has prospective owners for as many puppies as the litter may contain, lest you find yourself with several fast-growing young dogs and no homes in which to place them.

THE BROOD BITCH

Bitches should not be mated earlier than their second season, by which time they should be from fifteen to eighteen months old. Many breeders prefer to wait and finish the championships of their show bitches before breeding them, as pregnancy can be a disaster to a show coat and getting the bitch back in shape again takes time. When you have decided what will be the proper time, start watching at least several months ahead for what you feel would be the perfect mate to best complement your bitch's quality and bloodlines. Subscribe to the magazines which feature your breed exclusively and to some which cover all breeds in order to familiarize yourself with outstanding stud dogs in areas other than your own, for there is no necessity nowadays to limit your choice to a local dog unless you truly like him and feel that he is the most suitable. It is quite usual to ship a bitch to a stud dog a distance away, and this generally works out with no ill effects. The important thing is that you need a stud dog strong in those features where your bitch is weak, a dog whose bloodlines are compatible with hers. Compare the background of both your bitch and the stud dog under consideration, paying particular attention to the quality of the puppies from bitches with backgrounds similar to your bitch's. If the puppies have been of the type and quality you admire, then this dog would seem a sensible choice for yours, too.

Stud fees may be a few hundred dollars, sometimes even more under special situations for a particularly successful sire. It is money well spent, however. *Do not* ever breed to a dog because he is less expensive than the others unless you honestly believe that he can sire the kind of puppies who will be a credit to your kennel and your breed.

Contacting the owners of the stud dogs you find interesting will bring you pedigrees and pictures which you can then study in relation to your bitch's pedigree and conformation. Discuss your plans with other breeders who are knowledgeable (including the one who bred your own bitch). You may not always receive an entirely unbiased opinion (particularly if the person giving it also has an available stud dog), but one learns by discussion so listen to what they say, consider their opinions, and then you may be better qualified to form your own opinion.

As soon as you have made a choice, phone the owner of the stud dog you wish to use to find out if this will be agreeable. You will be asked about the bitch's health, soundness, temperament, and freedom from serious faults. A copy of her pedigree may be requested, as might a picture of her. A discussion of her background over the telephone may be sufficient to assure the stud's owner that she is suitable for the stud dog and that she is of type, breeding, and quality herself, capable of producing the kind of puppies for which the stud is noted. The owner of a top-quality stud is often extremely selective in the bitches permitted to be bred to his dog, in an effort to keep the standard of his puppies high. The owner of a stud dog may require that the bitch be tested for brucellosis, which should be attended to not more than a month previous to the breeding.

Check out which airport will be most convenient for the person meeting and returning the bitch, if she is to be shipped, and also what airlines use that airport. You will find that the airlines are also apt to have special requirements concerning acceptance of animals for shipping. These include weather limitations and types of crates which are acceptable. The weather limits have to do with extreme heat and extreme cold at the point of destination, as some airlines will not fly dogs into temperatures above or below certain levels, fearing for their safety. The crate problem is a simple one, since, if your own crate is not suitable, most of the airlines have specially designed crates available for purchase at a fair and moderate price. It is a good plan to purchase one of these if you intend to be shipping dogs with any sort of frequency. They are made of fiberglass and are the safest type to use for shipping.

Normally you must notify the airline several days in advance to make a reservation, as they are able to accommodate only a certain number of dogs on each flight. Plan on shipping the bitch on about her eighth or ninth day of season, but be careful to avoid shipping her on a weekend when schedules often vary and freight offices are apt to be closed. Whenever you can, ship your bitch on a direct flight. Changing planes always carries a certain amount of risk of a dog being overlooked or wrongly routed at the middle stop, so avoid this danger if at all possible. The bitch must be accompanied by a health certificate which you must obtain from your veterinarian before taking her to the airport. Usually it will be necessary to have the bitch at the airport about two hours prior to flight time. Before finalizing arrangements, find out from the stud's owner at what time of day it will be most convenient to have the bitch picked up promptly upon arrival.

It is simpler if you can bring the bitch to the stud dog yourself. Some people feel that the trauma of the flight may cause the bitch to not conceive; and, of course, undeniably there is a slight risk in shipping which can be avoided if you are able to drive the bitch to her destination. Be sure to leave yourself sufficient time to assure your arrival at the right time for her for breeding (normally the tenth to fourteenth day following the first signs of color); and remember that if you want the bitch bred twice, you should allow a day to elapse between the two matings. Do not expect the stud's owner to house you while you are there. Locate a nearby motel that takes dogs and make that your headquarters.

Just prior to the time your bitch is due in season, you should take her to visit your veterinarian. She should be checked for worms and should receive all the booster shots for which she is due plus one for parvovirus, unless she has had the latter shot fairly recently. The brucellosis test can also be done then, and the health certificate can be obtained for shipping if she is to travel by air. Should the bitch be at all overweight, now is the time to get the surplus off. She should be in good condition, neither underweight nor overweight, at the time of breeding.

The moment you notice the swelling of the vulva, for which you should be checking daily as the time for her season approaches, and the appearance of color, immediately contact the stud's owner and settle on the day for shipping or make the appointment for your arrival with the bitch for breeding. If you are shipping the bitch, the stud fee check should be mailed immediately, leaving ample time for it to have been received when the bitch arrives and the mating takes place. Be sure to call the airline, making her reservation at that time, too.

Do not feed the bitch within a few hours before shipping her. Be certain that she has had a drink of water and been well exercised before closing her in the crate. Several layers of newspapers, topped with some shredded newspaper, make a good bed and can be discarded when she arrives at her destination; these can be replaced with fresh newspapers for her return home. Remember that the bitch should be brought to the airport about two hours before flight time, as sometimes the airlines refuse to accept late arrivals.

If you are taking your bitch by car, be certain that you will arrive at a reasonable time of day. Do not appear late in the evening. If your arrival in town is not until late, get a good night's sleep at your motel and contact the stud's owner first thing in the morning. If possible, leave children and relatives at home, as they will only be in the way and perhaps unwelcome by the stud's owner. Most stud dog owners prefer not to have any unnecessary people on hand during the actual mating.

After the breeding has taken place, if you wish to sit and visit for awhile and the stud's owner has the time, return the bitch to her crate in your car (first ascertaining, of course, that the temperature is comfortable for her and that there is proper ventilation). She should not be permitted to urinate for at least one hour following the breeding. This is the time when you attend to the business part of the transaction. Pay the stud fee, upon which you should receive your breeding certificate and, if you do not already have it, a copy of the stud dog's pedigree. The owner of the stud dog does not sign or furnish a litter registration application until the puppies have been born.

Upon your return home, you can settle down and plan in happy anticipation a wonderful litter of puppies. A word of caution! Remember that although she has been bred, your bitch is still an interesting target for all male dogs, so guard her carefully for the next week or until you are absolutely certain that her season has entirely ended. This would be no time to have any unfortunate incident with another dog.

THE STUD DOG

Choosing the best stud dog to complement your bitch is often very difficult. The two principal factors to be considered should be the stud's conformation and his pedigree. Conformation is fairly obvious; you want a dog that is typical of the breed in the words of the Standard of perfection. Understanding pedigrees is a bit more subtle since the pedigree lists the ancestry of the dog and involves individuals and bloodlines with which you may not be entirely familiar.

To a novice in the breed, the correct interpretation of a pedigree may at first be difficult to grasp. Study the pictures and text of this book and you will find many names of important bloodlines and members of the breed. Also make an effort to discuss the various dogs behind the proposed stud with some of the more experienced breeders, starting with the breeder of your own bitch. Frequently these folks will be familiar with many of the dogs in question, will be able to offer opinions of them, and may have access to additional pictures which you would benefit by seeing. It is very important that the stud's pedigree be harmonious with that of the bitch you plan on breeding to him. Do not rush out and breed to the latest winner with no thought of whether or not he can produce true quality. By no means are all great show dogs great producers. It is the producing record of the dog in question, and the dogs and bitches from which he has come, that should be the basis on which you make your choice.

Breeding dogs is never a money-making operation. By the time you pay a stud fee, care for the bitch during pregnancy, whelp the litter, and rear the puppies through their early shots, worming, and so on, you will be fortunate to break even financially once the puppies have been sold. Your chances of doing this are greater if you are breeding for a show-quality litter which will bring you higher prices, as the pups are sold as show prospects. Therefore, your wisest investment is to use the best dog available for your bitch regardless of the cost; then you should wind up with more valuable puppies. Remember that it is equally costly to raise mediocre puppies as it is top ones, and your chances of financial return are better on the latter. Breeding to the most excellent, most suitable stud dog you can find is the only sensible thing to do, and it is poor economy to quibble over the amount you are paying in a stud fee.

It will be your decision as to which course you follow when you breed your bitch, as there are three options: linebreeding, inbreeding, and outcrossing. Each of these methods has its supporters and its detractors! Linebreeding is breeding a bitch to a dog belonging originally to the same canine family, being descended from the same ancestors, such as half brother to half sister, grandsire to granddaughter, niece to uncle (and vice-versa) or cousin to cousin. Inbreeding is breeding father to daughter, mother to son, or full brother to sister. Outcross breeding is breeding a dog and a bitch with no or only a few mutual ancestors.

Linebreeding is probably the safest course, and the one most likely to bring results, for the novice breeder. The more sophisticated inbreeding should be left to the experienced, longtime breeders who throroughly know and understand the risks and the possibilities involved with a particular line. It is usually done in an effort to intensify some ideal feature in that strain. Outcrossing is the reverse of inbreeding, an effort to introduce improvement in a specific feature needing correction, such as a shorter back, better movement, more correct head or coat, and so on.

It is the serious breeder's ambition to develop a strain or bloodline of their own, one strong in qualities for which their dogs will become distinguished. However, it must be realized that this will involve time, patience, and at least several generations before the achievement can be claimed. The safest way to embark on this plan, as previously mentioned, is by the selection and breeding of one or two bitches, the best you can buy and from top-producing kennels. In the beginning you do *not* really have to own a stud dog. In the long run it is less expensive and sounder judgement to pay a stud fee when you are ready to breed a bitch than to purchase a stud dog and feed him all year; a stud dog does not win any popularity contests with owners of bitches to be bred until he becomes a champion, has been successfully Specialed for a while, and has been at least moderately advertised, all of which adds up to quite a healthy expenditure.

The wisest course for the inexperienced breeder just starting out in dogs is to keep the best bitch puppy from the first several litters. After that you may wish to consider keeping your own stud dog, if there has been a particularly handsome male in one of your litters that you feel has great potential or if you know where there is one available that you are interested in, with the feeling that he would work in nicely with the breeding program on which you have embarked. By this time, with several litters already born, your eye should have developed to a point enabling you to make a wise choice, either from one of your own litters or from among dogs you have seen that appear suitable.

The greatest care should be taken in the selection of your own stud dog. He must be of true type and highest quality as he may be responsible for siring many puppies each year, and he should come from a line of excellent dogs on both sides of his pedigree which themselves are, and which are descended from, successful producers. This dog should have no glaring faults in conformation; he should be of such quality that he can hold his own in keenest competition within his breed. He should be in good health, be virile and be a keen stud dog, a proven sire able to transmit his correct qualities to his puppies. Need one say that such a dog will be enormously expensive unless you have the good fortune to produce him in one of your own litters? To buy and use a lesser stud dog, however, is downgrading your breeding program unnecessarily since there are so many dogs fitting the description of a fine stud whose services can be used on payment of a stud fee.

You should *never* breed to an unsound dog or one with any serious disqualifying faults according to the breed's standard. Not all champions by any means pass along their best features; and by the same token, occasionally you will find a great one who can pass along his best features but never gained his championship title due to some unusual circumstances. The information you need about a stud dog is what type of puppies he has produced, and with what bloodlines, and whether or not he possesses the bloodlines and attributes considered characteristic of the best in your breed.

If you go out to buy a stud dog, obviously he will not be a puppy, but rather a fully mature and proven male with as many of the best attributes as possible. True, he will be an expensive investment, but if you choose and make his selection with care and forethought, he may well prove to be one of the best investments you have ever made.

Of course, the most exciting of all is when a young male you have decided to keep from one of your litters, due to his tremen-

Am., Ger., Int'l. Ch. Anbara Justa Teddy Bear, by Ch. San Jo Raaga Looki Mei, ROM, ex Ch. Anbara's Abra-Ka-Dabra, ROM, was bred and owned and handled by Barbara Wood to finish with two Specialty wins. The sire of Best in Show Ch. Anbara-Rimar's Grin 'N Bear It.

Multiple Group winning Ch. Gyal Kham-Nag of San Jo, ROM, an inbred son of the first registered Lhasa and foundation stud for San Jo. Marianne Nixon, owner, San Jo Kennels, Bellevue, Washington.

dous show potential, turns out to be a stud dog such as we have described. In this case he should be managed with care, for he is a valuable property that can contribute inestimably to this breed as a whole and to your own kennel specifically.

Do not permit your stud dog to be used until he is about a year old, and even then he should be bred to a mature, proven matron accustomed to breeding who will make his first experience pleasant and easy. A young dog can be put off forever by a maiden bitch who fights and resists his advances. Never allow this to happen. Always start a stud dog out with a bitch who is mature, has been bred previously, and is of even temperament. The first breeding should be performed in quiet surroundings with only you and one other person to hold the bitch. Do not make it a circus, as the experience will determine the dog's outlook about future stud work. If he does not enjoy the first experience or associates it with any unpleasantness, you may well have a problem in the future.

Your young stud must permit help with the breeding, as later there will be bitches who will not be cooperative. If right from the beginning you are there helping him and praising him, whether or not your assistance is actually needed, he will expect and accept this as a matter of course when a difficult bitch comes along.

Things to have handy before introducing your dog and the bitch are K-Y jelly (the only lubricant which should be used) and a length of gauze with which to muzzle the bitch should it be necessary to keep her from biting you or the dog. Some bitches put up a fight; others are calm. It is best to be prepared.

At the time of the breeding, the stud fee comes due, and it is expected that it will be paid promptly. Normally a return service is offered in case the bitch misses or fails to produce one live puppy. Conditions of the service are what the stud dog's owner makes them, and there are no standard rules covering this. The stud fee is paid for the act, not the result. If the bitch fails to conceive, it is customary for the owner to offer a free return service; but this is a courtesy and not to be considered a right, particularly in the case of a proven stud who is siring consistently and whose fault the failure obviously is *not*. Stud dog owners are always anxious to see their clients get good value and to have, in the ring, winning young stock by their dog; therefore, very few refuse to mate the second time. It is wise, however, for both parties to have the terms of the transaction clearly understood at the time of the breeding.

If the return service has been provided and the bitch has missed a second time, that is considered to be the end of the matter and the owner would be expected to pay a further fee if it is felt that the bitch should be given a third chance with the stud dog. The management of a stud dog and his visiting bitches is quite a task, and a stud fee has usually been well earned when one service has been achieved, let alone by repeated visits from the same bitch.

The accepted litter is one live puppy. It is wise to have printed a breeding certificate which the owner of the stud dog and the owner of the bitch both sign. This should list in detail the conditions of the breeding as well as the dates of the mating.

Upon occasion, arrangements other than a stud fee in cash are made for a breeding, such as the owner of the stud taking a pick-of-the-litter puppy in lieu of money. This should be clearly specified on the breeding certificate along with the terms of the age at which the stud's owner will select the puppy, whether it is to be a specific sex, or whether it is to be the pick of the entire litter.

The price of a stud fee varies according to circumstances. Usually, to prove a young stud dog, his owner will allow the first breeding to be quite inexpensive. Then, once a bitch has become pregnant by him, he becomes a "proven stud" and the fee rises accordingly for bitches that follow. The sire of championship quality puppies will bring a stud fee of at least the purchase price of one show puppy as the accepted "rule-of-thumb." Until at least one champion by your stud dog has finished, the fee will remain equal to the price of one pet puppy. When his list of champions starts to grow, so does the amount of the stud fee. For a top-producing sire of champions, the stud fee will rise accordingly.

Almost invariably it is the bitch who comes to the stud dog for the breeding. Immediately upon having selected the stud dog you wish to use, discuss the possibility with the owner of that dog. It is the stud dog owner's prerogative to refuse to breed any bitch deemed unsuitable for this dog. Stud fee and method of payment should be stated at this time and a decision reached on whether it is to be a full cash transaction at the time of the mating or a pick-of-the-litter puppy, usually at eight weeks of age.

If the owner of the stud dog must travel to an airport to meet the bitch and ship her for the flight home, an additional charge will be made for time, tolls, and gasoline based on the stud owner's proximity to the airport. The stud fee includes board for the day on the bitch's arrival through two days for breeding, with a day in between. If it is necessary that the bitch remain longer, it is very likely that additional board will be charged at the normal per-day rate for the breed.

Be sure to advise the stud's owner as soon as you know that your bitch is in season so that the stud dog will be available. This is especially important because if he is a dog being shown, he and his owner may be unavailable, owing to the dog's absence from home.

As the owner of a stud dog being offered to the public, it is essential that you have proper facilities for the care of visiting bitches. Nothing can be worse than a bitch being insecurely housed and slipping out to become lost or bred by the wrong dog.

If you are taking people's valued bitches into your kennel or home, it is imperative that you provide them with comfortable, secure housing and good care while they are your responsibility.

There is no dog more valuable than the proven sire of champions, Group winners, and Best in Show dogs. Once you have such an animal, guard his reputation well and do *not* permit him to be bred to just any bitch that comes along. It takes two to make the puppies; even the most dominant stud cannot do it all himself, so never permit him to breed a bitch you consider unworthy. Remember that when the puppies arrive, it will be your stud dog who will be blamed for any lack of quality, while the bitch's shortcomings will be quickly and conveniently overlooked.

Going into the actual management of the mating is a bit superfluous here. If you have had previous experience in breeding a dog and bitch, you will know how the mating is done. If you do not have such experience, you should not attempt to follow directions given in a book but should have a veterinarian, breeder friend, or handler there to help you with the first few times. You do not turn the dog and bitch loose together and await developments, as too many things can go wrong and you may altogether miss getting the bitch bred. Someone should hold the dog and the bitch (one person each) until the "tie" is made and these two people should stay with them during the entire act.

If you get a complete tie, probably only the one mating is absolutely necessary. However, especially with a maiden bitch or one that has come a long distance for this breeding, a follow-up with a second breeding is preferred, leaving one day in between the two matings. In this way there will be little or no chance of the bitch missing.

Once the tie has been completed and the dogs release, be certain that the male's penis goes completely back within its sheath. He should be allowed a drink of water and a short walk, and then he should be put into his crate or somewhere alone where he can settle down. Do not allow him to be with other dogs for a while as they will notice the odor of the bitch on him, and, particularly with other males present, he may become involved in a fight.

PREGNANCY, WHELPING, AND THE LITTER

Once the bitch has been bred and is back at home, remember

to keep an ever watchful eye that no other males get to her until at least the twenty-second day of her season has passed. Until then, it will still be possible for an unwanted breeding to take place, which at this point would be catastrophic. Remember that she actually can have two separate litters by two different dogs, so take care.

In other ways, she should be treated normally. Controlled exercise is good and necessary for the bitch throughout her pregnancy, tapering it off to just several short walks daily, preferably on lead, as she reaches her seventh week. As her time grows close, be careful about her jumping or playing too roughly.

The theory that a bitch should be overstuffed with food when pregnant is a poor one. A fat bitch is never an easy whelper, so the overfeeding you consider good for her may well turn out to be a hindrance later on. During the first few weeks of pregnancy, your bitch should be fed her normal diet. At four to five weeks along, calcium should be added to her food. At seven weeks her food may be increased if she seems to crave more than she is getting, and a meal of canned milk (mixed with an equal amount of water) should be introduced. If she is fed just once a day, add another meal rather than overload her with too much at one time. If twice a day is her schedule, then a bit more food can be added to each feeding.

A week before the pups are due, your bitch should be introduced to her whelping box so that she will be accustomed to it and feel at home there when the puppies arrive. She should be encouraged to sleep there but permitted to come and go as she wishes. The box should be roomy enough for her to lie down and stretch out in but not too large, lest the pups have more room than is needed in which to roam and possibly get chilled by going too far away from their mother. Be sure that the box has a "pig rail"; this will prevent the puppies from being crushed against the sides. The room in which the box is placed, either in your home or in the kennel, should be kept at about 70 degrees Fahrenheit. In winter it may be necessary to have an infrared lamp over the whelping box, in which case be careful not to place it too low or close to the puppies.

Newspapers will become a very important commodity, so start collecting them well in advance to have a big pile handy for the whelping box. With a litter of puppies, one never seems to have papers enough, so the higher pile to start with, the better off you will be. Other necessities for whelping time are clean, soft turkish towels, scissors, and a bottle of alcohol.

You will know that her time is very near when your bitch becomes restless, wandering in and out of her box and out of the room. She may refuse food, and at that point her temperature will start to drop. She will dig at and tear up the newspapers in her box, shiver, and generally look uncomfortable. Only you should be with your bitch at this time. She does not need spectators; and several people hanging over her, even though they may be family members whom she knows, may upset her to the point where she may harm the puppies. You should remain nearby, quietly watching, not fussing or hovering; speak calmly and frequently to her to instill confidence. Eventually she will settle down in her box and begin panting; contractions will follow. Soon thereafter a puppy will start to emerge, sliding out with the contractions. The mother immediately should open the sac, sever the cord with her teeth, and then clean up the puppy. She will also eat the placenta, which you should permit. Once the puppy is cleaned, it should be placed next to the bitch unless she is showing signs of having the next one immediately. Almost at once the puppy will start looking for a nipple on which to nurse, and you should ascertain that it is able to latch on successfully.

If the puppy is a breech (i.e., born feet first), you must watch carefully for it to be completely delivered as quickly as possible and for the sac to be removed quickly so that the puppy does not drown. Sometimes even a normally positioned birth will seem extremely slow in coming. Should this occur, you might take a clean towel, and as the bitch contracts, pull the puppy out, doing so gently and with utmost care. If, once the puppy is delivered, it shows little signs of life, take a rough turkish towel and massage the puppy's chest by rubbing quite briskly back and forth. Continue this for about fifteen minutes, and be sure that the mouth is free of liquid. It may be necessary to try mouth-to-mouth breathing, which is begun by pressing the puppy's jaws open and, using a finger, depressing the tongue which may be stuck to the roof of the mouth. Then place your mouth against the puppy's and blow hard down the puppy's throat. Rub the puppy's chest with the towel again and try artificial respiration, pressing the sides of the chest together slowly and rhythmically—in and out, in and out.

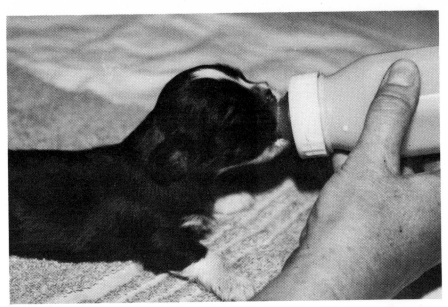

Mohican's All Things Wundfull at 10 days old enjoying a bit of lunch. Thelma Hartmann, owner, Mohican Lhasas, Fairfield, Connecticut.

"Poppi" with Lha Li, Ying Su and Fancy, her three-week-old puppies by Ch. Joyslyn's Piece of the Rock. Ruth M. Hatcher, owner, Roanoke, Virginia.

Keep trying one method or the other for at least twenty minutes before giving up. You may be rewarded with a live puppy who otherwise would not have made it.

If you are successful in bringing the puppy around, do not immediately put it back with the mother as it should be kept extra warm. Put it in a cardboard box on an electric heating pad or, if it is the time of year when your heat is running, near a radiator or near the fireplace or stove. As soon as the rest of the litter has been born, it then can join the others.

An hour or more may elapse between puppies, which is fine so long as the bitch seems comfortable and is neither straining nor contracting. She should not be permitted to remain unassisted for more than an hour if she does continue to contract. This is when you should get her to your veterinarian, whom you should already have alerted to the possibility of a problem existing. He should examine her and perhaps give her a shot of Pituitrin. In some cases the veterinarian may find that a Caesarean section is necessary due to a puppy being lodged in a manner making normal delivery impossible. Sometimes this is caused by an abnormally large puppy, or it may just be that the puppy is simply turned in the wrong position. If the bitch does require a Caesarean section, the puppies already born must be kept warm in their cardboard box with a heating pad under the box.

Once the section is done, get the bitch and the puppies home. Do not attempt to put the puppies in with the bitch until she has regained consciousness, as she may unknowingly hurt them. But do get them back to her as soon as possible for them to start nursing.

Should the mother lack milk at this time, the puppies must be fed by hand, kept very warm, and held onto the mother's teats several times a day in order to stimulate and encourage the secretion of milk, which should start shortly.

Assuming that there has been no problem and that the bitch has whelped naturally, you should insist that she go out to exercise, staying just long enough to make herself comfortable. She can be offered a bowl of milk and a biscuit, but then she should settle down with her family. Freshen the whelping box for her with newspapers while she is taking this respite so that she and the puppies will have a clean bed.

Unless some problem arises, there is little you must do for the puppies until they become three to four weeks old. Keep the box clean and supplied with fresh newspapers the first few days, but then turkish towels should be tacked down to the bottom of the box so that the puppies will have traction as they move about.

If the bitch has difficulties with her milk supply, or if you should be so unfortunate as to lose her, then you must be prepared to either hand-feed or tube-feed the puppies if they are to survive. Tube-feeding is so much faster and easier. If the bitch is available, it is best that she continues to clean and care for the puppies in the normal manner, excepting for the food supplements you will provide. If it is impossible for her to do this, then after every feeding you must gently rub each puppy's abdomen with wet cotton to make it urinate, and the rectum should be gently rubbed to open the bowels.

Newborn puppies must be fed every three to four hours around the clock. The puppies must be kept warm during this time. Have your veterinarian teach you how to tube-feed. You will find that it is really quite simple.

After a normal whelping, the bitch will require additional food to enable her to produce sufficient milk. In addition to being fed twice daily, she should be given some canned milk several times each day.

When the puppies are two weeks old, their nails should be clipped, as they are needle sharp at this age and can hurt or damage the mother's teats and stomach as the pups hold on to nurse.

Between three and four weeks of age, the puppies should begin to be weaned. Scraped beef (prepared by scraping it off slices of beef with a spoon so that none of the gristle is included) may be offered in very small quantities a couple of times daily for the first few days. Then by the third day you can mix puppy chow with warm water as directed on the package, offering it four times daily. By now the mother should be kept away from the puppies and out of the box for several hours at a time so that when they have reached five weeks of age she is left in with them only overnight. By the time the puppies are six weeks old, they should be entirely weaned and receiving only occasional visits from their mother.

Most veterinarians recommend a temporary DHL (distemper, hepatitis, leptospirosis) shot when the puppies are six weeks of age. This remains effective for about two weeks. Then at eight weeks of age, the puppies should receive the series of permanent shots for DHL protection. It is also a good idea to discuss with your vet the advisability of having your puppies inoculated against the dreaded parvovirus at the same time. Each time the pups go to the vet for shots, you should bring stool samples so that they can be examined for worms. Worms go through various stages of development and may be present in a stool sample even though the sample does not test positive in every checkup. So do not neglect to keep careful watch on this.

The puppies should be fed four times daily until they are three months old. Then you can cut back to three feedings daily. By the time the puppies are six months of age, two meals daily are sufficient. Some people feed their dogs twice daily throughout their lifetime; others go to one meal daily when the puppy becomes one year of age.

The ideal age for puppies to go to their new homes is between eight and twelve weeks, although some puppies successfully adjust to a new home when they are six weeks old. Be sure that they go to their new owners accompanied by a description of the diet you've been feeding them and a schedule of the shots they have already received and those they still need. These should be included with the registration application and a copy of the pedigree.

THE REGISTER OF MERIT (ROM)

The Register of Merit was established in 1973 by the American Lhasa Apso Club as a system for honoring dogs and bitches who have contributed outstandingly to the breed. Five champion offspring qualify a dog for this listing; three champion offspring qualify a bitch.

Star Producers

A very interesting system was recently developed by Norman and Carolyn Herbel by which one could rate the producing abilities of Lhasa Apso sires and dams. This information was first published in the breed magazine *Lhasa Tales*. We appreciate the Herbels sending us the rating data and the Star Producers list, which provides names and statistics on some of the most numerically

274

successful dogs and bitches.

In Lhasa pedigrees, one frequently notes one or more asterisks (*) following the name of a dog. These indicate the number of champions produced by that dog or bitch on the following basis:

Sires

One Star Producer (*) indicates 6-16 champion offspring
Two Star Producer (**) indicates 17-27 champion offspring
Three Star Producer (***) indicates 28-38 champion offspring
Four Star Producer (****) indicates 39-49 champion offspring
Five Star Producer (*****) indicates 50-60 champion offspring

Dams

One Star Producer (*) 4-6 champion offspring
Two Star Producer (**) 7-9 champion offspring
Three Star Producer (***) 10-12 champion offspring
Four Star Producer (****) 13-15 champion offspring
Five Star Producer (*****) 16-18 champion offspring

This is a tremendous help to prospective breeders, especially if they are newcomers to the fancy and not always familiar with dogs' and bitches' names when selecting breeding partners who are from proven successful backgrounds. Once again the Herbels have done the Lhasa breed an inestimable service. (It should be noted that some reasons for a Lhasa Apso's not being entitled to have an ROM added to his name may be that the owner is not an ALAC member, or is a member but has not applied for a title, or the owner of the qualified Lhasa was retired or deceased before the ROM System was established in 1973.)

As of January 1, 1986, the Herbels have found the all-time leading sires and dams in the breed to have been as follows:

Ch. Tabu's King of Hearts at age three years. An outstanding Lhasa owned by Stephen G.C. Campbell, Rimar Lhasa Apsos, Elizabeth, New Jersey.

Sires	Champions sired
Ch. Tibet of Cornwallis, ROM★★★★	48
Ch. Everglo Spark of Gold, ROM★★★★	44
Ch. Tabu's King of Hearts, ROM★★★	36
Ch. Cherryshores Bah Bieh Boi, ROM★★★	28
Ch. Wingsong's Gusto of Innsbrook, ROM★★	26
Ch. Chen Korum Ti, ROM★★	24
Ch. Orlane's Dulmo, ROM★★	24
Ch. Orlane's Intrepid★★	24
Ch. San Jo Shenanigan★★	22
Ch. Orlane's Inimitable★★	22
Ch. Everglo Zijuh Tomba★★	22
Ch. Chen Krisna Nor, ROM★★	21
Ch. Chen Nyun Ti, ROM★★	21
Ch. Zijuh Seng Tru, ROM★★	21
Ch. Arborhill's Bhran Dieh, ROM★★	20
Ch. Kham of Norbulingka, ROM★★	20

Dams	Champions produced
Ch. Chiz Ari Sehilot, ROM*****	16
Cordova SinSa, ROM****	13
Ch. Gindy of Norbulingka, ROM***	12
Chok's Joppa Bu Mo, ROM***	11
Ch. Ruffway Tashi***	11
Ch. Kinderland's San Po, ROM**	9
Ch. Kyi Chu Kira, C.D., ROM**	9
Ch. Shyr Lyz Miss Cun Tai Kai Lei, ROM**	9
Ch. Arborhill's Lee Sah, ROM**	8
Ch. Colarlie's Miss Shanda, ROM**	8
Hamilton Chang Tru**	8
Ch. Karma Rus Timala, ROM**	8
Kinderland's Ta Sen Isis, ROM**	8
Ch. Jyi Chu Kara Nor, ROM**	8
Miradel's Ming Fu Chia, C.D.**	8
Zijuh On Ba Zim Zim, ROM**	8

The great Ch. Tibet of Cornwallis winning one of his Bests in Show for Mr. and Mrs. Norman Herbel, Langhorne, Pennsylvania, in 1969. Handled by Jane Forsyth. By Karma Tharpa ex Lico's Cheti-La, Tibet was born in 1966, bred by Paul Williams.

We wish that space permitted us to give you the entire list of Star Producers, but hope that what we have provided explains how it works and how it can benefit your breeding programs. We strongly recommend that breeders, especially the novices, refer to

Ch. Karma Rustimala, ROM, dam of eight champions and a top producer Non-Sporting Bitch of 1970s. By Ch. Karma Mingma, Rustimala was very well known for the quality of her offspring and for their lovely disposition, beautiful heads and expression. One of the important bitches at Magestic Kennels, owned by Lois M. and Pamela Magette.

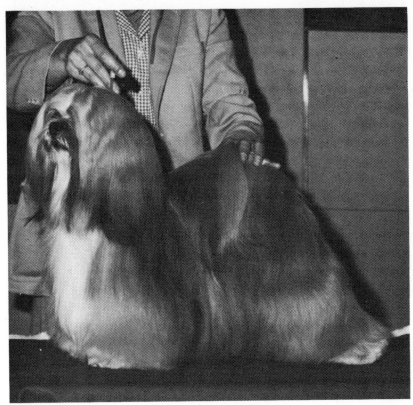

Multiple Best in Show and Best in Specialty Show winner, Ch. San Jo's Shindig, completed title in June 1982 at age 14 months, doing so at CLAF Specialty. Following day at the National, this young dog was Best Puppy in Futurity against his kennel mate San Jo's Kian A Pretty Penny, the Grand Futurity winner. A son of Ch. San Jo Shenanigan ROM ex Group Winning Ch. San Jo's Tabatha. Owner-handled by Leslie Ann Engen, bred and owned by San Jo Kennels, Bellevue, Washington.

these Star Ratings in the pedigrees of their dogs and of dogs to whom they may be considering breeding, to help make a sensible choice from the quality of production point of view. Many gorgeous dogs have never reproduced their own quality at all, which is why it is so important to give particular consideration to the breeding and producing records of dogs with whom you may be working.

Ch. Kimrik's Jeh Sah Cah, foundation bitch at Taglha Kennels, Norfolk, Virginia, owned by Mrs. Wilson J. Browning, Jr. Taking Best of Winners at Westminster in 1969, where Mrs. Browning purchased her under Jane Kay's advice.

Chapter 12

Traveling with Your Lhasa Apso

When you travel with your dog, to shows or on vacation or wherever, remember that everyone does not share your enthusiasm or love for dogs and that those who do not, strange creatures though they seem to us, have their rights too. These rights, on which you should not encroach, include not being disturbed, annoyed, or made uncomfortable by the presence and behavior of other people's pets. Your dog should be kept on lead in public places and should recognize and promptly obey the commands: "Down," "Come," "Sit," and "Stay."

Take along his crate if you are going any distance with your dog, and keep him in it when riding in the car. A crated dog has a far better chance of escaping injury than one riding loose in the car, should an accident occur or an emergency arise. If you do permit your dog to ride loose, never allow him to hang out a window, ears blowing in the breeze. An injury to his eyes could occur in this manner. He could also become overly excited by something he sees and jump out, or he could lose his balance and fall out.

Never, ever, under any circumstances, should a dog be permitted to ride loose in the back of a pick-up truck. Some people do transport dogs in this manner, which is cruel and shocking. How easily such a dog can be thrown out of the truck by sudden jolts or an impact! Doubtless many dogs have jumped out at the sight of something exciting along the way. Some unthinking individuals tie the dog, probably not realizing that were he to jump under those circumstances, his neck would be broken, he could be dragged alongside the vehicle, or he could be hit by another vehicle. If for any reason you are taking your dog in an open-back truck, please have sufficient regard for that dog to at least provide a crate for him; and then remember that, in or out of a crate, a dog riding under the direct rays of the sun in hot weather can suffer and have his life endangered by the heat.

If you are staying at a hotel or motel with your dog, exercise him somewhere other than in the flower beds and parking lot of the property. People walking to and from their cars really are not thrilled at "stepping in something" left by your dog. Should an accident occur, pick it up with a tissue or paper towel and deposit it in a proper receptacle; do not just walk off, leaving it to remain there. Usually there are grassy areas on the sides of and behind motels where dogs can be exercised. Use them rather than the more conspicuous, usually carefully tended, front areas or those close to the rooms. If you are becoming a dog show enthusiast, you will eventually need an exercise pen to take with you to the show. Exercise pens are ideal to use when staying at motels, too, as they permit you to limit the dog's roaming space and to pick up after him more easily.

Never leave your dog unattended in the room of a motel unless you are absolutely certain that he will stay there quietly and not damage or destroy anything. You do not want a long list of complaints from irate guests, caused by the annoying barking or whining of a lonesome dog in strange surroundings, or an overzealous watch dog barking furiously each time a footstep passes the door or he hears a sound from an adjoining room. And you certainly do not want to return to torn curtains or bedspreads, soiled rugs, or other embarrassing evidence of the fact that your dog is not really house-reliable after all.

If yours is a dog accustomed to traveling with you and you are positive that his behavior will be acceptable when left alone, that is fine. But if the slightest uncertainty exists, the wise course is to leave him in the car while you go to dinner or elsewhere; then

Ch. Rondelay's Zhu Danga, by America's Lhasa ex Promenade Sing a Ling, born January 1967, was bred by Ruth E. Deck and co-owned by Beverly and Donald Mayo and Ruth Deck, New York, New York. Handled by Jane Forsyth, this picture from Eastern Dog Club 1967.

bring him into the room when you are ready to retire for the night.

When you travel with a dog, it is often simpler to take along from home the food and water he will need rather than to buy food and look for water while you travel. In this way he will have the rations to which he is accustomed and which you know agree with him, and there will be no fear of problems due to different drinking water. Feeding on the road is quite easy now, at least for short trips, with all the splendid dry foods and high-quality canned meats available. A variety of lightweight, refillable water containers can be bought at many types of stores.

Always be careful to leave sufficient openings to ventilate your car when the dog will be alone in it. Remember that during the summer, the rays of the sun can make an inferno of a closed car within only a few minutes, so leave enough window space open to provide air circulation. Again, if your dog is in a crate, this can be done quite safely. The fact that you have left the car in a shady spot is not always a guarantee that you will find conditions the same when you return. Don't forget that the position of the sun changes in a matter of minutes, and the car you left nicely shaded half an hour ago can be getting full sunlight far more quickly than you may realize. So, if you leave a dog in the car, make sure there is sufficient ventilation and check back frequently to ascertain that all is well.

If you are going to another country, you will need a health certificate from your veterinarian for each dog you are taking with you, certifying that each has had rabies shots within the required time preceding your visit.

Index

285